Ethics in Management

Kenneth E. Goodpaster

Associate Professor of Business Administration

Division of Research   Harvard Business School   Boston

Course Module Series

Acknowledgments. *This Course Module, because it is a series of cases, draws upon two main resources: the companies, other organizations, and people who furnished information for the cases; and those who made possible their preparation and presentation.*

I am grateful to the corporations and individuals—disguised or not—who contributed time, thought, and information to the cases. Without these contributions, there would be neither course nor module.

For case preparation, I wish to thank Dekkers Davidson, John Keller, Richard Post, and David Whiteside, each of whom wrote or contributed to the writing of studies in this volume.

Finally, I would like to thank my colleague and friend, John B. Matthews, Joseph C. Wilson Professor of Business Administration, for his unselfish encouragement and example. Teaching ethics in management is an art, and there are few, if any, artists who could match his understanding of the casewriting process or skill in the use of the case method. I am pleased to dedicate this book to him.

K.G.

For information on other titles in the HBS Course Module Series, write HBS Publishing Division, Harvard Business School, Boston, Mass. 02163.

Library of Congress Catalog Card No. 84-12847
ISBN No. 0-87584-165-1

Contents

Editor's note: For easier reference, case items called *Exhibits* follow the case text. Those labeled *Tables* and *Figures* appear within the text.

Introduction

To many, the ethical aspects of management are both important and intractable. They are important because they pose fundamental questions about the decision making of executives and the human impact of corporate power. They are intractable because *values* are notoriously ill-defined and frequently in conflict with one another. Attempting to sort through the often divergent pronouncements of business leaders, management educators, and philosophers leads to a kind of paralysis: to make judgments seems imperious; to refuse to make them seems impossible.

This Course Module offers a set of cases and readings aimed at integrating ethical reflection with management decision making. All were designed for use in two second-year MBA courses at the Harvard Business School (an elective in ethics and a required course in business policy). In addition, most have been used in the School's executive education programs as well as in other academic and corporate settings.

Three criteria have guided the selection and organization of these materials: *topical relevance* to the practicing manager, *curricular relevance* to management education, and *analytical relevance* to applied ethics. Topically, they represent some of the most difficult management challenges of our time:

1. Learning the forms and limits of moral reasoning in business: "Some Avenues for Ethical Analysis in General Management."
2. Translating ethical ideals into policy and practice: "The Beliefs of Borg-Warner."
3. Recognizing employee rights and responsibilities: "Jim Sawyer" and "To Employers."
4. Sponsoring moral or amoral values in TV ads and programs: "Consolidated Foods Corporation" and "Note on the TV Controversy."
5. Minimizing ethical pressures from management incentive systems: "H. J. Heinz Company."
6. Implementing layoffs along with affirmative action policies: "Duke Power Company."
7. Confronting the ethics of bankruptcy: "Braniff International."
8. Managing product safety: "Note on Product Safety" and "The Ford Pinto."
9. Responding to conflicting standards in international business: "Note on the Export of Pesticides."

Further background for addressing these topics is presented in the two reprints included from the *Harvard Business Review*, "Can the Best Corporations Be Made Moral?" and "Can a Corporation Have a Conscience?"

From the point of view of the second criterion, curricular relevance, the selections display breadth and richness of a different kind. The prism diagram below illustrates the traffic between ethics and the various functional areas of management education, dispersed and integrated by general management.

(Each case or note mentioned above highlights one of these disciplines as the numerical correspondence indicates.)

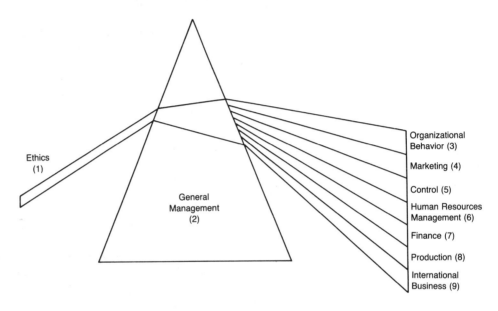

The third criterion governing the selection of case material for this module has been analytical relevance. There are three levels on which ethical analysis can be applied to business activity: The level of *personal behavior and character*; the level of *organizational policy and culture*; and the level of *systemic values* that define capitalism itself. Although each of the elements of the series raises issues on more than one of these levels, the emphasis can be seen to shift gradually from the personal (1, 2, 3) through the organizational (4, 5, 6) to the systemic (7, 8, 9).

This module is not presented with an ethical "bottom line," nor does it offer any kind of final word, either by the author or by the Harvard Business School. In the spirit of the case method, it is designed to create a realistic discussion environment for teaching and learning. It represents the opening, not the closing, of a dialogue.

One can hope, however, that the *process* of actively discussing these cases and readings will advance the understanding of those who participate. If so, then a step will have been taken toward joining moral insight to administrative wisdom.

Kenneth E. Goodpaster

Some Avenues for Ethical Analysis in General Management

Kenneth E. Goodpaster
prepared this note as a basis for
class discussion.

The general manager inevitably confronts ethical issues, whatever his or her location in the corporate structure and whatever the size and complexity of the organization. Sometimes the demands of responsible judgment and action are obvious; for example, when decisions involve clear, significant, and avoidable harms or indignities to persons inside or outside the organization. But often the demands of responsible judgment and action are not obvious. (One has only to consider the knot of problems surrounding the affirmative action and reverse discrimination controversy or the debate over business operations in South Africa.) Often what the general manager seeks and needs is a more or less orderly way of thinking through the moral implications of a policy decision—a perspective and a language for appraising the alternatives available from an ethical point of view.

This note will sketch only the broadest outlines of such a perspective and such a language, drawing upon the resources of ethics as a philosophical discipline. A fuller development of these topics is available elsewhere.[1]

The Dual Role of the General Manager

Janus, one of the principal gods of Roman mythology, was the god of beginnings. His image, often appearing at the gates of cities, had two faces on one head.[2] One face looked to the city within, while the other looked outward. This Janus-faced image is a convenient one for representing the dual role of the general manager in the modern corporation.

---

1. See course materials for Ethical Aspects of Corporate Policy, especially: "Ethical Frameworks for Management," HBS Case Services No. 384–105, and "Relativism in Ethics," Case No. 381–097.
2. Webster's *New Collegiate Dictionary* (Springfield, Mass.: G. & C. Merriam Company, 1977), p. 619, illustrates the Janus image.

Chester I. Barnard, in his classic *The Functions of the Executive*, writes:

> The survival of cooperation depends upon two interrelated and interdependent classes of processes: (a) those which relate to the system of cooperation as a whole in relation to the environment; and (b) those which relate to the creation or distribution of satisfactions among individuals.
>
> The instability and failures of cooperation arise from defects in each of these classes of processes separately, and from defects in their combination. The functions of the executive are those of securing the effective adaptation of these processes.[3]

Whether the task be policy formulation or policy implementation, Barnard goes on to argue that the executive or the general manager must attend constantly to both of these aspects of corporate life: the outward-looking and the inward-looking.

Beyond the great value of Barnard's reflections for the whole field of business policy, they also provide a gateway to the field of ethics as it relates to business policy. The study of ethics is the study of human action and its moral adequacy. Since the action of the executive has a dual aspect, we can expect the ethical responsibilities of the executive to have a dual aspect.

Transactions and the Moral Point of View

Many people have offered elaborate definitions of the subject matter of ethics, but the most useful for our present purposes is offered by philosopher Alan Gewirth. Ethics or morality, he observes,

> is primarily concerned with interpersonal actions, that is, with actions that affect persons other than their agents. I shall refer to such actions as *transactions*, and to the persons affected by them as *recipients*. I shall also say that both the agent and his recipients *participate* in transactions, although the former does so actively and the latter passively, by undergoing or being affected by the agent's action toward him.[4]

Gewirth goes on to point out that there are many kinds and degrees of "one person's affecting another," but that the morally relevant transactions are those

> where what is affected is the recipient's freedom and well-being, and hence his capacity for action. . . . Such modes of affecting in transactions can be most readily recognized in their negative forms: when one person coerces another, hence preventing him from participating purposively or with well-being in the transaction.[5]

If we join Gewirth's observations about the subject matter of ethics or morality with Barnard's observations about the dual role of the executive, we have the initial contours of a framework for analysis as shown below.

Figure A
Ethical Relevance of the General Manager's Functions or Roles

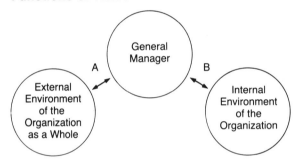

In this figure, A and B represent two broad classes of transactions that are both central to the functions of the general manager and ethically important in their own right. *A-transactions* have to do primarily with managing the organization's relationship with the wider social and natural environment in which it operates. Examples of ethical issues that fall under this heading include product safety, environmental protection, truth in advertising and marketing, responsibilities to investors and suppliers, and various other forms of local, national, and international corporate impact.

B-transactions have to do primarily with managing the internal environment of the organization, including interpersonal relations, authority, incentives, and structure. Examples of ethical issues that fall under this heading include worker health and safety; fairness in hir-

3. Chester I. Barnard, *The Functions of the Executive*, Thirtieth Anniversary Edition (Cambridge, Mass.: Harvard University Press, 1968), pp. 60–61.
4. Alan Gewirth, *Reason and Morality* (Chicago, Ill.: University of Chicago Press, 1978), p. 129.

5. Ibid.

ing, firing, and promotion; civil liberties for employees; and more subtle organizational pressures that affect either the general moral climate or culture of the corporation or the character of individuals as they rise through the ranks.

In A-transactions, the general manager views the corporation as a *moral agent* in the wider society, while in B-transactions, the general manager views the corporation as itself a *moral environment* to be managed with a view to the freedom and well-being of its members. Both types of transactions involve issues of policy formulation as well as policy implementation.

Figure B
Relating Business Policy, Ethics, and the Dual Role of the General Manager

	Corporation as Moral Agent	Corporation as Moral Environment
Business Policy Formulation		
Business Policy Implementation		

From the perspective of the history of ethics or moral philosophy, the foregoing represents an acknowledgment of the (modern) fact that the corporation is in some respects a microcosm of the community in which it operates and in other respects a macrocosm of the individual citizen living and working in that wider community. Insofar as the corporation resembles the wider community, ethical issues arise that are analogous to those in classical political philosophy: legitimacy of authority; rights and responsibilities associated with entry, exit, membership, promotion, and succession; civil liberties; moral climate. Insofar as the corporation resembles an individual "person" in the community, ethical issues arise that are analogous to classical issues of personal responsibility: duties and obligations to avoid harm, to respect the law, to further justice and the common good, and to provide for the least advantaged. There will be differences in each realm, of course, since the respective analogies are imperfect, but the similarities are strong enough to help order the ethical agenda of business policy.

The general manager, then, sits at the nexus of two broad regions of judgment and action that call not only for economic intelligence but also for ethical awareness. And just as the former calls for a healthy balance of analytical skill and intuition, so does the latter. Moral reasoning, despite the aspirations of some of the great thinkers of the past, is no more reducible to a mechanical decision procedure than is economic or administrative reasoning. Ethics, though not unscientific, is not a science.

The alternative, however, need not be thought of as anarchic: "There's no disputing tastes." Ethical judgment may not manifest the same kind of objectivity that we have come to expect of the natural sciences, but few would seriously contend that reason has no place in ethics. The history of philosophical as well as theological thought about ethics reveals, amidst much disagreement, a shared conviction that moral judgment can and should be rooted in what some have called the moral point of view and that this point of view governs and disciplines what are taken to be good and bad reasons, sound and unsound arguments, principles and intuitions. For many, the moral point of view has been understood in religious terms as the point of view that reflects God's will for humanity. For others, the moral point of view has been understood in more natural terms, not dependent for its authority on religious faith. But if one sets aside questions about its ultimate *source*, one finds significant consensus as to its general character. The moral point of view is seen as a mental and emotional standpoint from which all persons have a special dignity or worth, from which the Golden Rule derives its force, from which words like *ought* and *duty* derive their meaning.

In a later section, we shall outline the main types of reasoning that have been associated with this point of view. First, however, we must locate such moral reasoning within the wider territory of philosophical ethics.

Normative Ethics

Contemporary philosophers divide the field of ethics into three parts: descriptive ethics, normative ethics, and metaethics (see *Figure C*). Descriptive ethics is not, strictly speaking, a philosophical activity. It is more appropriately classified among the social sciences, since it is aimed at an empirical or neutral *description* of the values of individuals and groups. To say,

Figure C
Branches of Ethical Thinking

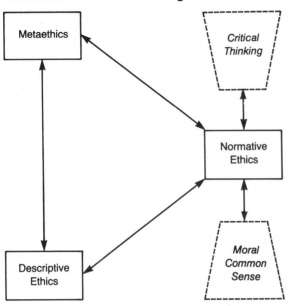

for example, that a business executive or an organization approves of bribery is to make a descriptive ethical claim, one that can be supported or refuted by pointing to factual evidence.

Normative ethics, by contrast, is not aimed at neutral factual claims about the ethical characteristics of individuals or groups. Normative ethical inquiry seeks to develop and defend judgments of right and wrong, good and bad, virtue and vice. For this reason, we will examine normative ethics more closely below. To say that a business executive or an organization approves of bribery *and* is wrong or bad for doing so is to add a normative ethical claim to a descriptive one. If it is to be supported or refuted, some sort of criteria of "wrongness" or "badness" must be provided.

Metaethics is concerned neither with describing values nor with advancing criteria for right and wrong, but with examining questions about the meaning and provability of ethical judgments. Metaethics is therefore a level of abstraction above normative ethics. At this remove, one might explore the differences among scientific, religious, and ethical judgments; the relation of legality to morality; the implications of cultural differences for ethical objectivity, and so forth.

It is important to keep descriptive ethical, normative ethical, and metaethical issues sepa-

rate, if for no other reason than that confusion results from failing to do so. To continue our example, consider a statement such as "For Americans, bribery is wrong, but for certain others it is not." On one reading, such a statement is simply a descriptive ethical remark: "Americans, as a matter of fact, generally disapprove of bribery while people in Society X do not." On another reading, however, the statement is normative: "Americans are wrong to pay bribes but people in Society X are not." On still a third reading, the implication of the statement might be metaethical: "There is no objective right or wrong about bribery, only social custom." Unless one is clear about which of these three possible interpretations of the original statement is intended, little progress will be made in any discussion of its merits.

Focusing now on normative ethics, the kind of inquiry most relevant to our present purposes, two sublevels need to be distinguished. First, and most familiar, is what we will call the level of *moral common sense*. Whether in our personal lives or in our professional or organizational lives, most of us operate with a more or less well-defined set of ethical values, principles, or rules of thumb that guide decision making. Seldom are such values or rules spelled out explicitly in a list, but if they were, the list would probably include such items as:

- Avoid harming others
- Respect the rights of others
- Do not lie or cheat
- Keep promises and contracts
- Obey the law
- Prevent harm to others
- Help those in need
- Be fair
- Reinforce these imperatives in others

In many decision situations, such a repertoire of common sense moral judgments is sufficient. It functions as an informal normative ethical framework, one that sometimes demands a lot from us but that we are prepared to live by both for the sake of others and for our own inner well-being.[6]

But problems arise—sometimes hypothetically, sometimes in practice. And when they arise, we seem to be forced into a second level

6. For a fuller discussion of what is called moral common sense here and of the differences in weight among the rules, see Bernard Gert, *The Moral Rules: A New Rational Foundation for Morality* (New York: Harper & Row, 1973).

of normative ethical thinking. The problems come from two main sources: (1) internal conflicts or unclarities about items on our own common sense lists, and (2) interpersonal conflicts in which we find that others' lists disagree (e.g., are longer, shorter, or differently weighted). How can I keep this promise and still avoid harm to others? What does it mean to be fair? If he or she doesn't (they don't) value honesty, how can or why should I (we)? What priorities are there among items on the list?

We are driven by such questions into a level of normative ethical thinking beyond moral common sense, to what philosophers call *critical thinking*. At this level, the search is for *criteria* that will justify the inclusion or exclusion of common sense norms, clarify their applicability in certain circumstances, and resolve conflicts among them.

Avenues of Critical Thinking in Ethics

A full-dress review of the many ways in which philosophers, past and present, have sought to organize what we are calling critical ethical thinking is beyond the scope of this note. It is possible, however, to sketch briefly three of the more important normative views that have been proposed. These three views will provide some avenues for ethical analysis in the sense that discussions of cases often exemplify, and can even be guided by, one or more of them.

Utilitarianism. One of the most influential normative ethical views, at least in the modern period, is utilitarianism. There are numerous variations and refinements, but the basic utilitarian message is that moral common sense is to be governed by a single dominant *goal*: maximizing net expectable utility (or happiness or pleasure or preference or welfare) for all parties affected by a decision or action. Critical thinking, according to utilitarians, consists in testing our ethical rules of thumb against the yardstick of social costs and benefits. It is in this way that we best achieve congruence between our decisions and the moral point of view.

Adopting a purely utilitarian ethic raises many questions and problems: How does one measure utility or happiness? For whom does one measure it (oneself only, one's group, one's society, all societies)? What about the tyranny of the majority in the calculation? Defenders of the view acknowledge such problems but insist that they can be resolved. "At least," they argue, "the utilitarian approach anchors ethical thinking in something resembling a scientific, empirical method."

In the context of general management, utilitarian reasoning frequently manifests itself as a commitment to the social virtues of the market system, both inside the organization and outside. The greatest good for the greatest number comes from competitive decision making, it is argued, and market forces can be relied upon to minimize social harm.

Contractarianism. A second influential approach to critical thinking in ethics is contractarianism. Again there are variations, but the central idea is that moral common sense is to be governed not by utility maximization, but by fairness. And fairness is explained as a condition that prevails when all individuals are accorded equal respect as participants in social arrangements. The idea of a social contract has appeal in this view because it emphasizes the *rights* of individuals to a veto in a way that utilitarianism does not.

Contractarianism in its various forms has been criticized, of course. Questions are raised about the clarity and sufficiency of its basic commitment to equality, about the practicality of its focus on rights, and about what some perceive to be its excessive emphasis on tolerance and individual liberties.

In general management settings, contractarian reasoning manifests itself in concerns about the implications of corporate policy for consumer rights, employee rights, and fair treatment of minorities. These rights-based arguments are often directly counter to utilitarian arguments on such topics.

Pluralism. The third approach to critical thinking in ethics is perhaps the least unified and systematic, even though it is widely held. We will refer to it as pluralism. The governing ethical idea in this view is *duty*. For the pluralist, critical thinking about the first-level duties suggested by our moral common sense leads not to some single outside umpire (such as utility or fairness) but to a more reflective examination of duty itself. One must try to economize on one's list of basic duties, subordinating some to others, relying in the end on one's faculty of moral perception (or intuition or conscience) for the resolution of hard cases. The pluralist focuses on the rightness or wrongness of actions as moral qualities that are distinct from extrinsic concerns such as consequences or rights. Fidelity and honesty are obligations not because they lead to more welfare or because others have a right to expect them, they are just basic duties. Not to live by such duties is simply to be corrupt, bad-willed, to lack moral integrity.

Those unsympathetic with pluralism point to problems about securing interpersonal agreement about basic duties (either what they are or how to weight them) and claim that pluralism does not take us far enough beyond moral common sense (the point of critical thinking in the first place). Defenders acknowledge these difficulties but insist that our convictions about basic duties and obligations are more trustworthy than our convictions about avenues that try too hard to systematize them.

Pluralistic reasoning in general management is evidenced by appeals to principle. Basic obligations—such as honesty, integrity, and consistency—are cited. Rights are viewed as shorthand devices for corresponding duties to respect others and utilitarian reasoning is identified with expediency. Some actions, it is argued, are just wrong whatever the consequences. These three avenues are summarized in the figure below.

Figure D
Three Avenues of Critical Thinking

Avenue	Type	Managing Moral Common Sense
Utilitarianism	Goal-based	What action or policy maximizes benefit/cost?
Contractarianism	Rights-based	What action or policy most fairly respects rights?
Pluralism	Duty-based	What action or policy reflects the stronger duty?

Each of these three isms could be pursued at great length, both conceptually and historically. For our present purposes, however, it is enough to see them as concentrations of effort at critical thinking in ethical matters. Each represents a worthwhile perspective from which specific moral issues might be addressed, if not resolved. All have in common a serious concern with improving the clarity and consistency of ethical judgment.

The debate over the moral acceptability or unacceptability of euthanasia affords a particularly striking example of how the three avenues can come into play at once. Both proponents *and* opponents of euthanasia argue on the basis of social utility (or disutility), on the basis of rights (of the living and of the dying), and on the basis of duties (to alleviate suffering or not to kill). Too often, perhaps, the parties to such arguments either fail to examine the full implications of the critical avenue they adopt or fail to appreciate that others are adopting a different avenue.

Getting Down to Cases

What are some of the implications of the foregoing in the context of case analysis? Can the study of ethics-related management problems be improved through the use of such categories?

If these questions are interpreted as requests for decision procedures, the answers will be disappointing. But analytical *guidance* is present and accounted for. The following sets of questions offer a way to structure study and discussion:

1. Are there ethical issues involved in this case? Centrally or peripherally? Is a decision required?
2. If there are ethical issues involved, under which of the two broad roles of the general manager do they fall (A-transactions or B-transactions)? Or are both involved? How? What, precisely, are the ethical issues in each category?
3. From a descriptive ethical perspective, what appear to be the critical ethical assumptions or values shown by the persons or organizations in the case?
4. From the point of view of maximizing utility for those affected, what is the best course of action? What facts in the case support this conclusion?
5. From the point of view of fairness or concern for individual rights, what is the best course of action? Again, what facts support this conclusion?
6. From the point of view of setting priorities among duties and obligations, what should be done? Why?
7. Do the three avenues converge on a course of action or do they diverge?
8. If they diverge, which avenue should override?

9. Are there ethically relevant considerations in the case that are not captured by any of the three avenues? What are they?
10. What is the decision or action plan?

These questions are not exhaustive, but analysis based on them will almost certainly enhance the kind of learning that case discussion affords. The result may be a convergence of opinion or not; when it is not, explanations should be pursued. In either case, the moral point of view will have been sought out and joined to the administrative point of view. Sound leadership demands no more and no less.

Selected Bibliography

Brandt, Richard B. *A Theory of the Good and the Right*. London: Oxford University Press, 1979.

Dworkin, Ronald. *Taking Rights Seriously*. Cambridge: Harvard University Press, 1978.

Frankena, William K. *Ethics*. 2d ed., Englewood Cliffs, N.J.: Prentice-Hall, 1973.

Fried, Charles. *Right and Wrong*. Cambridge: Harvard University Press, 1978.

Hare, R. M. *Moral Thinking*. London: Oxford University Press, 1981.

Rawls, John. *A Theory of Justice*. Cambridge: Harvard University Press, 1971.

The Beliefs of Borg-Warner

*Dekkers L. Davidson,
research associate, prepared this
case under the supervision of
Kenneth E. Goodpaster as a
basis for class discussion rather
than to illustrate either effective
or ineffective handling of an
administrative situation.*

It was May 19, 1982, the last day of Borg-Warner's 1982 chairman's meeting, and CEO James Beré closed the final session of the meeting by speaking about the development of "The Beliefs of Borg-Warner":

> For some time, Borg-Warner has been a company in search of an identity. I am not sure that during most of the half-century of our history we ever really ourselves questioned what we stood for, what needs we fulfill, or where we were going. But before we can know surely where we are going, we must first know *what* we are. So we are beginning a long reexamination. Why now? Because right now we are at a turning point in a long and massive transition in this company . . . because in a sea of violent change, guidelines are vital to avoid being swamped . . . because values and profits are inseparable.

He also talked about what the "Beliefs" meant and how they would affect the company:

> With this formal document, we are saying, both as a corporation and as individuals, that we believe that inherent values are as applicable in our work as in our personal lives. In fact, these values may be even more important on the job, since our business actions affect far more people than do our personal affairs.
>
> So if it sounds familiar, please do not dismiss it. These are not one-day-a-week precepts—they are basic guidelines to the day-to-day running of a business.
>
> We know we are not going to change our activities and our personality overnight. It has taken us a full decade to shift

---

Note: References throughout the case to company history and documents come from H. Lee Geist's *Borg-Warner: The First Fifty Years* (Chicago, Borg-Warner Corporation, 1978).

"The Beliefs of Borg-Warner: To Reach Beyond the Minimal"

Any business is a member of a social system, entitled to the rights and bound by the responsibilities of that membership. Its freedom to pursue economic goals is constrained by law and channeled by the forces of a free market. But these demands are minimal, requiring only that a business provide wanted goods and services, compete fairly, and cause no obvious harm. For some companies, that is enough. It is not enough for Borg-Warner. We impose upon ourselves an obligation to reach beyond the minimal. We do so convinced that by making a larger contribution to the society that sustains us, we best assure not only its future vitality, but our own.

This is what we believe.

We believe in the dignity of the individual.

However large and complex a business may be, its work is still done by people dealing with people. Each person involved is a unique human being, with pride, needs, values, and innate personal worth. For Borg-Warner to succeed, we must operate in a climate of openness and trust, in which each of us freely grants others the same respect, cooperation, and decency we seek for ourselves.

We believe in our responsibility to the common good.

Because Borg-Warner is both an economic and social force, our responsibilities to the public are large. The spur of competition and the sanctions of the law give strong guidance to our behavior, but alone do not inspire our best. For that we must heed the voice of our natural concern for others. Our challenge is to supply goods and services that are of superior value to those who use them; to create jobs that provide meaning for those who do them; to honor and enhance human life; and to offer our talents and our wealth to help improve the world we share.

We believe in the endless quest for excellence.

Though we may be better today than we were yesterday, we are not as good as we must become. Borg-Warner chooses to be a leader—in serving our customers, advancing our technologies, and rewarding all who invest in us their time, money, and trust. None of us can settle for doing less than our best, and we can never stop trying to surpass what already has been achieved.

We believe in continuous renewal.

A corporation endures and prospers only by moving forward. The past has given us the present to build on. But to follow our visions to the future, we must see the difference between traditions that give us continuity and strength, and conventions that no longer serve us—and have the courage to act on that knowledge. Most can adapt after change has occurred; we must be among the few who anticipate change, shape it to our purpose, and act as its agents.

We believe in the commonwealth of Borg-Warner and its people.

Borg-Warner is both a federation of businesses and a community of people. Our goal is to preserve the freedom each of us needs to find personal satisfaction while building the strength that comes from unity. True unity is more than a melding of self-interests; it results when values and ideals also are shared. Some of ours are spelled out in these statements of belief. Others include faith in our political, economic, and spiritual heritage; pride in our work and our company; the knowlege that loyalty must flow in many directions, and a conviction that power is strongest when shared. We look to the unifying force of these beliefs as a source of energy to brighten the future of our company and all who depend upon it.

from a stodgy manufacturing company dominated by the auto industry to the degree of balance that we have now. Events move faster today—but it would still be a mistake to expect us to become something radically different very quickly.

But we know we *will* change. We have a very strong base of people, and operations, and financial structure to build upon. With an equally strong framework of shared values to guide and strengthen us, I believe we can become *anything* we want to.

Beré ended his speech by asking the company's managers to commit themselves to the "Beliefs" and to make them meaningful through their own words and actions: "One of the noble houses of England has as its motto a Latin phrase that translates essentially as, 'What I promise, I will do.' This statement today is our promise to the future. Please join me in that promise."

The Chairman's Meeting

Once every two years the 100 senior managers of Borg-Warner, along with spouses, would gather at the chairman's meeting to discuss important long-range issues. Whereas the annual president's meeting afforded a regular opportunity to discuss operating business issues, the chairman's meeting was viewed as a special session that allowed a retreat from the daily pressures of management so that participants could reflect on the company's health and direction. With a theme of shared values, the 1982 chairman's meeting had concluded with the release of "The Beliefs of Borg-Warner."

The development of this statement of beliefs had begun long before the 1982 chairman's meeting was even scheduled. While the "Beliefs" had only come to fruition after 10 months of intensive work, they were also the product of the company's long history, its culture, and the ideals of its chief executive officer.

Company History

Borg-Warner Corporation was born at a time when America's love affair with the automobile was in full bloom. A whole new social, economic, and transportation pattern had developed around the motorized wheels. Yet, despite the big annual increases in car production during the 1920s, the industry was going through a stage of consolidation.

Early acquisitions. On June 5, 1928, Borg-Warner was created when four established auto parts manufacturers agreed to consolidate their assets in a holding company. "What we want," said George Borg, first president of Borg-Warner, "is a corporation which cannot be made or broken by the fortunes of any single division, or the market for any one product." Each of the participants maintained its identity and operating methods while the corporation supplied the "fiscal glue."

In just over a year Borg-Warner added five more operations, thus establishing itself as a major force in the automotive industry. A published company history explained developments:

These nine tribal fiefdoms were to remain the heart of Borg-Warner for almost 25 years. . . . The nine companies had the same customers and parallel technology in common—but little else. Each considered itself as still independent. . . . Borg-Warner was not considered as a parent—it was known as the "central office." The charter of the corporation stated that: "individual divisions retain all powers not expressly limited to the central corporation."

The philosophies that were to guide, or to dominate the operations of Borg-Warner through much of its history, and to be the roots of both its strengths and its weaknesses were really established from the day the merger began.

Charles S. Davis, Borg-Warner's chairman, served as a referee who helped maintain the growth of the independent divisions. In an effort to lessen Borg-Warner's dependence on the automotive industry, Davis helped acquire an electric refrigeration business, a small chemical operation, and an aviation supply firm.

In 1950 Roy C. Ingersoll, an entrepreneurial division executive, became CEO. Whereas Davis had been content in his role as central banker, Ingersoll wanted to *run* the corporation. He was frustrated, however, as were his successors, by the organization of the company: 44 people reported directly to him—35 division heads and an assortment of staff people—representing a wide spectrum of activities and policies and a wider range of operations. There was little time for communication, and, given the tradition of decentralization and divisional autonomy, there seemed little that Ingersoll could do about the organization. A company document stated that "the central office had only two real controls over a division: it could refuse to allocate further capital funds, or it could fire the division president." Ingersoll eventually presided over the first restructuring in the company's history, thus improving communication within the organization.

Period of redevelopment. Once a consensus developed that Borg-Warner needed to reduce its dependence on Detroit (a full two-thirds of the company's business was going to the automotive industry), Roy Ingersoll set the transition in motion. Existing operations—the electric refrigeration and chemical businesses—were rebuilt and expanded. New operations—oilfield supply-service and air conditioning businesses—were acquired.

In 1961 Robert Ingersoll became CEO only after his father reluctantly agreed to step aside at age 73. While Roy Ingersoll had instinctively been a dynasty builder, his son offered a different style of leadership. "Bob Ingersoll was a new type at Borg-Warner. Neither a driver like his father, nor a negotiator like Davis, he was probably a better manager than either one."

Robert Ingersoll succeeded in grouping the divisions more along business lines, and set up group administrations through vice presidents who would have responsibility for compatible industries—such as automotive, chemical, construction, industrial, and so forth. By 1964 his new group organization was in place and attitudes slowly started to change. Communication between divisions and the corporate office improved and it became possible to find out what the divisions were doing ahead of time, rather than after the fact. The corporate office knew how earnings projections were arrived at and which "losers" among division products had been maintained and protected. The central office was referred to as a central bank and sometimes as a management consultant.

Robert Ingersoll introduced a new policy by ending the tradition that the company acquired operations but never got rid of them. Long-term commitment to an operation was a great ideal—but he insisted on justification for that commitment. Although a large number of persons objected to any divestiture, Robert Ingersoll sold the electric refrigeration business—it was the first real divestiture the company had ever had in its 40-year history. Other smaller

divestitures followed and included companies that had been acquired under his father's direction. He oversaw other fundamental changes in the character of the company. International operations accelerated and the chemical operation spawned a highly successful plastics business that held great promise.

The Beré Years

In 1972 Robert Ingersoll left the company when President Richard M. Nixon appointed him U.S. ambassador to Japan. James F. Beré was chosen to be the next CEO, representing yet another style of leadership. As a company observer noted: "Beré was the company's first professional manager, one with strong humanistic overtones, as keenly aware of a big company's obligations to society in general as to its stockholders. He was also the first chief executive with no personal connection to the 'early days'—and probably the first one to make decisions on a basis of company needs rather than company traditions." Beré joined Borg-Warner in 1961 as a seasoned business executive, and in an unusual move he was immediately named president of an automotive parts division. Subsequently, he occupied the group vice president's chair, acting as an ombudsman between the divisions and corporate staff. He established his reputation as an operating manager even though it was not his strong point. This reputation did, however, help him win the confidence of Robert Ingersoll and eventually gain the position as Borg-Warner's president. He had only been with Borg-Warner for seven years, but his lack of experience with the company was viewed as one of his assets in getting the job. Beré preferred to involve himself in long-term policy and strategic matters, while Chairman Ingersoll consistently involved himself in the day-to-day division affairs. Even though Ingersoll remained the boss until he left, the two men had apparently worked out an unconscious role reversal, one which made their working relationship strong. When Ingersoll stepped down, Beré was ready to assume the formal title of CEO.

After the shock of the 1974–1975 economic downturn, Beré realized that he had to improve communications between corporate staff and division management. In late 1975 Borg-Warner introduced a strategic planning system that involved many more people than previously, including division-level people all the way down to individual product areas. The operating manager now had to ask hard questions: What business am I really in? What future does the business have? Should we be in it at all? The discipline of such self-examination forced groups and divisions to make their own hard decisions about how to allocate their resources to the areas providing or promoting the best return. For the first time, the operating people aimed for clearer goals other than just next week, next month, or at most, next year.

By 1976 Borg Warner's nonproductive activities had been shed and modern management systems installed. The transportation equipment business remained the largest segment of the company, accounting for one-third of total earnings. The air conditioning, chemical and plastics, and finance operations had helped to diversify the corporation's earnings base. Beré continued to believe the company needed some new directions.

Recognizing that consumption of services was beginning to exceed consumption of manufactured products in the economy at large, Borg-Warner's management began to think about adding a service business. In 1977 the company acquired Baker Industries and gained a substantial foothold in the protective services industry. During late 1978 Borg-Warner and Firestone Tire and Rubber Company, with annual sales twice those of Borg-Warner, mutually agreed to consider a merger of their companies.

After serious negotiations, each company decided to retain its independence and the merger talks ended. In mid-1982 Borg-Warner acquired Burns International Security Services and thereby became the largest protective services operation in the world.

In 1982 Borg-Warner Corporation was a diverse, multinational corporation that was listed among the 500 largest industrial corporations in the United States. According to *Fortune*, it ranked 154 with sales of $2,761.2 million, 117 with net earnings of $172.1 million, and 71 with 55,700 employees. (*Exhibits 1* and *2* present a corporate profile and selected financial data). *Table A* illustrates the change in the character of the company over the 1970–1980 decade.

Early Attempts at Developing a Corporate Creed

Borg-Warner's first attempt to formally articulate a statement of beliefs occurred in 1970. During Robert Ingersoll's administration, the public relations department drafted a "Borg-Warner Creed" that mentioned the company's obligations to shareholders, employees, customers, suppliers—and society (see *Exhibit 3*). While many U.S. companies publicly adopted similar codes of ethics around this time, Borg-Warner was unable to achieve a consensus on any such statement. Initial efforts fizzled in the company's policy committee.

Ingersoll had frequently urged company management to reexamine attitudes and beliefs about work and the role of the corporation in

Table A
Changing Corporate Business Mix

	Early 1970s	Early 1980s
Net Earnings	$50 million	$170 million
Manufacturing: Air conditioning group, chemicals and plastics group, energy and industrial equipment group, and transportation equipment group	88%	40%
Services: Financial services group and protective services group	10%	27%
Affiliates: Major equity investments including a 19% interest in Hughes Tool Company, a 22% interest in Echlin, and a 24% interest in Amedco	2%	33%

Source: Borg-Warner's Investor Facts, 1982.

modern society. As a company document explained:

> He was the bridge between the old attitude that an employee was literally nothing but a cents-per-hour cost, and the current belief that the employee, at all levels, has an individual personality and individual rights.
>
> When he interviewed someone for an upper level job—he often started the interview with a thoroughly unexpected question: "What is your philosophy of life?" He was looking for honesty and a sense of dedication to company and customer, rather than followers of the old tradition of "make a buck any way you can."

While Ingersoll's beliefs were well known, his successor had to formalize a corporate statement of ethics. During a visit to a Texas Instruments' facility in early 1974, Beré had been handed a copy of its code of ethics and was impressed. He decided the time had come for Borg-Warner to articulate a statement of values and beliefs.

"Borg-Warner's Ethics." After several drafts, "Borg-Warner's Ethics" was published as a booklet for senior management review. As its foreword suggested, this was food for larger thought. It asked such questions as: "What ultimate standards do we cling to at Borg-Warner?" "In conflicts of purpose, how do we expect you to choose [what is best]?" The booklet was meant to offer guidance to managers wrestling with ethical dilemmas. The seven parts dealt with the law, company policy, affirmations of ethics, employee relations, consumer affairs, community relations, and corporate "sociology."

Although a senior management committee recommended that "Borg-Warner's Ethics" should eventually be published in a book, it suggested that management first establish a foothold for such a standard of ethical conduct. The committee thought the company had not yet attained the standards set forth in the drafted statements. Like the earlier effort, therefore, this attempt also sputtered.

Beré's concerns about corporate ethics. Following widespread reports of illegal and improper conduct during the first half of the 1970s by employees of public companies, Beré rekindled the discussion about corporate ethics in mid-1976. In a letter to all company employees, Beré stated

that "Borg-Warner does not want you to act in any way contrary to your ethical principles." He urged employees to seek guidance from their supervisors or co-workers if in doubt about the morality of a certain action (see *Exhibit 4*).

The 1976 annual report included a discussion about the social responsibility of business, along with the usual reporting of sales and earnings results. Beré began to speak more frequently about "building the character of our company," and he argued that Borg-Warner had to manage its business so as to create public confidence by considering the "economic *and* social needs of its constituents."

At the 1977 annual shareholders' meeting, Beré delivered a special "Report on the Non-economic Side of the Business," addressing the public's dissatisfaction with big business:

> Americans are dissatisfied with business, not because of complaints about its economic performance, but because they see corporations and their managers as too self-serving, too remote, too purely economic in our approach to human needs.
>
> The public today judges corporations more by our social performance—that is, by the effect of our routine conduct of business on the quality of life of people we touch: our employees, the people in our plant communities, our customers and the ultimate users of our products or services.

In the future, managers of Borg-Warner's businesses would be required to assess and respond to the needs of their customers, general public, and civic officials as part of the strategic planning process. At a senior management conference in late 1977 Beré declared that managers would be judged on their ability to meet social performance goals. As he put it, "Our objective will be to generate public approval based upon a sense of commitment to the company, employees, and society."

According to one corporate officer, "Beré had the right idea [about a code of ethics] but the timing was wrong. There were powerful people around Borg-Warner who still gave only lip service to the concept. The 'snicker index' was simply too high." Since Beré's own thoughts had solidified, he believed that some progress could finally be made to articulate a corporate statement of ethics. One senior manager noted that Beré was still quite vague about what such a statement would actually say. "But," he said,

"Beré was determined to develop one—soon." Beré was often heard to say that "when we have a code of beliefs it should include. . . ."

Developing a statement of beliefs. In summer 1981 Beré made another attempt to develop a corporate statement of beliefs. During an officer's meeting then, he reviewed his own initial attempts to develop a corporate statement:

I did not have the nerve to issue a statement of beliefs in the mid-1970s. I had gone to some of our senior managers with the concept and they told me it was a stupid idea because, as they said, "we have actions in our company that cannot measure up to a standard of ethics." I finally became mature enough to realize, that regardless of any past mistakes, a norm was essential to this company. Others, like our public relations people, believed it was a good idea, but were dubious that we could live up to it. Some also felt it would detract from the business of running the company.

When asked why such a project should be attempted under such difficult economic conditions, he talked about the things that had prompted him to proceed:

Why do it in 1981? There is a mosaic of factors that has triggered my actions.

First, I attended a seminar sponsored by the American Enterprise Institute and was moved by the words of one of the speakers, Michael Novak. Novak was convinced that we had a leadership dilemma in our society. Political leaders, he felt, would not speak from an ethical point of view—because it was not in their self-interest. The church, he argued, was divided and had lost its way—it was not providing people with needed guidance. Schools had lost their capability of providing an ethical norm for society. The family structure was in a state of decay. Novak made a strong plea: "If we are going to have true beliefs in the business sector, you, as business leaders, better stand up and realize that it is time to decide what your culture is—and give it some beliefs." I was convinced he was right! There had been a deterioration of ethics in our society. The norm was gone, and people were looking for leadership—but they wanted *quality* leadership.

Secondly, I have been CEO long enough so there is no way people are going to detach my actions from what I plan to publish.

Thirdly, I have confidence in our corporate communications department. They are the professional communicators and I know they will have to play a major role in shaping this document. When they appeared receptive to the idea, I felt confident we could proceed.

Lastly, when I visited our management training sessions, I heard a lot of our managers, particularly the younger ones, say they wanted to identify with a company that stands for something, that has a vision about what it is doing. For many of them, something was missing.

Beré was convinced that business could provide quality leadership by developing norms and went on to talk about the duties and rights of the modern corporation:

I think I have an obligation as a corporate leader to establish standards. I do *not* think I have a right to be so exclusive that I become a bigot. But I do think I have a right to not deal with the extreme 10 percent in society. My job is to cater to the middle 80 percent in society—any person with qualifications, regardless of background, is permitted to come. But we are not going to take the whole range of society. What I am saying is . . . we have a right to have beliefs in a company, to tell you what they are, before you join us.

A corporate statement of beliefs can give people a norm . . . it is similar to athletics. The best athletic events all have rules. You do not play basketball without a set of rules. I happen to think that people in business, which is also highly competitive, really admire a person who has made it big . . . as long as they have played by the rules. They absolutely despise a person who has cheated.

While we have an obligation as leaders to establish that norm, we must remain humble enough to realize that the norm may be wrong. It is not something that is fixed in concrete.

By mid-1981 a great deal of spadework had already been done to develop a corporate statement of beliefs. Yet, as one company officer put it, "We were shooting arrows and drawing the target around the points where they landed." Few understood what a corporate statement of beliefs was going to say and do.

Developing Shared Values

In September 1981, Beré put the task of developing a set of corporate beliefs before the company's senior managers. Speaking at the annual president's meeting, he talked about the company's strategy and performance:

> In the business world, there is a tendency to think of strategy as some cosmic approach that somehow takes place on the top floor of a corporate headquarters. We've had a certain amount of confusion about it in this company, too. For instance, we've said we wanted to reduce our dependence on the highly cyclical automotive market. We've said that with the country swinging steadily toward a service economy, we had to direct more interest to the service sector ourselves. Well, we've done both of these things.

He believed the company's view of strategic planning had to be enlarged:

> Now I think it may be time to redefine our understanding of what strategy should mean to Borg-Warner. Part of that goes back to the original meaning of the word *company*. [It is] a group of persons with common interests banded together to achieve a common goal. Common interests. Common goals . . . I am not sure we ever really had enough of them.
>
> To my mind, shared values—a company-wide set of principles against which all business decisions can be measured and tested—must be the base upon which concrete long-term objectives are built.

The Japanese, he argued, offered a model worthy of emulation but not outright imitation:

> In large Japanese companies, for instance, there is an understanding, often unspoken, but spread through the ranks, of where the company wants to go, what it wants to be, and what it will do, and how to gain those results. That really is possible here, too.
>
> I do not believe that the Japanese style of management by consensus really holds promise for close imitation in the United States. There is a homogeneity of approach and tradition in Japan that carries over from the culture to the work place. I hope Americans never lose the sense of drive, of individual achievement, that made this country great in the first place.
>
> But I do believe that in the American system, there is a great deal of room and flexibility for individual achievement within the larger framework of group achievement—room for both independence and interdependence.

As he finished his speech, Beré started the clock ticking toward the next gathering of Borg-Warner's senior management: "We are going to raise our strategic sights now . . . we are going to try to codify and publish the values that will guide us . . . all of you must be involved. . . . The theme of our chairman's meeting next May is going to be where we stand, what we believe, what our shared values really are. We would like to have our compendium (of beliefs) ready by then if we can."

Management's Response to Drafting a Statement of Beliefs

Only seven months remained to discuss, develop, and publish the actual words for a company statement of beliefs. Beré asked each manager to think about the actual contents of such a corporate statement and to write to him with suggestions. (*Exhibit 5* presents excerpts from some of the 40 responses out of about 90 managers who attended the meeting.) It was critical for Beré and the company to achieve wide participation. Otherwise, he felt the beliefs would mean very little to the company's employees. To do this, Beré looked to Robert Morris, vice president of communications, for assistance.

Morris was familiar with the work of other companies that had undertaken similar efforts—notably, his previous employer, IBM. He began by spending a great deal of time talking with Beré to flesh out what he was asking for. Although the quantity of responses from management had been fairly good, the content of the letters indicated that there was considerable confusion about Beré's request for help in drafting a statement of beliefs.

Morris advocated more discussion with the company's management. He solicited more letters from division management; he also considered setting up field interviews and roundtable "rap sessions" to widen the discussion. When he realized that his department lacked the resources to undertake such an effort, he went outside the corporation for help.

In early January 1982 Management Analysis Center (MAC) was retained to interview a select group of 35 managers and to analyze their responses on the proposed statement of beliefs. According to Morris, MAC did a good job of categorizing the issues and, most importantly, helped build the perception that this statement was being developed in a democratic fashion.

Beré's List. Meanwhile, Beré was developing his own list of items that he thought should be in the statement of beliefs: He kept an index card in his pocket during the day and would often jot down words or phrases that he felt belonged with the company's philosophy. His words were then combined with the suggestions generated by management. For Morris, Beré's list proved critical in drafting a specific statement from what was originally an abstract concept:

Sense of belonging
Work ethic
Competitive zeal
Company loyalty
Rational decision making
Employee ideas
Risk taking
Agents of change
Citizenship
Share power
Gratitude
Belief in the economic system
The whole person
Diversity

Morris and his staff worked feverishly to prepare a draft of the beliefs since only a few months remained to the chairman's meeting. When Beré resisted words in one draft that were attributable to Socrates, Morris and his staff had to begin anew. Beré insisted that the statement be grounded in Judeo-Christian values.

To arouse enthusiasm for the development of the beliefs, Morris had an expert on corporate culture address an officers' luncheon on the subject of institutional values. It turned out to be a disaster. The top circle of management left the session more confused than ever about how values and beliefs would affect their strategic thinking.

Morris enlisted help from a philosopher at a well-known university whose teaching and research centered on ethics and business. The philosopher helped Beré and his staff find a historical springboard for each of the principles included in the draft statement. Beré later said: "He was a real catalyst—he boosted my confidence that we could finally articulate a meaningful statement of philosophy for Borg-Warner."

The chairman's meeting. By early March the agenda for the May 1982 chairman's meeting had been established (see *Exhibit 6*). Guests would hear prominent speakers from industry and academia address issues on shared values and corporate policy. Yet the beliefs, to be released at that meeting's conclusion, were still not fully formulated.

When the actual principles in the statement started to come together, Beré realized that a preamble—a philosophical foundation—was needed to properly introduce the company's beliefs. Two approaches were considered: one could talk about how an enterprise making money could do good things for the community; or, conversely, one could talk about how an enterprise could do good things for the community and then expect to find profits flow as a natural consequence of its behavior. When Borg-Warner settled on the second choice, the statement of beliefs was ready to be presented at the chairman's meeting.

Important questions were raised during the three-day session. Division management was concerned that a corporatewide statement of philosophy might reduce division autonomy. Beré was convinced that the sharing of common values would allow operating personnel to make difficult decisions *without* looking to headquarters for help. Centralization, he insisted, came when people relied too heavily upon the "mystical powers" of their leader. In this instance, he thought, the "Beliefs" would give power to a broader base of management—sharing beliefs meant sharing power.

When asked what steps would follow the chairman's meeting, Beré talked in general terms:

The starting point for communicating these beliefs begins here—how I practice what is written down in this statement "to reach beyond the minimal."

These beliefs are signposts, guides, goals—a vehicle for discussion. We must tell our people that these are *not* schoolroom rules—after all, they are *not* a bunch of kids. We need to start a training program to explain why we have beliefs. We need to continue to discuss the operating implications of these beliefs—how it will affect management behavior. We will have to become a lot more selective in the type of people we bring in [to Borg-Warner]. We must come up forward to tell people—this is the culture of our company, this is what we believe in!

Lastly, we have to make this a living document of our company activity—no different than our accounting system. To me, the "Beliefs" are another professional tool of management to be utilized to reach our common goals.

He also reminded everyone of the relationship between philosophy and profit making:

I contend that unless you do what we are doing in terms of beliefs, you will *not* have a profitable company. Therefore, to those who attack me and say "this is none of your business—your job is to make money for the stockholders,"—I say I am optimizing the stockholder's holdings. If I do what I am now doing, I will attract talent and release creativity to the point of making this a better company. This is what I believe.

The chairman's meeting was termed a great success. The invited speakers had triggered thoughtful management discussions on the subject of corporate philosophy and ethics. As the company's senior managers filed out of the conference room following the closing remarks, each received a portfolio of the "Beliefs," per-

sonally signed by Beré. It was a gratifying moment for Beré and his staff. Yet, he knew that the real job of sharing and communicating the "Beliefs" had just begun.

Incorporating the "Beliefs." A plan would have to be developed over the next several months that would move "The Beliefs of Borg-Warner" beyond the status of high-sounding rhetoric. Steps would need to be taken to clarify, communicate, and put into practice such phrases as "to reach beyond the minimal." It was important, as one officer put it, "that these words not disappear like spit on sand."

Almost everyone in the company recognized that Beré was deeply committed to the "Beliefs," but many wondered how such principles could meaningfully be shared in a large and decentralized organization whose divisions treasured their operating independence.

The axiom that policy formulation is empty without careful attention to implementation was something that Beré understood very well; however, the "Beliefs" of Borg-Warner were not just ordinary policies.

Exhibit 1
Corporate Profile

In 1982 Borg-Warner was a $2.7 billion diversified manufacturing and services company involved in eight markets basic to the world's economy: transportation, construction, consumer products, machinery, agribusiness, energy, financial, and protective services. Borg-Warner had operations in 20 countries on 6 continents. Its more than 100 operating units were organized into six product and service groups, described below.

Air Conditioning

This group manufactured a broad range of air conditioning, refrigeration, and heating equipment under the York®, Fraser-Johnston®, Luxaire® and Moncrief® brand names. These included engineered systems for large buildings; industrial refrigeration equipment for the petrochemicals, food and other process industries; commercial air conditioning equipment for small buildings, schools, factories and apartment buildings; and residential air conditioning systems, heat pumps and furnaces. In 1981 sales for the group were $571 million and operating profit was $30 million.

Chemicals and Plastics

Borg-Warner Chemicals was the largest producer of ABS—a family of engineering thermoplastics used in a growing variety of applications around the world. Borg-Warner Chemicals also was in the specialty chemicals business with a growing line of intermediates, additives and alkylphenols. The group produced styrene monomer for Cycolac® ABS and for sale on the open market. Group sales in 1981 were $664 million; operating profit was $61 million.

Energy and Industrial Equipment

Major products in this group included centrifugal pumps for power plants, petroleum production, processing and pipelines, agriculture and general industrial applications; precision seals for pumps and compressors; valves; chains; bearings; and other power transmission products for general industrial applications. The group also made a.v. educational systems. In 1981 sales were $480 million and operating profit was $36 million.

Financial Services

Borg-Warner Acceptance Corporation (BWAC), the twelfth largest independent U.S. finance company in 1981, was the group's major unit. With more than 330 branches throughout the world, BWAC was the largest consumer durables floor-planning organization in the country, excluding captive automobile finance companies. BWAC also provided commercial, industrial and leveraged lease financing; insurance premium financing and other insurance-related services to businesses; it also provided marine, agribusiness, and automotive financing. The unconsolidated units which made up the financial services group contributed $32 million of net earnings in 1981.

Protective Services

Acquired in 1977, Baker Industries offered the broadest range of protective services in the security field. It provided Wells Fargo® alarm, guard and armored services; Pony Express® courier service, and Pyrotronics fire and smoke detection and extinguishment systems. In mid-1982, Borg-Warner also acquired Burns International Security Services. The combined Burns and Baker operations made Borg-Warner the largest protective services entity in the world, with the world's largest security guard service operation. On an annual basis, the group's revenue approached $700 million. In 1981, before the Burns acquisition, revenues were $364 million (not included in the consolidated financial data) and operating profit was $33 million.

Transportation Equipment

This group supplied component products to the manufacturers of automobiles, trucks, and off-highway vehicles and to replacement part distributors. Included were transmissions and transmission parts, clutches, axles, four-wheel-drive units, electronic sensors, control devices, and engine-timing components. Sales for the group in 1981 were $1.02 billion and operating profit was $78 million.

Exhibit 2
Selected Financial Data, 1971–1981

	1981	1980	1979	1978‡	1977	1976	1975	1974	1973	1972	1971
Earnings Year ended December 31											
(millions of dollars except per share data)											
Sales and other income:											
Net sales	$2,761.2	$2,673.3	$2,717.4	$2,326.0	$2,031.9	$1,862.4	$1,639.0	$1,767.6	$1,546.8	$1,283.2	$1,148.2
Other income	35.1	15.7	9.7	12.6	12.5	18.3	8.8	4.8	4.2	3.3	4.2
	2,796.3	2,689.0	2,727.1	2,338.6	2,044.4	1,880.7	1,647.8	1,772.6	1,551.0	1,286.5	1,152.4
Costs and expenses:											
Cost of sales	2,179.6	2,134.3	2,133.8	1,780.7	1,554.8	1,440.2	1,308.2	1,419.9	1,179.8	973.0	885.4
Depreciation	73.8	64.4	59.6	55.2	50.9	43.4	42.8	43.1	40.5	37.3	34.7
Selling, general and administrative expenses	375.0	334.9	310.2	290.8	252.6	231.3	206.4	206.3	182.3	153.5	131.8
Interest expense	23.0	31.4	20.9	16.7	16.7	16.6	24.3	31.1	16.7	13.1	13.6
Finance charges from related companies	19.1	17.6	12.2	10.0	9.1	9.4	12.1	7.0	5.0	4.0	3.8
Minority interests	5.1	4.3	2.6	3.0	2.6	2.7	2.1	2.0	2.0	1.2	.9
Provision for income taxes	56.5	47.1	68.2	81.3	71.4	66.8	21.0	21.9	61.6	52.8	40.2
	2,732.1	2,634.0	2,607.5	2,237.7	1,958.1	1,810.4	1,616.9	1,731.3	1,487.9	1,234.9	1,110.4
Earnings from consolidated operations	64.2	55.0	119.6	100.9	86.3	70.3	30.9	41.3	63.1	51.6	42.0
Equity in earnings of affiliates	62.9	35.3	8.7	6.9	4.9	.8	5.5	1.5	1.4	1.4	.4
Earnings from manufacturing operations	127.1	90.3	128.3	107.8	91.2	71.1	36.4	42.8	64.5	53.0	42.4
Earnings from financial services companies	32.0	27.2	21.1	16.1	12.8	10.6	8.1	8.0	6.8	6.2	5.0
Earnings from protective services companies	13.0	8.6	6.2	1.9							
Net earnings+	$ 172.1	$ 126.1	$ 155.6	$ 125.8	$ 104.0	$ 81.7	$ 44.5	$ 50.8*	$ 71.3	$ 59.5**	$ 47.4
Per common share	1981	1980	1979	1978	1977	1976	1975	1974	1973	1972	1971
Net earnings+	$ 4.00	$ 2.93	$ 3.63	$ 2.94	$ 2.47	$ 2.11	$ 1.15	$ 1.33*	$ 1.85	$ 1.52**	$ 1.23
Operating data Year ended December 31	1981	1980	1979	1978	1977	1976	1975	1974	1973	1972	1971
Return on sales	6.2%	4.7	5.7%	5.4%	5.1%	4.4%	2.7%	2.9%*	4.6%	4.6%**	4.1%
Return on sales from consolidated operations	2.3	2.1	4.4	4.3	4.2	3.8	1.9	2.3*	4.1	4.0*	3.7
Dividends	$ 53.9	$ 49.6	$ 43.8	$ 39.3	$ 34.5	$ 27.5	$ 26.4	$ 26.1	$ 26.4	$ 24.6	$ 24.5
Per common share paid+	1.28	1.17	1.04	.93	.83	.71	.68	.68	.68	.63	.63
Capital expenditures	175.8	134.2	130.7	115.3	77.0	36.0	55.9	83.0	69.6	62.8	55.2
Research and development expense	66.5	63.9	55.8	49.1	45.3	44.2	42.2	42.2	41.2	42.7	39.2
Financial data December 31	1981	1980	1979	1978	1977	1976	1975	1974	1973	1972	1971
Current assets	$ 826.8	$ 757.9	$ 851.9	$ 795.8	$ 648.7	$ 688.5	$ 589.5	$ 687.5	$ 641.9	$ 528.3	$ 502.1
Current liabilities	560.4	446.2	460.1	401.3	315.5	318.6	243.5	264.2	291.4	188.0	168.7
Net working capital	266.4	311.7	391.8	394.5	333.2	369.9	346.0	423.3	350.5	340.3	333.4
Current ratio	1.48 to 1	1.70 to 1	1.85 to 1	1.98 to 1	2.06 to 1	2.16 to 1	2.42 to 1	2.60 to 1	2.20 to 1	2.81 to 1	2.98 to 1
Investments and advances	664.1	519.1	393.9	351.5	343.8	209.5	188.6	166.3	113.1	97.7	75.8
Property, plant and equipment, net	673.2	606.7	556.0	493.7	443.5	423.6	397.6	412.8	400.8	377.8	364.8
Total assets	2,191.2	1,908.3	1,823.4	1,658.7	1,450.2	1,340.3	1,192.5	1,284.6	1,171.5	1,021.4	963.0
Notes payable and long-term debt	258.1	226.4	219.1	194.6	171.3	206.1	180.9	301.5	214.6	178.3	183.2
Debt to equity ratio	20.9%	19.8	20.5%	20.3%	19.6%	27.8%	26.3%	45.0%	33.4%	28.6%	31.9%
Shareholders' equity	1,235.9	1,145.7	1,068.9	958.1	872.2	742.3	689.1	670.0	642.4	610.4	574.9
Return on average equity	14.5%	11.4*	15.4%	13.7%	12.9%	11.4%	6.6%	7.7%*	11.4%	10.0%**	8.4%
Book value per common share+	29.52	27.06	25.30	22.63	20.54	19.18	17.76	17.31	16.74	15.47	14.70
Other data *(thousands)*											
Average number of common shares outstanding+	43,030	43,088	42,890	42,832	42,186	38,828	38,532	38,214	38,544	39,280	38,658
Number of stockholders at year end	47.0	50.0	53.6	55.9	57.0	58.6	63.3	63.7	61.6	60.8	64.3
Average number of employees	55.7	55.2	55.4	47.0	38.9	38.9	39.6	46.5	46.3	42.9	41.4

+Adjusted for two-for-one stock split effective November 25, 1981.
‡Includes net expense of $20.5 million, or $.54 per share of common stock, resulting from accounting changes, principally to reflect the cost of substantially all domestic inventories at LIFO (last-in, first-out).

*Restated for accrual of compensated absences.
**After extraordinary items, net of tax, of $260 thousand or one cent per share of common stock.

Source: Borg-Warner Corporation, 1981 annual report.

Exhibit 3
Proposed Borg-Warner Creed, 1970

Borg-Warner Corporation is owned by the shareholders who supply its capital funds, but is responsible also to employees, customers, suppliers, and to society. Operating within a free enterprise economy, the corporation acknowledges its obligations to the following groups:

Obligations to Shareholders

To earn a return on their investment that compares favorably with other leading companies in our industries, enhancing over the long term the value of that investment. To pay out a fair proportion of income in dividends, consistent with the corporation's continuing need for capital for growth.

Obligations to Employees

To pay an adequate wage to each employee commensurate with his individual contribution to the corporation's work, and at least at the average level of the community where he is employed. To provide the best and safest possible working conditions. To give each Borg-Warner employee equal opportunity for personal achievement and recognition for such achievement. To provide a work environment in which initiative and creativity are recognized and rewarded.

Obligations to Customers

To develop, through skill, innovation and enterprise, products and services of the highest quality for the purpose intended, and sell them at a price competitive with other producers. To be guided in developing products by the needs of present and prospective customers. To strive always to be a reliable supplier, justifying a reputation for dependability and good service.

Obligations to Suppliers

To be a reliable customer, working with suppliers as business partners to ensure mutually satisfactory standards of quality and schedules for delivery. To follow business practices that are fair and responsible.

Obligations to Society

Shareholders, employees, customers and suppliers all are people who live within a society. To provide for the interests of all these groups, Borg-Warner is obligated to preserve that which it considers good for society, and to take the necessary steps, including the commitment of corporate resources, to improve it when practical.

Source: Draft company proposal, September 16, 1970.

Exhibit 4
Beré's Letter to Employees

Borg-Warner Corporation   June 23, 1976
200 South Michigan Avenue
Chicago, Illinois 60604
Telephone: (312) 663-2060

To: Borg-Warner Employees

In view of widespread reports of illegal or improper conduct by employees of public companies, you may have asked yourself: What standard of conduct does Borg-Warner expect of me as its representative?

In the past we have stated that our policy is to comply with the letter and spirit of all laws, wherever we operate. In addition, we will soon issue an expanded statement that reaffirms this policy and deals with political contributions and improper payments.

Such policies are concerned with laws and regulations, and therefore are relatively specific. However, the question itself is broader, relating to the ethical aspects of actions we take on Borg-Warner's behalf that might violate no law, but could violate our personal codes and consciences.

Borg-Warner's philosophy of management puts a premium on individual judgment. We believe most decisions should be made by managers close to the action—not by corporate decree. However, you should know what we expect of you in dealing with the moral and ethical content of decisions.

Briefly stated, it is this: *In Carrying Out Your Duties, Borg-Warner Does Not Want You To Act In Any Way Contrary To Your Ethical Principles.*

I realize that business is conducted by people whose personal standards vary widely. However, at Borg-Warner, we traditionally seek to hire only people of high moral standards and, believing we have done so, we trust you to maintain those standards in your service with us.

Should there be any doubt about the morality of any action you are considering on Borg-Warner's behalf, ask yourself these questions:

> Would I be willing to tell my family about the actions I am contemplating?
> Would I be willing to go before a community meeting, a congressional hearing, or any public forum, to describe the action?

In any case, if you would not be willing to do so, Borg-Warner would not want you to go ahead with the action on the assumption it would help the company.

I might make a final suggestion, based on the variations in interpreting ethical conduct, even among well-meaning people.

If you apply the above test and still have doubt about what to do, discuss it with others in the company for whom you have respect—whether peers, subordinates or superiors. I am sure this will help to guide you.

In summary: Your actions in representing Borg-Warner should be always lawful and proper, always capable of withstanding public disclosure, and always guided by your personal code of conduct.

I am confident each of you will abide by that standard.

Very truly yours,

James F. Beré
Chairman and Chief Executive Officer

Exhibit 5
Excerpts from Management Letters

There are several areas that I feel should be addressed in this policy statement:

1. The philosophy should be customer oriented so that the policy will clearly support our new "marketing" orientation and can serve as a sales tool.
2. The philosophy should as clearly as possible describe the kinds of businesses and products we wish to have in our corporate lineup.
3. Clearly define the financial objectives of the corporation.
4. Describe the interaction between the employee and the corporation. What is expected of the employee and what the employee can expect should be described at least in general terms.

I have purposely excluded a discussion of business ethics since our current policy seems completely clear on the subject.

— *a manager, Transportation Equipment Group*

In response to this request, I submit the following:

To create an environment which will assure the *long-term viability* of Borg-Warner or its successors by supplying *quality goods* and *services* in world markets that generate adequate capital to finance *growth* in *new, existing and emerging markets.*

— *a manager, Transportation Equipment Group*

Bill Kieschnick, Atlantic Richfield's new president, made the following value statements during a recent speech:

"Atlantic Richfield Company believes that to serve its owners, employees and society well, it must have a consistent and coherent set of values on which it premises all of its policies and actions."

— *a manager, Energy Equipment Group*

As management's relationship with employees is such an important ingredient in any formula for success, I propose to limit my further comments to one particular aspect that worries me—the apparent conflict between the company's support for QWL [quality of worklife] programmes and its policy of divestment where a business unit is not considered to fit into its long-term business strategy.

The fact is that, especially in Europe, there are large numbers of employees very worried and insecure about their future because they surmise that their units are up for sale or may be closed. The attitude of these employees is not unnaturally tempered by the circumstances, but would, I'm sure, be greatly improved if they could be assured that divestment is always the action of last resort.

Although probably a question of policy rather than philosophy, I do feel that a code of divestment practice is needed that employees will accept as fair and reasonable. As mentioned earlier, I also feel that an essential element of such a code would be that divestiture or closure will be an act of last resort, authorised only when every possible effort has been made to effect a "cure" by some other eans.

— *a manager, overseas corporate office*

(continued next page)

Exhibit 5 (continued)

In response to your request at the president's meeting that we set down some suggestions for "Principles of Borg-Warner," I have distilled my thoughts to the following:

Philosophy

Borg-Warner wants to be the *best company* in any area in which it operates. It wants to be *flexible* in attainment of its strategies. *Decisions* are to be made at the *lowest level* (i.e., nearest to the facts) with an *acceptance* of the fact that taking risks sometimes entails making errors.

The company's people will have a *trust* in each other and *share* in its successes and failures. *The company, through its people, will be dedicated to balanced service to its several constituencies*, i.e., stockholders, customers, suppliers, community and employees. Its people will *contribute* as they are able and be *credited* according to their contributions.

Goals

The company shall have goals of *profitable growth* in the value of its stockholders' investment, *personal development* of its people and a strong orientation to *improving service to its customers*.

— *a manager, Transportation Equipment Group*

Obviously, as an outside director, the potential for a meaningful contribution is limited, so I hope you will not be disappointed by my thin offering.

You have sponsored a high regard for the individual and good participation by all parties—as evidenced by the procedures in this program. There seems ample evidence of decentralization and participation, and perhaps more importantly, of a human face to the entire organization.

There is one area where I believe focus and consistency could be greater. As a descendant of a parts manufacturing operation, it is not surprising that Borg-Warner does not appear to demonstrate a high degree of marketing sensitivity. What seems to happen is that you at the center supply the strategic insights on market potential, which leads to acquisitions and divestitures. But in a way, these rather severe approaches are a substitution for marketing sensitivity and responsiveness in the traditional units. Perhaps organizational evolution and modernization would be a smoother process if it were more organic.

Accordingly, I suggest that somewhere in the beliefs and practices you have a fundamental statement of purpose that you succeed by finding customer needs and by responding to them with unique quality, service, and price.

— *an outside director*

Exhibit 6
Agenda for 1982 Chairman's Meeting

Monday, May 17		Tuesday, May 18		Wednesday, May 19	
7:45 A.M.	Continental breakfast	7:45 A.M.	Continental breakfast	7:45 A.M.	Continental Breakfast
8:30 A.M.	General meeting session Peter Valli, moderator	8:30 A.M.	General meeting session Bill Blalock, moderator	8:30 A.M.	General meeting session Len Harvey, moderator
	"Shared Values" Jim Beré		"Choices" Jerry Dempsey		"What Businesses Can Do" Amitai Etzioni, professor of sociology George Washington University, founder and director of Center for Policy Research
	"The Power of Belief" Professor John R. Hale University College, London		"What Americans Believe" Florence Skelly, president Yankelovich, Skelly & White, Inc.		
	"The Spirit of Democratic Capitalism" Michael Novak American Enterprise Institute		"Running Scared" Thomas J. Watson, Jr., chairman emeritus, IBM Corporation		"Beliefs at Work" Robert Patchin Director of productivity programs Northrop Corporation
	"Personal Values" Dr. Robert Kelly professor and consultant to business		"Gossamer Aircraft and Creativity" Dr. Paul MacCready, founder and president, AeroVironment, Inc.		"The Entrepreneurial Spirit" Bob LaRoche
					"Marketing and Moral Vision" Professor Peter E. Gibson Harvard University
	Lunch and afternoon free		Lunch and afternoon free		Closing remarks Jim Beré
					Lunch and afternoon free
6:00 P.M.	Reception	5:45 P.M.	Trip to Rawhide	6:00 P.M.	Reception
7:00 P.M.	Mexican fiesta			7:00 P.M.	Dinner dance

Jim Sawyer (A)

Dekkers L. Davidson,
research associate, prepared this
case under the supervision of
Kenneth E. Goodpaster as a
basis for class discussion rather
than to illustrate either effective
or ineffective handling of an
administrative situation.
Names of persons, institutions,
and locations have been
disguised.

It had been a long, hot summer day and Robert Taylor, vice president of finance, United Industries' Plastics Division (UIPD), was troubled and confused. An incident earlier that day had led him to file the following disciplinary report with Richard Hammond, UIPD's vice president of personnel.

To: Personnel file of Jim L. Sawyer

Date: July 9, 1980

After lunch (about 1:00 P.M.) I looked for Jim to discuss a problem. He was not back from lunch so I tried several times later and he still had not returned. At 3:20 P.M., on a hunch, I walked down to Gino's Bar and found Jim and Art Wentworth having an extended lunch, including beer, and enjoying some kind of dice game. I told them I wanted to speak with them in my office. I told Jim his behavior (extended lunch hour) was not in keeping with his position as a manager and that it was totally unacceptable. He apologized and admitted that he had been doing this at times over the past year. He said it would not recur.

E. M. Sanchez will speak with Art about this problem on July 10.

R. J. Taylor

Company Background

United Industries was a multinational corporation with headquarters in Cleveland, Ohio. Sales for 1980 were $2.36 billion with net earnings after taxes of $112.8 million. Sales resulted from four major operating groups: Air Conditioning ($520m), Automotive Equipment ($788m), Industrial Products ($458m), and Plastics ($594m). Because of its diversified activities, United Industries was a highly decentralized operation with many policy decisions delegated to each of the operating companies, particularly those associated with product development and personnel.

United Industries Plastics Division exemplified the independent spirit found within the corporation. Headquartered along the Ohio River in Huntington, Kentucky, UIPD was proud of its accomplishments. Its sales and earnings growth were at the top of its industry; furthermore, the company had recently introduced a new line of highly profitable plastic resins. Though the division was successfully driven by its marketing department, UIPD executives were especially proud of its employee orientation. As UIPD President Gordon Marshall put it, "The business *is* the people . . . my job is to get them excited about our goals."

Many people liked the fact that United Industries was a paternalistic employer. With over half of the 3,500 UIPD employees located in Huntington, United Industries was the town's major employer. Even though many of its competitors were closely located along the river, the town was a friendly place. The people enjoyed the business rivalry, and the competition actually fostered a strong spirit of community cooperation. It was a working town of 50,000 people who appreciated its rural identity and relative isolation.

Many people spent their entire lives in the Huntington area. After completing school, graduates could usually choose from a number of opportunities among local plastics manufacturers. Like its competition, United had a high percentage of home-grown personnel. UIPD was certainly not tied to the idea of only hiring local talent, however, and it often recruited outside the area for technical and managerial positions. Furthermore, United's corporate staff had always encouraged some interdivisional transfers to develop the management ranks in each of the company's divisions.

Gordon Marshall, 53, a Canadian by birth and educated as a chemical engineer, had spent 28 years with the firm before being named worldwide UIPD president in early 1980. He served the community as a director for the Huntington

Chamber of Commerce and the Huntington National Bank. He also acted as an adviser to a number of local small business enterprises. (See *Figure A* for the individuals described and their working relationships.)

Richard Hammond, 54, served as Marshall's second-in-command. He had been with the company for 18 years, serving in a variety of functional areas before being named vice president in 1972. Hammond was personally involved with almost every hiring decision as well as every employee termination. No UIPD employee could be fired until Hammond and Marshall were certain that the decision was a fair and just one. Hammond would often act as an advocate for the employee during such performance reviews. Because of this unusual high-level review, hiring choices were made with utmost care and consideration. Hammond believed that a decision to terminate an employee was the most drastic job decision any United manager would ever make. Hammond insisted that dismissals should never come as a surprise to any employee. He demanded that UIPD managers explicitly note and discuss performance weaknesses with employees during appraisal sessions. Then each worker would be given an honest chance to overcome weak points and to succeed at United.

Robert Taylor, 48, had spent 18 years with UIPD, serving in various accounting and financial positions. Edward Sanchez, 30, a Harvard Business School graduate, had joined UIPD in 1973 and served as controller, reporting to Robert Taylor. Jim Sawyer, 40, who also joined UIPD in 1973, was control evaluation manager and likewise reported directly to Taylor.

Jim Sawyer

Jim Sawyer was considered an intelligent and highly ambitious individual who had potential for growth at United Industries. He joined UIPD in March 1973 after nine years of related industrial experience and assumed the job of business analyst within the finance department. Within three years, Sawyer was promoted to credit manager responsible for managing new and existing credit accounts. Although he was seen as a capable credit manager, his aggressive manner alienated some clients accustomed to a more easygoing relationship with people at UIPD. When antagonisms developed between Sawyer and his supervisor at that time, Barbara

Figure A
Partial Organization Chart, Plastics Division

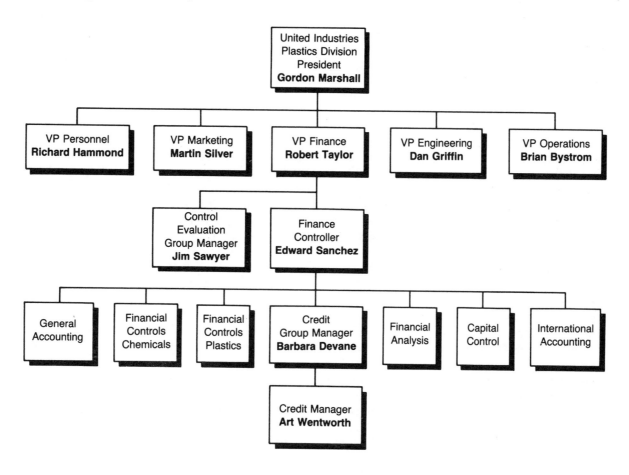

Devane, Taylor decided to transfer him to another group within the department. Sawyer had expressed some interest in securing a marketing assignment, but management believed that his career would develop with additional experience in the finance area.

In March 1979 Sawyer was appointed control evaluation manager reporting directly to Taylor. He was responsible for managing a small task force assigned to audit and review UIPD's operations and policies. According to Taylor, the group required minimal supervision from him, thus permitting Sawyer a great deal of individual discretion and freedom.

Signposts

The July incident at Gino's had irritated Taylor. He had not enjoyed an especially warm relationship with Sawyer, but nevertheless he recognized that Sawyer had significant potential for development. Jim was a quick thinker who was good with numbers and had a lot to offer the finance department. Inexplicably, however, his performance had begun to falter; he was not meeting deadlines and his work was barely meeting management's expectations.

Taylor had heard that Sawyer was having domestic difficulties and wondered whether this personal distraction explained his failure to meet certain business obligations. He also wondered if Sawyer was feeling trapped in his job; Taylor thought that Sawyer might still be angry about the lateral transfer from the previous year. He knew from experience that Sawyer was an intense person who could easily become frustrated. Sawyer had once written United's CEO imploring him to exert more pressure on corporate executives to implement the quality-of-work-life (QWL) program. This kind of end run around divisional management had been viewed as an impulsive act that had embarrassed both Sawyer and the company. As the summer progressed, Taylor became more alarmed as Sawyer missed work deadlines and occasionally arrived late for work on Monday mornings. Taylor wondered what Sawyer's problem was.

In addition to filing his July memorandum, Taylor had sought Hammond's professional guidance in trying to reverse Sawyer's performance setbacks. Hammond lived near Sawyer's home and had known his family since their arrival in Huntington. He had a polite relationship with Sawyer but they rarely met socially outside of the office. Hammond was fond of Sawyer's children, having come to know them in their teenage years as neighborhood newspaper carriers. He had occasionally talked with Sawyer's wife, Marion, when out for a walk around the neighborhood.

Hammond suspected that the trouble ran deeper than family problems. He recalled seeing Sawyer at a community meeting, where his breath smelled of whiskey. Hammond sometimes had lunch at Gino's and he remembered seeing the same group at the bar with a long line of beer cans before them. He also noticed Sawyer's lateness on Monday mornings and was concerned about performance slips. In addition, Hammond thought he detected a change in Sawyer's physical appearance; his palms and cheekbones appeared red and blotched. Something, Hammond realized, had gone wrong. Taylor and Hammond kept their apprehensions about Sawyer to themselves. They had talked with each other frequently in an effort to find the causes of Sawyer's difficulties, but neither was totally certain about what should or could be done to rectify the situation.

In mid-August 1980 Taylor departed for an overseas business trip and left Edward Sanchez in charge of the finance department. Meanwhile, Hammond continued to investigate the problem of alcoholism and sought professional advice from several public and private alcoholic treatment centers. Hammond had recently been forced to terminate a high-level clerical employee who had faltered on the job because of a drinking problem. The employee had denied having a problem with alcohol abuse and refused to accept any help or treatment. Fi-

nally, after repeated performance lapses, he was fired. Hammond distinctly remembered the words of one professional counselor: "People who are having problems with alcohol abuse don't wear a badge that tells everyone they are alcoholic. Correctly identifying the disease of alcoholism is the first step toward successful treatment." (*Exhibits 1, 2, and 3 contain literature about alcoholism that Hammond had obtained from local alcoholic treatment centers.*)

Friday afternoon before the Labor Day weekend Sawyer could not be found, and his desk had been left strewn with work papers. Sanchez had called an impromptu meeting to review a report for the corporate staff and he needed Sawyer's input. A secretary recalled seeing Sawyer earlier in the day but had no idea where he had gone. After searching UIPD's headquarters, Sanchez went to see Hammond. Hammond told Sanchez to stop searching while he took responsibility for locating Sawyer.

Hammond found Sawyer with another UIPD employee at Gino's Bar. Hammond walked into Gino's, made eye contact with Sawyer, then turned around and walked out the door. Sawyer's lunch partner, sensing trouble, ran back to his office to remind his supervisor, Sanchez, that he was on a legitimately scheduled vacation day. Sawyer, however, never returned to his desk that day.

Taylor returned from his overseas trip during the long Labor Day weekend. Hammond believed that the time had come to confront Sawyer with his suspicions. To prepare for their encounter once business resumed following the holiday, Hammond telephoned Taylor at home to tell him about the second incident at Gino's. Taylor was furious: "Why should I be concerned about Jim's problem when he doesn't appear concerned about it! I just don't need this problem. I know he's having personal difficulties, but how many chances can I give him?" Hammond shared this sense of exasperation but believed that the company should try to help Sawyer and his family.

It was Labor Day, September 1, 1980. Taylor and Hammond had to decide what to do about Jim Sawyer when he reported to work the next day. If they could not reach an agreement, they would have to take the matter directly to Marshall.

Exhibit 1
Facts on Alcoholism

Alcohol is America's favorite recreational drug. It is also the nation's number one drug of abuse. Alcohol is a mood changer, as are tranquilizers, heroin, cocaine, barbiturates, and amphetamines. The chronic alcoholic is physically and psychologically addicted.

In 1956, alcoholism was recognized by the American Medical Association as a disease with identifiable and progressive symptoms. This position is endorsed by the American Hospital Association, the American Bar Association, the American Psychiatric Association, and the World Health Organization.

Fifty-two percent of all male admissions to state mental hospitals suffer from alcohol-related problems.

There are an estimated 12-15 million alcoholic persons in America today. Of the 100 million persons in this country who drink, one in ten is prone to alcoholism.

Alcoholism is one of the top three killer diseases, along with cancer and heart disease. Persons afflicted with alcoholism are sick, as are people who suffer from heart disease or cancer. If not treated, alcoholism ends in permanent mental damage, physical incapacity, or early death.

The average alcoholic is in his or her mid-forties with a responsible job and a family. Fewer than 5 percent of all alcoholics are found on Skid Row. Ninety-five percent are employed or employable, like many people you see every day.

Fifty percent of all fatal accidents occurring on the roads involve alcohol, and half of these involve an alcoholic.

Alcoholism involves both sexes and crosses all ethnic, religious, economic and sociocultural groups. While there are as many women alcoholics as there are men, only 25 percent of the women receive treatment.

Thirty-one percent of those who take their own lives are alcoholics. The suicide rate among alcoholics is 58 times that of the general population.

Alcoholism costs the nation $54.1 billion annually. Industry alone picks up a $25.2 billion tab for lost work time, health and welfare service benefits, property damage, medical expenses, and overhead costs of insurance and wage losses.

Eighty percent of all violence in the American home is alcohol related.

Children of alcoholic parents are 50 percent more likely to marry an alcoholic person.

Alcoholism is a treatable disease.

Education, early detection, and community treatment facilities are the greatest forces operating today for the control and reduction of alcoholism. Prevention and intervention through programs of information and education have been primary objectives of the National Council on Alcoholism since its founding in 1944.

Source: Statistics were taken from material published by the National Institute on Alcohol Abuse and Alcoholism (NIAAA) 1977–1978.

Exhibit 2

The Progression and Recovery of the Alcoholic in the Disease of Alcoholism

To be read from left to right.

Progression

Urgency of First Drinks
Feelings of Guilt
Memory Blackouts Increase
Drinking Bolstered with Excuses
Grandiose and Aggressive Behavior
Efforts to Control Fail Repeatedly
Tries Geographical Escapes
Family and Friends Avoided
Loss of Ordinary Will Power
Tremors and Early Morning Drinks
Decrease in Alcohol Tolerance
Onset of Lengthy Intoxications
Moral Deterioration
Impaired Thinking
Drinking with Inferiors
Indefinable Fears
Unable to Initiate Action
Obsession with Drinking
Vague Spiritual Desires
All Alibis Exhausted
Complete Defeat Admitted

Occasional Relief Drinking
Constant Relief Drinking Commences
Increase in Alcohol Tolerance
Onset of Memory Blackouts
Surreptitious Drinking
Increasing Dependence on Alcohol
Unable to Discuss Problem
Decrease of Ability to Stop Drinking When Others Do So
Persistent Remorse
Promises and Resolutions Fail
Loss of Other Interests
Work and Money Troubles
Unreasonable Resentments
Neglect of Food
Physical Deterioration

Crucial Phase

Chronic Phase

Obsessive Drinking Continues in Vicious Circles

Recovery

Enlightened and Interesting Way of Life Opens Up with Road Ahead to Higher Levels than Ever Before

Increasing Tolerance
Contentment in Sobriety
Confidence of Employers
Appreciation of Real Values
Rebirth of Ideals
New Interests Develop
Adjustment to Family Needs
Desire to Escape Goes
Return of Self-Esteem
Diminishing Fears of the Unknown Future
Appreciation of Possibilities of New Way of Life

Group Therapy and Mutual Help Continue
Rationalizations Recognized
Care of Personal Appearance
First Steps Towards Economic Stability
Increase of Emotional Control
Facts Faced with Courage
New Circle of Stable Friends
Family and Friends Appreciate Efforts
Natural Rest and Sleep
Realistic Thinking
Regular Nourishment Taken

Rehabilitation

Start of Group Therapy
Onset of New Hope
Physical Overhaul by Doctor
Spiritual Needs Examined
Right Thinking Begins
Takes Stock of Self
Meets Normal and Happy Former Addicts
Stops Taking Alcohol
Told Addiction Can be Arrested
Learns Alcoholism is an Illness
Honest Desire for Help

Source: Comprehensive Care Corporation, Copyright © 1982. Reprinted by permission.

Exhibit 3

Alcoholism is hurting your business

It cost business $54.2 billion a year

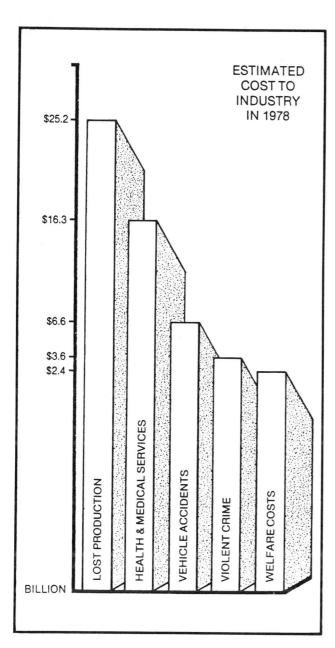

ESTIMATED COST TO INDUSTRY IN 1978

$25.2
$16.3
$6.6
$3.6
$2.4

LOST PRODUCTION — HEALTH & MEDICAL SERVICES — VEHICLE ACCIDENTS — VIOLENT CRIME — WELFARE COSTS

BILLION

All the alcoholics in the world aren't on Skid Row. One out of every 10 employed persons is an alcoholic.

It means:

Inefficiency
Increased absenteeism
Overtime pay
Faulty decision making
More on-the-job accidents
Low employee morale

The effects of alcoholism can cost your company an additional 25 percent of each alcoholic employee's salary. Despite the extra costs, however, alcoholic employees are often the most valued in the organization. They usually average 15-30 years with the company, and the cost to replace their skills, expertise and experience is incalculable.

Like cancer and diabetes, alcoholism is a disease. It is not a moral issue. Alcoholism can be treated and controlled.

Treating and retaining the alcoholic employee is good business. Every dollar your company invests in employee assistance programs for the problem drinker yields at least a $17 return. Alcoholic treatment expenses are covered by most health insurance policies. For the price of the premium you are probably already paying, you can correct the damage done to the bottom line of your profit and loss statement by alcoholism.

Source: Comprehensive Care Corporation, Copyright © 1982. Reprinted by permission.

Harvard Business School

383—074

To Employers

"To Employers" is a reprint of chapter 10 from Alcoholics Anonymous, the "blue book" that has served as a basic text for A.A. members since it was originally published in 1939. It should be read in that context. Alcoholics Anonymous is a fellowship of men and women whose primary purpose is to help its members stay sober and to help other alcoholics achieve sobriety. A.A. is a self-supporting group that is open to anyone who has a desire to stop drinking. A.A. is not allied with any sect, denomination, political group, organization, or institution.

Among many employers nowadays, we think of one member who has spent much of his life in the world of big business. He has hired and fired hundreds of men. He knows the alcoholic as the employer sees him. His present views ought to prove exceptionally useful to businessmen everywhere.

But let him tell you:

I was at one time assistant manager of a corporation department employing sixty-six hundred men. One day my secretary came in saying that Mr. B— insisted on speaking with me. I told her to say that I was not interested. I had warned him several times that he had but one more chance. Not long afterward he had called me from Hartford on two successive days, so drunk he could hardly speak. I told him he was through—finally and forever.

My secretary returned to say that it was not Mr. B— on the phone; it was Mr. B—'s brother, and he wished to give me a message. I still expected a plea for clemency, but these words came through the receiver: "I just wanted to tell you Paul jumped from a hotel window in Hartford last Saturday. He left us a note saying you were the best boss he ever had, and that you were not to blame in any way."

Another time, as I opened a letter which lay on my desk, a newspaper clipping fell out. It was the obituary of one of the best salesmen I ever had. After two weeks of drinking, he had placed his toe on the trigger of a loaded shotgun—the barrel was in his mouth. I had discharged him for drinking six weeks before.

Still another experience: A woman's voice came faintly over long distance from Virginia. She wanted to know if her husband's company insurance was still in force. Four days before he had hanged himself in his woodshed. I had been obliged to discharge him for drinking, though he was brilliant, alert, and one of the best organizers I have ever known.

Note: Reprinted with permission from Alcoholics Anonymous World Services, Inc., New York, N.Y., Copyright © 1939, 1955, 1976. All rights reserved.

Here were three exceptional men lost to this world because I did not understand alcoholism as I do now. What irony—I became an alcoholic myself! And but for the intervention of an understanding person, I might have followed in their footsteps. My downfall cost the business community unknown thousands of dollars, for it takes real money to train a man for an executive position. This kind of waste goes on unabated. We think the business fabric is shot through with a situation which might be helped by better understanding all around.

Nearly every modern employer feels a moral responsibility for the well-being of his help, and he tries to meet these responsibilities. That he has not always done so for the alcoholic is easily understood. To him the alcoholic has often seemed a fool of the first magnitude. Because of the employee's special ability, or of his own strong personal attachment to him, the employer has sometimes kept such a man at work long beyond a reasonable period. Some employers have tried every known remedy. In only a few instances has there been a lack of patience and tolerance. And we, who have imposed on the best of employers, can scarcely blame them if they have been short with us.

Here, for instance, is a typical example: An officer of one of the largest banking institutions in America knows I no longer drink. One day he told me about an executive of the same bank who, from his description, was undoubtedly alcoholic. This seemed to me like an opportunity to be helpful, so I spent two hours talking about alcoholism, the malady, and described the symptoms and results as well as I could. His comment was, "Very interesting. But I'm sure this man is done drinking. He has just returned from a three-months leave of absence, has taken a cure, looks fine, and to clinch the matter, the board of directors told him this was his last chance."

The only answer I could make was that if the man followed the usual pattern, he would go on a bigger bust than ever. I felt this was inevitable and wondered if the bank was doing the man an injustice. Why not bring him into contact with some of our alcoholic crowd? He might have a chance. I pointed out that I had had nothing to drink whatever for three years, and this in the face of difficulties that would have made nine out of ten men drink their heads off. Why not at least afford him an opportunity to hear my story? "Oh, no," said my friend, "This chap is either through with liquor, or he is minus a job. If he has your will power and guts, he will make the grade."

I wanted to throw up my hands in discouragement, for I saw that I had failed to help my banker friend understand. He simply could not believe that his brother-executive suffered from a serious illness. There was nothing to do but wait.

Presently the man did slip and was fired. Following his discharge, we contacted him. Without much ado, he accepted the principles and procedure that had helped us. He is undoubtedly on the road to recovery. To me, this incident illustrates lack of understanding as to what really ails the alcoholic, and lack of knowledge as to what part employers might profitably take in salvaging their sick employees.

If you desire to help it might be well to disregard your own drinking, or lack of it. Whether you are a hard drinker, a moderate drinker or a teetotaler, you may have some pretty strong opinions, perhaps prejudices. Those who drink moderately may be more annoyed with an alcoholic than a total abstainer would be. Drinking occasionally, and understanding your own reactions, it is possible for you to become quite sure of many things which, so far as the alcoholic is concerned, are not always so. As a moderate drinker, you can take your liquor or leave it alone. Whenever you want to, you control your drinking. Of an evening, you can go on a mild bender, get up in the morning, shake your head and go to business. To you, liquor is no real problem. You cannot see why it should be to anyone else, save the spineless and stupid.

When dealing with an alcoholic, there may be a natural annoyance that a man could be so weak, stupid and irresponsible. Even when you understand the malady better, you may feel this feeling rising.

A look at the alcoholic in your organization is many times illuminating. Is he not usually brilliant, fast-thinking, imaginative and likeable? When sober, does he not work hard and have a knack of getting things done? If he had these qualities and did not drink would he be worth retaining? Should he have the same consideration as other ailing employees? Is he worth salvaging? If your decision is yes, whether the reason be humanitarian or business or both, then the following suggestions may be helpful.

Can you discard the feeling that you are dealing only with habit, with stubbornness, or a weak will? If this presents difficulty, re-reading chapters two and three, where the alcoholic sickness is discussed at length might be worth while. You, as a business man, want to know the necessities before considering the result. If you concede that your employee is ill, can he be forgiven for what he has done in the past? Can his past absurdities be forgotten? Can it be appreciated that he has been a victim of crooked thinking, directly caused by the action of alcohol on his brain?

I well remember the shock I received when a prominent doctor in Chicago told me of cases where pressure of the spinal fluid actually ruptured the brain. No wonder an alcoholic is strangely irrational. Who wouldn't be, with such a fevered brain? Normal drinkers are not so affected, nor can they understand the aberrations of the alcoholic.

Your man has probably been trying to conceal a number of scrapes, perhaps pretty messy ones. They may be disgusting. You may be at a loss to understand how such a seemingly above-board chap could be so involved. But these scrapes can generally be charged, no matter how bad, to the abnormal action of alcohol on his mind. When drinking, or getting over a bout, an alcoholic, sometimes the model of honesty when normal, will do incredible things. Afterward, his revulsion will be terrible. Nearly always, these antics indicate nothing more than temporary conditions.

This is not to say that all alcoholics are honest and upright when not drinking. Of course that isn't so, and such people often may impose on you. Seeing your attempt to understand and help, some men will try to take advantage of your kindness. If you are sure your man does not want to stop, he may as well be discharged, the sooner the better. You are not doing him a favor by keeping him on. Firing such an individual may prove a blessing to him. It may be just the jolt he needs. I know, in my own particular case, that nothing my company could have done would have stopped me for, so long as I was able to hold my position, I could not possibly realize how serious my situation was. Had they fired me first, and had they then taken steps to see that I was presented with the solution contained in this book, I might have returned to them six months later, a well man.

But there are many men who want to stop, and with them you can go far. Your understanding treatment of their cases will pay dividends.

Perhaps you have such a man in mind. He wants to quit drinking and you want to help him, even if it be only a matter of good business. You now know more about alcoholism. You can see that he is mentally and physically sick. You are willing to overlook his past performances. Suppose an approach is made something like this:

State that you know about his drinking, and that it must stop. You might say you appreciate his abilities, would like to keep him, but cannot if he continues to drink. A firm attitude at this point has helped many of us.

Next he can be assured that you do not intend to lecture, moralize, or condemn; that if this was done formerly, it was because of misunderstanding. If possible express a lack of hard feeling toward him. At this point, it might be well to explain alcoholism, the illness. Say that you believe he is a gravely ill person, with this qualification—being perhaps fatally ill, does he want to get well? You ask, because many alcoholics, being warped and drugged, do not want to quit. But does he? Will he take every necessary step, submit to anything to get well, to stop drinking forever?

If he says yes, does he really mean it, or down inside does he think he is fooling you, and that after rest and treatment he will be able to get away with a few drinks now and then? We believe a man should be thoroughly probed on these points. Be satisfied he is not deceiving himself or you.

Whether you mention this book is a matter for your discretion. If he temporizes and still thinks he can ever drink again, even beer, he might as well be discharged after the next bender which, if an alcoholic, he is almost certain to have. He should understand that emphatically. Either you are dealing with a man who can and will get well or you are not. If not, why waste time with him? This may seem severe, but it is usually the best course.

After satisfying yourself that your man wants to recover and that he will go to any extreme to do so, you may suggest a definite course of action. For most alcoholics who are drinking, or who are just getting over a spree, a certain amount of physical treatment is desirable, even imperative. The matter of physical treatment should, of course, be referred to your own doctor. Whatever the method, its object is to thoroughly clear mind and body of the effects of alcohol. In competent hands, this seldom takes long nor is it very expensive. Your man will fare better if placed in such physical condition that he can think straight and no longer craves liquor. If you propose such a procedure to him, it may be necessary to advance the cost of treatment, but we believe it should be made plain that any expense will later be deducted from his pay. It is better for him to feel fully responsible.

If your man accepts your offer, it should be pointed out that physical treatment is but a small part of the picture. Though you are providing him with the best possible medical attention, he should understand that he must undergo a change of heart. To get over drinking will require a transformation of thought and attitude. We all had to place recovery above everything, for without recovery we would have lost both home and business.

Can you have every confidence in his ability to recover? While on the subject of confidence, can you adopt the attitude that so far as you are concerned this will be a strictly personal matter, that his alcoholic derelictions, the treatment about to be undertaken, will never be discussed without his consent? It might be well to have a long chat with him on his return.

To return to the subject matter of this book: It contains full suggestions by which the employee may solve his problem. To you, some of the ideas which it contains are novel. Perhaps you are not quite in sympathy with the approach we suggest. By no means do we offer it as the last word on this subject, but so far as we are concerned, it has worked with us. After all, are you not looking for results rather than methods? Whether your employee likes it or not, he will learn the grim truth about alcoholism. That won't hurt him a bit, even though he does not go for this remedy.

We suggest you draw the book to the attention of the doctor who is to attend your patient during treatment. If the book is read the moment the patient is able, while acutely depressed, realization of his condition may come to him.

We hope the doctor will tell the patient the truth about his condition, whatever that happens to be. When the man is presented with this volume it is best that no one tell him he must abide by its suggestions. The man must decide for himself.

You are betting, of course, that your changed attitude plus the contents of this book will turn the trick. In some cases it will, and in others it may not. But we think that if you persevere, the percentage of successes will gratify you. As our work spreads and our numbers increase, we hope your employees may be put in personal contact with some of us. Meanwhile, we are sure a great deal can be accomplished by the use of the book alone.

On your employee's return, talk with him. Ask him if he thinks he has the answer. If he feels free to discuss his problems with you, if he knows you understand and will not be upset by anything he wishes to say, he will probably be off to a fast start.

In this connection, can you remain undisturbed if the man proceeds to tell you shocking things? He may, for example, reveal that he has padded his expense account or that he has planned to take your best customers away from you. In fact, he may say almost anything if he has accepted our solution which, as you know, demands rigorous honesty. Can you charge this off as you would a bad account and start fresh with him? If he owes you money you may wish to make terms.

If he speaks of his home situation, you can undoubtedly make helpful suggestions. Can he talk frankly with you so long as he does not bear business tales or criticize his associates? With this kind of employee such an attitude will command undying loyalty.

The greatest enemies of us alcoholics are resentment, jealousy, envy, frustration, and fear. Wherever men are gathered together in business there will be rivalries and, arising out of these, a certain amount of office politics. Sometimes we alcoholics have an idea that people are trying to pull us down. Often this is not so at all. But sometimes our drinking will be used politically.

One instance comes to mind in which a malicious individual was always making friendly little jokes about an alcoholic's drinking exploits. In this way he was slyly carrying tales. In another case, an alcoholic was sent to a hospital for treatment. Only a few knew of it at first but, within a short time, it was billboarded throughout the entire company. Naturally this sort of thing decreased the man's chance of recovery. The employer can many times protect the victim from this kind of talk. The employer cannot play favorites, but he can always defend a man from needless provocation and unfair criticism.

As a class, alcoholics are energetic people. They work hard and they play hard. Your man should be on his mettle to make good. Being somewhat weakened, and faced with physical and mental readjustment to a life which knows no alcohol, he may overdo. You may have to curb his desire to work sixteen hours a day. You may need to encourage him to play once in a while. He may wish to do a lot for other alcoholics and something of the sort may come up during business hours. A reasonable amount of latitude will be helpful. This work is necessary to maintain his sobriety.

After your man has gone along without drinking for a few months, you may be able to make use of his services with other employees who are giving you the alcoholic run-around—provided, of course, they are willing to have a third party in the picture. An alcoholic who has recovered, but holds a relatively unimportant job, can talk to a man with a better position. Being on a radically different basis of life, he will never take advantage of the situation.

Your man may be trusted. Long experience with alcoholic excuses naturally arouses suspicion. When his wife next calls saying he is sick, you might jump to the conclusion he is drunk. If he is, and is still trying to recover, he will tell you about it even if it means the loss of his job. For he knows he must be honest if he would live at all. He will appreciate knowing you are not bothering your head about him, that you are not suspicious nor are you trying to run his life so he will be shielded from temptation to drink. If he is conscientiously following the program of recovery he can go anywhere your business may call him.

In case he does stumble, even once, you will have to decide whether to let him go. If you are sure he doesn't mean business, there is no doubt you should discharge him. If, on the contrary, you are sure he is doing his utmost, you may wish to give him another chance. But you should feel under no obligation to keep him on, for your obligation has been well discharged already.

There is another thing you might wish to do. If your organization is a large one, your junior executives might be provided with this book. You might let them know you have no quarrel with the alcoholics of your organization. These juniors are often in a difficult position. Men under them are frequently their friends. So, for one reason or another, they cover these men, hoping matters will take a turn for the better. They often jeopardize their own positions by trying to help serious drinkers who should have been fired long ago, or else given an opportunity to get well.

After reading this book, a junior executive can go to such a man and say approximately this, "Look here, Ed. Do you want to stop drinking or not? You put me on the spot every time you get drunk. It isn't fair to me or the firm. I have been learning something about alcoholism. If you are an alcoholic, you are a mighty sick man. You act like one. The firm wants to help you get over it, and if you are interested, there is a way out. If you take it, your past will be forgotten and the fact that you went away for treatment will not be mentioned. But if you cannot or will not stop drinking, I think you ought to resign."

Your junior executive may not agree with the contents of our book. He need not, and often should not show it to his alcoholic prospect. But at least he will understand the problem and will no longer be misled by ordinary promises. He will be able to take a position with such a man which is eminently fair and square. He will have no further reason for covering up an alcoholic employee.

It boils right down to this: No man should be fired just because he is alcoholic. If he wants to stop, he should be afforded a real chance. If he cannot or does not want to stop, he should be discharged. The exceptions are few.

We think this method of approach will accomplish several things. It will permit the rehabilitation of good men. At the same time you will feel no reluctance to rid yourself of those who cannot or will not stop. Alcoholism may be causing your organization considerable damage in its waste of time, men and reputation. We hope our suggestions will help you plug up this sometimes serious leak. We think we are sensible when we urge that you stop this waste and give your worthwhile man a chance.

The other day an approach was made to the vice president of a large industrial concern. He remarked: "I'm mighty glad you fellows got over your drinking. But the policy of this company is not to interfere with the habits of our employees. If a man drinks so much that his job suffers, we fire him. I don't see how you can be of any help to us for, as you see, we don't have any alcoholic problem." This same company spends millions for research every year. Their cost of production is figured to a fine decimal point. They have recreational facilities. There is company insurance. There is a real interest, both humanitarian and business, in the well-being of employees. But alcoholism—well, they just don't believe they have it.

Perhaps this is a typical attitude. We, who have collectively seen a great deal of business life, at least from the alcoholic angle, had to smile at this gentleman's sincere opinion. He might be shocked if he knew how much alcoholism is costing his organization a year. That company may harbor many actual or potential alcoholics. We believe that managers of large enterprises often have little idea how prevalent this problem is. Even if you feel your organization has no alcoholic problem, it might pay to take another look down the line. You may make some interesting discoveries.

Of course, this chapter refers to alcoholics, sick people, deranged men. What our friend, the vice president, had in mind was the habitual or whoopee drinker. As to them, his policy is undoubtedly sound, but he did not distinguish between such people and the alcoholic.

It is not to be expected that an alcoholic employee will receive a disproportionate amount of time and attention. He should not be made a favorite. The right kind of man, the kind who recovers, will not want this sort of thing. He will not impose. Far from it. He will work like the devil and thank you to his dying day.

Today I own a little company. There are two alcoholic employees, who produce as much as five normal salesmen. But why not? They have a new attitude, and they have been saved from a living death. I have enjoyed every moment spent in getting them straightened out.

Consolidated Foods Corporation (A)

Kenneth E. Goodpaster
*prepared this case as the basis
for class discussion rather than
to illustrate either effective or
ineffective handling of an
administrative situation.*

Much like individual citizens, Consolidated Foods has an obligation to act in a socially responsible manner. In addition, we are keenly aware of the votes cast each day by consumers through their purchase decisions in our extremely competitive marketplace. Thus, your comments are taken seriously into account.

Corporate response to consumer ad complaint

It was mid-June 1981 and top management at Consolidated Foods Corporation (CFC) in Chicago was concerned about consumer complaints and threatened boycotts. Some of these concerns related to the TV and print ad content of its recently acquired Hanes division and others related to sponsoring TV programs thought to portray excessive sex or violence. The tactics of the organized groups had become progressively more sophisticated, evolving from simple letter-writing campaigns to elaborate TV monitoring and publicity efforts. In addition the targets of the groups had shifted from the networks to advertisers and their parent companies.

John H. Bryan, Jr., chief executive officer of CFC, had been receiving numerous individual consumer complaint letters as well as communications from organized groups. Like many of the people in the civic and religious groups forming the coalition, Bryan was raised in the conservative Christian South. He shared many of the protesters' values. Yet his corporate role demanded that he look at the issues more broadly. He did not watch much television, though on occasion he had been dismayed by what was passing for entertainment on the networks. Sex and violence were being depicted with increasing boldness to attract viewers and ultimately to sell consumer products.

On his desk were several documents, including a copy of the fall 1980 results of a TV monitoring campaign organized by the National Federation for Decency. Though Consolidated Foods was not mentioned among the sponsors of offending programs, it received top billing among "Users of Sex in Commercials," and Bryan's name and home address were listed with those of other chief executive officers (see *Exhibit 1*). There was also a memorandum from the recently formed Coalition for Better Television listing Consolidated Foods interim scores in the latest monitoring effort (see *Exhibit 2*). The memorandum clearly implied that a boycott was likely for those whose scores did not measure up. Finally, there was a copy of a policy statement on advertising that had just been passed by the Public Responsibility Committee of Consolidated's board of directors (see *Exhibit 3*).

Bryan reflected on these materials before him, wondering what course of action to take: What could or should the corporation do that it had not already done? Obviously, it was not in the interest of Consolidated Foods or any of its operating units to advertise in ways that would lose rather than gain sales. General guidelines pertaining to truthfulness and good taste in ads and media had been in place for years in several of the operating units. Moreover elaborate consumer testing of ads, though not directly aimed at measuring variables like offensiveness, was almost certain to pick up information that would signal any of these problems. As a general rule, Bryan believed that direct corporate involvement in division-level policy on such matters was inappropriate and that the Hanes division was doing a responsible job. He also believed that the threat of a well-orchestrated boycott of Hanes products, and possibly other Consolidated Foods products, was a serious matter.

Corporation Background

Consolidated Foods Corporation had grown during its 42-year history from a small Baltimore distributor of sugar, coffee, and tea to a $5.6 billion diversified company active in three major business segments: consumer packaged goods, food services, and consumer direct sales. Its founder, Nathan Cummings, guided the company through complex acquisitions and divestitures for nearly 30 years, retiring to the role of honorary chairman of the board in 1968. (See *Exhibit 4* for a brief chronology of the company.)

Years of uninterrupted gains came to a halt during the 1973–1974 fiscal year; then in FY 1975, earnings fell dramatically. The stock, which had traded as high as $51 a few years previously, bottomed out at $10½. The chairman resigned in February 1975 and Bryan, age 38, president of the company, became chief executive officer. Bryan had come to CFC's headquarters on April 1, 1974, from the position of president of the Mississippi-based Bryan Foods division. John J. Cardwell, who joined the company in mid-1976 as president, spoke of Bryan in an interview: "[He] took a number of write-downs, established an internal audit group at the headquarters, sold off a few furniture companies and otherwise set the stage for the subsequent turnaround." FY 1976 already began to show the results of the new strategy. In FY 1977 67% of the operating units were generating a return on net operating assets below 24%. By FY 1982, fewer than 16% of the operating units would be earning below the 24% return rate. At about the midpoint of the turnaround period, 1976–1981, Consolidated Foods added a major element to its consumer product mix by acquiring the Hanes Corporation of Winston-Salem, North Carolina.

Hanes Group

Hanes Corporation was formed in 1965 by the merger to two successful companies, Hanes Hosiery Mills and P. H. Hanes Knitting Company, both headquartered in Winston-Salem. A market-oriented consumer products company, its line included women's seamless hosiery, support hosiery, and panty hose; brassieres, girdles, swim wear, and cosmetics; men's and boys' underwear, casual wear, knit sport shirts, sweaters, and socks. Among the better-known brand names for Hanes products were Hanes and L'eggs hosiery, Bali bras, L'erin cosmetics, and Hanes underwear.

Hanes Corporation had 5 operating units, 23 manufacturing plants, and more than 13,000 employees in North Carolina, South Carolina, Virginia, Pennsylvania, New Mexico, Puerto Rico, Mexico, and the Dominican Republic. The corporation also operated an extensive system of customer service centers and warehouses in strategic locations throughout the United States, as well as New York sales offices. International trade specialists conducted export sales, overseas market development, and foreign licensing for Hanes products.

Hanes hosiery was a pioneer in the production and marketing of seamless nylon hosiery for women and was generally credited with being the principal force in the industry's change from full-fashioned (seamed) to seamless hosiery. Similarly, Hanes hosiery was credited with being the first major hosiery manufacturer and marketer to recognize the potential of a first-quality, nationally advertised brand of hosiery products in food and drug stores. This brand, L'eggs, was introduced into four test markets in March 1970, and in less than two years, it became the leading U.S. manufacturer's brand. By 1979 L'eggs enjoyed a 30% share of the $1.5 billion hosiery market.

Consolidated Foods' annual report for 1979 described the Hanes acquisition: "[It provides] a strong consumer packaged goods company that fits well with the corporation's other packaged goods businesses. Its orientation is toward high margin products with strong brand identification, supported by heavy advertising and aggressive promotion. In addition, Hanes capitalizes on the trend of women purchasing more nongrocery items at the grocery store."

At the completion of the acquisition in January 1979, Hanes Corporation was combined with Aris (gloves), Canadelle (brassieres), and Sirena (swimwear) to form the Hanes Group. Robert E. Elberson, former president and chief executive officer of Hanes Corporation, was made an executive vice president and a director of Consolidated Foods, with responsibility for the Hanes Group and three other operating units. (Financial information on CFC and an organization chart appear as *Exhibits 5* and *6*.)

By 1981 Consolidated Foods had met most of its turnaround goals and was planning modest shifts in corporate organization that would signal less emphasis on acquisition and more corporate participation in guiding internal growth. In an interview Cardwell described this new orientation:

All our businesses are more execution-sensitive than strategy-sensitive. (Maybe all businesses are.) But that means, if we are fully to discharge our corporate responsibilities, that the corporate center must have a considerable involvement in execution, and not limit itself to providing only broad direc-

tion and ex-post review. In effect, we have completed the first phase of corporate redirection, and are now in our "second act." That act focuses almost exclusively on growth from within; hence the necessity of now paying greatly increased attention to execution; hence the requirement for a more directive style of management and a more prominent corporate presence.

Advertising at Hanes

For many years advertising had played a central role in the marketing of Hanes products. And with the acquisition of Hanes, advertising began to be a much more important factor in the business of Consolidated Foods. Hanes expenditures on advertising and promotion represented about one-third of total corporate spending in this category.

The development and placement of TV commercials and print ads at Hanes followed a pattern widely used among consumer packaged goods companies. Strategic marketing decisions at company headquarters in Winston-Salem led to product-related positioning statements that were shared with advertising agency teams in New York.

Dancer, Fitzgerald, Sample (DFS), for example, was one of a small number of major agencies used by the Hanes Group. It had responsibility for several Hanes products, including L'eggs hosiery. Using the positioning statements from Hanes, DFS would develop more focused advertising copy and creative ideas for both TV commercials and print ads; then Hanes management would select from DFS's proposals. At this stage a typical TV commercial was presented as a storyboard—a series of 10–20 drawings depicting image and voice messages to guide further production.

Selected storyboards were then rendered animatics—cartoon-like videotapes suitable for market testing. This stage was important because it kept investment manageable ($5,000–10,000) by comparison with finished commercials ($100,000–150,000).

Animatics were then market tested in various ways. "Ad labs" were convened in which groups (women in the case of Hanes hosiery) would be asked to give their reactions to the animated commercials. If testing results at this stage were positive, then a commercial would be produced in final (nonanimated) form. Further local broadcast testing of the final commercial assessed impact and recall before advertising placement, the last phase of the process, was completed.

Hanes management turned to DFS for guidance on ad placement. Demographic statistics and target, frequency, and reach information would be used to determine appropriate local and network time slots. Prime-time network programming would also be prescreened (when possible) by DFS staff to assure compliance with Hanes advertising guidelines. Finally, the commercial would run in its carefully selected program environment.

Corporate and Group Advertising Policies

Since October 1977 Consolidated Foods had a Public Responsibility Committee (PRC) of the board of directors. Beyond responsibility for corporate contributions, the "Statement of Purpose" of the committee provided that "oversight and guidance" be exercised "in the areas of employee safety and equal employment opportunity programs and performance." The committee also undertook any activities "deemed necessary and advisable to monitor or improve the corporation acting in the public interest."[1]

At its August 1980 meeting, the PRC reviewed existing advertising guidelines at three operating companies with a view toward preparing a general corporate advertising policy. It was thought that such a statement could be used in answering inquiries or complaints on advertising. A statement was approved by the PRC at its January 1981 meeting and was to be conveyed to key operating unit managers by Bryan.

Since the mid-1970s Hanes Corporation had maintained its own written guidelines on advertising placement, pertaining to both TV programming and print media. The implementation of these guidelines was left primarily to the advertising agencies employed by the corporation, but the agencies were advised that from time to time they would be requested to demonstrate "that their judgment coincides with that of Hanes Corporation senior management." (The guidelines in effect in June 1981 are reproduced as *Exhibit 7.*)

---

1. Minutes of Public Responsibility Committee meeting, April 1978.

Pressures During 1980

During 1980 Hanes management as well as Bryan at corporate headquarters received increasing numbers of consumer complaints. Some of the letters dealt with ad content, expressing offense at commercial themes like "Gentlemen Prefer Hanes" and "Show Us Your Underalls." Others dealt with Hanes sponsorship of various TV programs thought to be too violent or too sexually permissive (e.g., "Dallas," "Charlie's Angels," "Three's Company," and certain TV movies). Similarities in style, content, and timing among some of the complaints made it clear that they were occasioned by organized groups' newsletters like those of the Joelton Church of Christ and the National Federation for Decency. Each letter received a formal response from top managers at Hanes as well as a response from communications staff at corporate headquarters.

In November 1980 Hanes management received a warning letter from the Reverend John Hurt, leader of the Joelton, Tennessee, Clean Up TV campaign. In essence, the letter threatened a boycott similar to one called by Rev. Hurt against General Foods and American Home Products. It referred to eight TV programs, several of which Hanes had sponsored in the past, implying that future sponsorship would result in a boycott of Hanes and other CFC products. The letter read in part:

> During the coming months, the shows . . . will continue to be monitored, and on a selected date, the first (suitable) sponsor whose ad is first to appear on each of these shows will immediately be selected and a nationwide boycott of all of their products begun without further warning. (In order to clarify this point, if a beer commercial, for example, is put on first, we shall simply bypass it and instead select the first suitable company whose ad appears on each program. Parent companies will also be held accountable for ads placed by their divisions.)
>
> Since our records indicate that your company has advertised on one or more of these shows within the past several months, this is your formal notice of our intended action. In view of the fact that the names of all of the companies who continue to help support these programs will probably also be made public even when a boycott is not involved, it would be to your advantage to

give serious consideration to selecting other programs which will not be in the public spotlight. Monitors from almost every state, however, will also regularly report on companies who help to sponsor any of the new shows which contain similar offensive material and appropriate action will be taken. This will include morally offensive movies and TV specials.

We are very hopeful that your company will see fit to make clear your genuine concern for moral decency and for the feelings of a very large segment of the public. The purpose of the campaign is not to remove programs from the air but to insist that they improve the moral content of their presentations.

Paul Fulton, general manager of the Hanes Group, did not respond to the letter, but subsequently no ads for Hanes products appeared on any of the eight programs. In an interview Fulton spoke of how he expressed his concern to corporate headquarters as well as to his immediate division subordinates: "I reviewed the situation in detail with Dancer-Fitzgerald-Sample with regard to its present impact and possible future implications. We are very concerned about what could develop out of this campaign, particularly if the Moral Majority becomes involved." Fulton went on to observe that avoidance of the eight programs in question would not "significantly limit our ability to effectively reach our consumers" so that reducing company exposure seemed to be the best course. "This position will obviously have to be reevaluated," he added, "if objectionable programs expand significantly."

Bryan had heard from the Reverend Donald Wildmon once before in September 1980 when he had written to Bryan about a specific program, "The Women's Room," that Consolidated Foods had helped sponsor. Bryan had not seen the program, but he could remember having inquired about its content and found that he shared Rev. Wildmon's dismay. Bryan could also remember thinking long and hard about

whether and how to reply to his letter. (The letter and reply appear as *Exhibits 8* and *9*.)

Pressures Mount, 1981

The wide distribution given to the fall 1980 ratings resulted in a new wave of complaint letters to both CFC and Hanes during March and April 1981. The number more than doubled from the previous year, and many of the letters were being sent directly to Bryan's home address.

Bryan was perplexed. He felt strongly that advertisers, for self-interest if for no other motive, had to exercise great care in choosing both ads and programs for sponsorship. Good taste and social awareness were essential to the marketing effectiveness of any consumer goods company. On the other hand, the products (women's hosiery) and target markets of the Hanes division seemed to demand a somewhat "sexy" image and a programming policy that reached the right customers. Nielsen ratings were important indicators of what the relevant public apparently enjoyed watching. The consumer was, in some sense, getting no more and no less than he or she wanted in this domain. Was it a corporation's place to do anything but follow the market? He knew that these organized efforts for better television would not just disappear. The social and political environment was ripe for a reaffirmation of traditional values. Yet as sympathetic as he was to some of the complaints about the quality of TV programming and even TV advertising, he did not think that the values of Consolidated Foods or its operating units differed from any but the most narrowly conservative values.

The idea of Consolidated Foods or Hanes being singled out for criticism by CBTV or any other group was not appealing. Neither was the idea of caving in to this kind of pressure. Bryan reread the documents on his desk as he thought about how to respond to the threat of a boycott.

Exhibit 1
Report of the Fall 1980 TV Monitoring Program—National Federation for Decency

SEX INCIDENTS PER HOUR

	1980	1979
ABC	9.38	5.64
CBS	7.44	5.51
NBC	4.11	4.96
Total Avg. Per Programming Hour	6.97	

83.74% of all sex depicted outside marriage. Using intercourse and comments only viewers are exposed to 13,213 incidents over a period of one year of prime-time viewing. Using intercourse and comments and skin scenes viewers are exposed to 23,921 incidents. 73.87% of all programs contained sexual content. 59.87% of all programs contained profanity. 48.75% of all programs contained sex and profanity. 85% of all programs contained either sex and/or profanity.

TOP USERS OF SEX IN COMMERCIALS

1. Consolidated Foods	53
2. Ford Motor Company	19
3. Avon Products	15
4. Gulf & Western Industries	10
4. Revlon	10

TEN TOP SEX-ORIENTED PROGRAMS

1. It's A Living	43.00	ABC
2. Three's Company	40.90	ABC
3. Ladies Man	33.60	CBS
4. Soap	32.50	ABC
5. Laverne & Shirley	32.22	ABC
6. Happy Days	22.25	ABC
6. Taxi	22.25	ABC
7. One Day At A Time	19.25	CBS
8. Love Boat	16.68	ABC
9. Too Close For Comfort	15.20	ABC

Note: Prime-Time Viewing Sept. 14 - Dec. 6, 1980

TEN LEAST SEX-ORIENTED PROGRAMS

1. Wonderful World of Disney	0.0835	NBC
1. NBC Sports	0.0833	NBC
2. Little House On The Prairie	0.1904	NBC
3. The Waltons	0.3333	CBS
4. ABC Sports	0.4677	ABC
5. Those Amazing Animals	0.5833	ABC
6. Quincy	1.000	NBC
7. That's Incredible	1.083	ABC
8. NBC Magazine	1.250	NBC
9. The Incredible Hulk	1.375	CBS
10. Games People Play	1.428	NBC

TOP SPONSORS OF SEX

1. Revlon	18.50
2. Noxell	17.92
3. Beecham	16.28
4. Gulf & Western	15.30
5. American Motors	15.26
6. Carnation	14.95
7. Heublein	14.62
8. Clorox	14.60
9. Pfizer	13.58
10. Warner-Lambert	13.14

LEAST SPONSORS OF SEX

1. Timex	1.74
2. Hallmark	2.13
3. Philip Morris	2.53
4. Nissan Motors	3.62
5. I T & T	4.25
6. Zenith	4.97
7. RCA	5.09
8. Hershey	5.28
9. Eastman Kodak	5.44
10. General Mills	5.50

CONSTRUCTIVE PROGRAMS & SPONSORS

TOP TEN CONSTRUCTIVE PROGRAMS
(Based on minimum 120 minutes air time)

1. NBC Sports	9.000	NBC
2. Little House on the Prairie	8.730	NBC
3. Wonderful World of Disney	8.680	NBC
4. Those Amazing Animals	8.550	ABC
5. Quincy	8.220	NBC
6. 60 Minutes	8.183	CBS
7. The Waltons	7.933	CBS
8. NBC Magazine	7.513	NBC
9. Trapper John M.D.	7.440	CBS
10. CBS Specials	7.394	CBS

TEN LEAST CONSTRUCTIVE PROGRAMS
(Based on minimum 120 minutes air time)

1. Ladies Man	2.480	CBS
2. Soap	2.640	ABC
3. It's A Living	2.850	ABC
4. Taxi	3.050	ABC
5. Three's Company	3.164	ABC
6. Flo	3.980	CBS
7. Laverne & Shirley	4.033	ABC
8. WKRP In Cincinnati	4.264	CBS
9. Vegas	4.289	ABC
10. The Dukes of Hazzard	4.300	CBS

TEN MOST CONSTRUCTIVE PROGRAMMING SPONSORS

1. Timex	7.624
2. Hallmark	6.595
3. Kelloggs	6.506
4. Eastman Kodak	6.494
5. Hershey	6.493
6. General Electric	6.479
7. PepsiCo	6.475
8. Philip Morris	6.434
9. Polaroid	6.420
10. American Telephone & Telegraph	6.320

TEN LEAST CONSTRUCTIVE PROGRAMMING SPONSORS

1. Revlon	4.718
2. Dow Chemical	4.958
3. Noxell Corporation	5.083
4. Gulf & Western	5.131
5. Beecham	5.182
6. American Motors	5.277
7. Nestle Company	5.363
8. Richardson-Merrell	5.363
9. Warner-Lambert	5.443
10. Sterling Drug	5.469

Partial List of Addresses

AMERICAN HOME PRODUCTS
Chrm. W. F. LaPorte
435 East 52nd St.
New York, NY 10022
212-986-1000
Anacin, Easy-Off, Woolite

CONSOLIDATED FOODS CORP.
Chrm. John H. Bryan, Jr.
140 Melrose
Kenilworth, IL 60043
312-726-6414
Hanes hosiery, L'eggs, Underalls, Shasta beverages, Tyco toys

KELLOGG CO.
Chrm. Joe E. Lonning
222 Lincoln Hill Dr.
Battle Creek, MI 49015
616-966-2000
Cereals, Mrs. Smith's Pies

REVLON, INC.
Chrm. Michael C. Bergerac
767 5th Avenue
New York, NY 10022
212-522-5000
Charlie, Jontue, Flex balsam, cosmetics, Tums

BRISTOL-MYERS CO.
Chrm. Richard L. Gelb
1060 Fifth Avenue
New York, NY 10028
212-644-2100
Tickle, Clairol, Bufferin, Excedrin, Vanish

GENERAL MILLS, INC.
Chrm. Robert E. Kinney
1520 Xanthus Lane
Wayzata, MN 55391
612-540-2311
Cheerios, Betty Crocker, Wheaties, Cocoa Puffs

MILTON BRADLEY
Chrm. James J. Shea, Jr.
1500 Main St.
Springfield, MA 01115
413-525-6411
Toys, Playskool

VOLKSWAGEN OF AMERICA, INC.
Chrm. Toni Schmuecker
27621 Parkview Blvd.
Warren, MI 48092
313-574-3300
Automobiles

CARNATION CO.
Chrm. H. E. Olson
448 N. Las Palmas Ave.
Los Angeles, CA 90004
213-931-1911
Friskies, Come and Get It dogfood, Carnation foods

HALLMARK CARDS, INC.
Chrm. Joyce C. Hall
2501 McGee
Kansas City, MO 64108
816-274-5111
Cards, giftwrap, books

POLAROID CORP.
Chrm. Edwin H. Land
Brattle Street
Cambridge, MA 02139
617-864-6000
Cameras & Film

WM. WRIGLEY JR. CO.
Pres. William Wrigley
60 North Lake Shore Drive
Lake Geneva, WI 53147
312-644-2121
Doublemint, Juicy Fruit, Spearmint, Big Red gum

Exhibit 2
Memorandum
Coalition for Better Television

April 10, 1981

To: Network Advertisers
Re: Monitoring Results

Below are scores for your company for the first four weeks of monitoring which includes March 1–28. We felt you might be interested in them. To get an idea of where your company stands figure that a combined total of your ad ratio for sex, violence and profanity of 14 or more would put you in the top sponsors of sex, violence and profanity. If your constructive rating is less than 4.400 then you would fall in the bottom of constructive sponsors. The higher your combined ad ratio score the poorer your practice and the lower the constructive rating the poorer your practice.

If you desire more complete information on how to interpret the scores feel free to contact us. Remember that the scores are based on the first four weeks of monitoring. Several companies are making a serious effort to bring their scores down which means that companies on the borderline who don't make an effort will move up.

Company ___CONSOLIDATED FOODS___

Sex Score
     Volume ___162___
     Ad Ratio ___4.15___

Profanity Score
     Volume ___211___
     Ad Ratio ___5.41___

Violence Score
     Volume ___176___
     Ad Ratio ___4.51___

Constructive Rating ___4.549___

Sincerely,

Donald E. Wildmon

Exhibit 3
Corporate Policy and Procedures Memorandum

April 20, 1981

Department/Division: Corporate Affairs
Subject: Advertising Policy

Consolidated Foods Corporation has, and will continue to subscribe to, a philosophy of responsible corporate citizenship. This responsibility requires that advertisements representing the products and services of Consolidated Foods Corporation be truthful and free of statements, illustrations or implications offensive to reasonable standards of good taste.

Consolidated Foods Corporation is opposed to the placement of its advertisements in publications or broadcast programs which make gratuitous, exploitive or excessive use of violence or sexual themes, as well as those that demean human dignity or abuse particular segments of society. However, the corporation is unable to exercise control over the representation of its products which may infrequently appear as a result of editorial use.

The monitoring of advertising policies and placement of advertisements, including the use of randomly placed spot broadcast advertisements, remains the responsibility of the senior executive at each operating company, regardless of whether internal or agency advertising resources are utilized.

Source: Company files

Exhibit 4
Consolidated Foods Chronology

1939	Nathan Cummings purchased C. D. Kenny Co., a small wholesale distributor of sugar and packager of coffee and tea, located in Baltimore.
1942	Acquisition of Sprague Warner Co., located in Chicago, and distributor of the famous Richelieu brand of fine foods.
1945	Acquisition of Reid, Murdoch and Co., nationally recognized for its Monarch quality brand. Company entered food processing business. Name changed to Consolidated Grocers Corporation.
1946	Landmark year for company; stock offered to the public for the first time and company sales grew to $123 million.
1951	Acquisition of Union Sugar.
1954	Name changed to Consolidated Foods Corporation. Acquisition of Piggly Wiggly and Eagle Food Centers.
1956	Acquisition of Kitchens of Sara Lee.
1959–early 1960s	Acquisition of Lawson's, Shasta, Booth Fisheries, Popsicle, Kahn's, PYA, and Hollywood Brands.
1962	First overseas acquisition of Jonker Fris.
1966	Federal Trade Commission ordered division of food manufacturing and retail activities. Company sold Eagle. Acquisition of nonfood companies, such as Electrolux, Fuller Brush and Oxford Chemicals, began.
1967	Sales reached $1 billion.
1968	Founder Nathan Cummings retired and became honorary chairman of the board and chairman of the executive committee. Acquisition of Bryan Foods.
1976	John Bryan moved up from president to chairman of the corporation; John Cardwell named president.
1978	Investment of 65% controlling interest in Douwe Egberts. Acquisition of Chef Pierre.
1979	Acquisition of Hanes Corporation. Fiscal year sales reached $4.7 billion.

Source: In-house newsletter.

Exhibit 5
Consolidated Foods Corporation and Subsidiaries
Operating Results by Industry Segment, 1976–1981

(in millions)	1981 Sales	1981 Pre-Tax Income	1980 Sales	1980 Pre-Tax Income	1979 Sales	1979 Pre-Tax Income	1978 Sales	1978 Pre-Tax Income	1977 Sales	1977 Pre-Tax Income	1976[4] Sales	1976[4] Pre-Tax Income
Consumer Packaged Goods												
Beverages	$1,348	$ 88	$1,402	$ 97	$1,112	$ 84	$ 597	$ 58[3]	$ 181	$ 10	$ 173	$ 9
Hanes Group	792	46	715	44	397	6[2]	76	9	61	7	51	6
Specialty Meats	874	45	743	43	699	32	534	26	459	23	441	20
Frozen Foods	643	28	598	32	551	35	496	34	428	30	396	26
Other Consumer Products	417	46	437	32	542	30	603	40	684	45	677	43
Total Consumer Packaged Goods	4,074	253	3,895	248	3,301	187	2,306	167	1,813	115	1,738	104
Food Services	1,075	31	978	39	902	35	739	26	643	25	601	25
Consumer Direct Sales	543	57	536	47	575	65	545	69	522	68	497	57
Total	5,692	341	5,409	334	4,778	287	3,590	262	2,978	208	2,836	186
Intersegment Sales	(78)	–	(66)	–	(58)	–	(54)	–	(45)	–	(48)	–
Interest, net	–	(28)	–	(41)	–	(34)	–	(14)	–	(10)	–	(11)
Unallocated Corporate Expense	–	(30)	–	(28)	–	(18)	–	(15)	–	(18)	–	(17)
Net Sales and Pre-Tax Income	$5,614	$283	$5,343	$265	$4,720	$235	$3,536	$233	$2,933	$180	$2,788	$158

[1] Sales by segment include sales to outside customers and sales between segments. Intersegment sales are at transfer prices which are equivalent to market value.

[2] Reduced by $30 as a result of valuing Hanes' inventory at fair market value at the date of acquisition.

[3] Increased by $24 as a result of valuing Douwe Egberts' inventory acquired net of deferred taxes at the date of acquisition.

[4] Fifty-three week accounting year.

Included in the above table are sales and pre-tax income of businesses sold as follows:

(in millions)	1981 Sales	1981 Pre-Tax Income	1980 Sales	1980 Pre-Tax Income	1979 Sales	1979 Pre-Tax Income	1978 Sales	1978 Pre-Tax Income	1977 Sales	1977 Pre-Tax Income	1976 Sales	1976 Pre-Tax Income
Other Consumer Products	$ 63	$ 7	$ 132	$ (1)	$ 262	$ 7	$ 350	$ 21	$ 443	$ 22	$ 435	$ 17
Food Services	–	–	–	–	–	–	–	–	53	3	51	2
Consumer Direct Sales	–	–	33	2	79	6	73	5	68	4	64	4

Description of Industry Segments

The corporation is a diversified company primarily engaged in the manufacture and distribution of a broad range of branded products and services. These products and services have been classified into the following three industry segments:

Consumer Packaged Goods. This segment manufactures and distributes hot and cold beverages; hosiery, undergarments, gloves, swimwear, and cosmetics; processed and fresh meats; frozen baked goods, fish, seafood, potatoes and confection products; and personal care products, sugar and a variety of canned and processed fruits and vegetables.

Food Services. This segment distributes food and related grocery products to volume feeding operations and operates restaurants and convenience retail food stores.

Consumer Direct Sales. This group produces and sells home cleaning appliances, household and personal care products, specialty chemicals and commercial vehicle cleaning equipment, and provides building maintenance and security services.

The Notes to Financial Statements should be read in conjunction with the Operating Results by Industry Segment.

Source: 1981 annual report

Exhibit 6
Organization Chart, June 1981

```
                    ┌─────────────────────────┐
                    │ Chairman and            │
                    │ Chief Executive Officer │
                    │ J.H. Bryan, Jr.         │
                    └─────────────────────────┘
                                 │
          ┌──────────────────────┼──────────────────────┐
          │                                              │
┌──────────────────┐                         ┌────────────────────────┐
│ Executive VP      │                         │ Senior VP              │
│ Chief Financial   │                         │ Secretary and          │
│ and Administrative│                         │ General Counsel        │
│ Officer           │                         │ G.H. Newman            │
│ M.E. Murphy       │                         └────────────────────────┘
└──────────────────┘
```

Executive VP Chief Financial and Administrative Officer M.E. Murphy

- VP Corporate Affairs
- VP and Treasurer
- VP Financial Planning and Control
- VP Tax and Insurance
- VP and Corporate Controller

President and Chief Operating Officer J.J. Cardwell

- Senior VP Human Resources
- VP Corporate Planning
- VP International Development

Executive VP R.E. Elberson
- Senior VP Hanes Group P. Fulton, Jr.
- Senior VP Specialty Apparel Group
- Senior VP Frozen Sweet Goods Group
- Group VP Booth/Idaho Group

Executive VP
- Chairman and CEO Kahn's Group
- President Bryan Foods

Executive VP
- Chairman and CEO Electrolux U.S.
- President Electrolux Canada

Executive VP
- President Shasta
- Senior VP PYA/Monarch
- President Douwe Egberts
- Senior VP Lawson
- Senior VP Diversified Products Group

53

Exhibit 7
Hanes Corporation Advertising Guidelines, March 31, 1978

Scope: The primary purpose of this document is to establish advertising placement guidelines which respond to public concern over the display of violence and sensitive moral issues on television and lack of good taste in magazines.

Television

1. *Violence*

   Hanes Corporation will avoid commercial participation in all TV programs judged to be excessively or gratuitously violent under any of the following criteria:

   - *Violence for the Sake of Violence.* Portrayals of violent actions not necessary to either story or character development.

   - *Glorification of Violent Acts.* Programming which makes the committing of violent actions appear to be appealing or which appears to condone the use of more than necessary violence on the part of the police, soldiers, etc., in the line of their duty.

   - *Overly Graphic Violence.* Portrayals which dwell on violent actions for excessively long periods or are unnecessarily descriptive in describing their effects either visually or verbally.

2. *Controversial Moral Issues*

   Hanes Corporation will avoid commercial participation in TV programming that may be offensive to a significant proportion of the population.

   Specifically, Hanes Corporation will avoid programs which:

   - Graphically depict sexual behavior—this is defined as full or partial nudity, explicit visual and verbal sexual descriptions/language and excessively passionate lovemaking.

   - Deal with polarizing moral issues such as abortion and homosexuality as major or minor themes.

   - Involve aberrant sexual behavior such as incest and sodomy even in a minor way.

   - Deal with any of the following subjects as primary themes or major subplots—nymphomania, statutory rape or prostitution.

   - May be offensive to large numbers of people in specific religious or ethnic groups.

Magazines

Magazine readership is generally restricted to adults or to a select audience by virtue of magazine availability. Therefore, advertising placement standards for magazines can provide wider ranges of tolerance. General standards of good taste provide a suitable editorial environment for Hanes products. Hanes Corporation will avoid advertising in all magazines which go beyond these standards. Specifically proscribed are: (a) frontal male nudity; (b) simulated sexual activities; (c) excessive use of verbal obscenities; and (d) an overwhelming sexual environment created editorially and/or by a preponderance of sexually oriented advertising.

In judging new magazines, no commitment will be made until there is time to evaluate the first one or two issues to determine whether the new magazine will violate the above standards.

Exhibit 7 (continued)

Implementation

1. Advertising media buyers will be supplied with the above guidelines and will advise the TV networks and magazine publishers of this policy. Primary responsibility for judging which programs or magazines comply with the above guidelines will rest with the advertising agency.

2. In the case of TV advertising, the TV networks will be periodically supplied with lists of specific programming deemed unacceptable.

3. Prescreening should be utilized for all prime time TV programming. (Prime time is defined as the period between 8:00 P.M. and 11:00 P.M.) Evaluation of non-prime time programs must be based on the title, reputation or random checking due to their magnitude.

4. Each advertising agency employed by Hanes will be requested, from time to time, to demonstrate through specific examples that its judgment coincides with that of Hanes Corporation senior management.

Exhibit 8
National Federation for Decency Letter

P.O. Box 1398
Tupelo, Mississippi 38801
Phone: (601) 844-5036

September 18, 1980

Mr. John H. Bryan, Jr.
140 Melrose
Kenilworth, IL 60043

Dear Mr. Bryan:

   Last Sunday evening, September 14, ABC aired a program entitled "The Women's Room" which Consolidated Foods helped sponsor. All the advance reviews of the program indicated it to be a vicious attack on marriage and the family. I must confess that it was exactly that. ABC said the purpose of the film was to "make people angry." I must confess, also, that it did that.

   We plan to run a list of the sponsors and their products in our next NFD Newsletter. If you care to explain your reason behind helping sponsor "The Women's Room" we would be happy to share it with our readers and supporters. Since much of our paper is reprinted in several hundred local and regional newsletters, I feel you might desire to share the reason why you chose to help sponsor such an obviously biased and prejudicial movie.

   I look forward to hearing from you. I am sure your media people can bring you up to date on this program.

Sincerely,

Donald E. Wildmon

Exhibit 9
Executive Offices' Corporate Response

October 8, 1980

Mr. Donald E. Wildmon
Executive Director
National Federation for Decency
P.O. Box 1398
Tupelo, Mississippi 38801

Dear Mr. Wildmon:

Mr. John Bryan has asked me to respond to your recent letter regarding a L'erin cosmetics commercial that aired during ABC's "The Women's Room." While neither Mr. Bryan or myself saw the program, the information we have received indicates that your concern about it being an attack on marriage and the family structure is well founded.

I would like first to explain the manner in which our companies operate. They have a great deal of autonomy, and, because of the variety of products marketed, have the responsibility for developing and implementing their own advertising programs.

L'erin cosmetics, as part of our Hanes Group, has in effect specific advertising guidelines relating to TV program content and the purchase of commercial time. L'erin's advertising agency has the responsibility to prescreen TV programs and movies shown during prime time. The agency is instructed not to place commercials on programs that relate predominately and specifically to sex and violence. The guidelines, as they now stand, do not specifically address programs which may be antifamily or marriage, or, for that matter antibusiness, antilabor, etc. On the surface, the agency did not believe "The Women's Room" violated the guidelines, thus a commercial for L'erin did air in certain local markets.

Your letter has prompted us to reexamine whether more expansive guidelines concerning matters of this type should be developed. In any case, I am forwarding copies of your letter and this response to Mr. John F. Ward, president of L'erin cosmetics, who, I'm sure, will be interested in your comments.

Your point of view concerning this specific program is well taken and we thank you for taking the time to bring this matter to our attention.

Very truly,

Richard D. Kemplin
Vice President–Corporate Affairs

cc: John F. Ward

Note on the TV Advertising and Programming Controversy, 1981

Kenneth E. Goodpaster prepared this note based on a student report by John Keller, MBA '82.

We take the view that television is now teaching—even advancing—a particular moral viewpoint. . . . Just look at any of the shows Norman Lear produces. Extramarital sex is OK; the practice of homosexuality is OK; booze, you name it . . . and now and then they throw in a couple hours of "Little House on the Prairie" to satisfy the moralist part of the audience. We're not saying that viewpoint should never be treated. Conservatives like sex as much as anybody else—maybe even more. What we are talking about is balance. The Norman Lear people have their influence, and we want to have ours, too.

With these comments Cal Thomas, vice president–communications of the Moral Majority, fired one of the opening salvos of a battle that would occupy the attention of TV networks, advertising agencies, corporate advertisers, and the American public in 1980 and 1981.[1]

Organized efforts to change the quality of TV programming were not new to the American scene. Groups as diverse as the Knights of Columbus (a Roman Catholic fraternal society), the National Council of Churches (representing mainstream Protestantism), the Anti-Defamation League (representing the Jewish faith), the National Federation for Decency (a conservative Christian group), and the National PTA Action Center (an association devoted to close communication between parents and teachers on the educational environment of the young) had all attempted to influence what enters American homes in the form of TV entertainment.

The efforts of 1980 and 1981, however, bore the imprint of increased organization and a concerted drive to influence TV programming through direct appeals and threats to those advertisers

---

1. Mark Miller, "New Move to Bridle TV," *Marketing and Media Decisions*, January 1981, Vol. 16, No. 1, p. 58. Reprinted by permission.

whose sponsorship made such programming possible. These appeals and threats were couched in terms of boycotts whereby religious groups claimed the ability to deliver large numbers of consumers who would refuse to patronize the products or services of sponsors of offending programs.

The threat of a TV boycott itself was also not new to the American public. In 1978, for example, the National Federation for Decency attempted to exert boycott pressure on Sears, Roebuck and Company for sponsoring programs allegedly containing excessive sex, violence, and profanity. Other early targets of boycott efforts had been General Foods and American Home Products (in this case, by Clean Up TV, a group sponsored by the National Churches of Christ).

In response to these earlier efforts, General Foods' representatives had pointed out they annually dropped 100 programs that did not meet corporate standards regarding sex and violence, and that only 3% of General Foods' advertising budget went into shows which Clean Up TV found objectionable. The company maintained, however, that "we're in the market to buy time, and not everything we buy will please every viewer. . . . We don't believe any one group should be able to dictate to all others what their choices should be."[2] This response was not adequate for the church groups and a boycott ensued.

The church groups, however, were emboldened by the response of another major corporation to these early boycott threats. Warner-Lambert reported dropping several shows as a result of Clean Up TV's campaign. A Warner-Lambert spokesperson observed:

> We had a policy since 1971 that . . . we should be associated with wholesome entertainment—programs that don't exploit sex or violence, or demean human dignity. And to carry out that policy, we have a practice of prescreening everything that we're on. For instance, we were advertising on "Saturday Night Live," which of course is impossible to prescreen because it is broadcast live. We stopped advertising on that show—not because of a moral judgment, but because we couldn't prescreen. In fact, we're now off a number of shows

that we had been on. You might say that our sensitivity to the matter has been heightened.[3]

On November 9, 1980, the *New York Times* reported that Warner-Lambert had dropped sponsorship of "The Newlywed Game," "The Dating Game," "Three's Company," and "Saturday Night Live." All of these programs had been on Clean Up TV's target list.

1981 Boycott, Spring Phase

With some initial success behind them, and encouraged by what many perceived as a shift of mood within the American public away from liberal social standards toward more traditional ones, church groups prepared a major assault on advertisers and programming for 1981. Leading the assault was the Coalition for Better Television (CBTV), a group headed by the Reverend Donald Wildmon of Tupelo, Mississippi, and supported by the following groups: the Moral Majority of the Reverend Jerry Falwell, the Church of Christ, the American Life Lobby, Concerned Women for America, and the Eagle Forum (Phyllis Schlafly's group). CBTV reported that it had scores of volunteers across the country who were monitoring all TV programming for offensive content. The output of this monitoring effort would be a list of those advertisers who consistently sponsored programs that CBTV rated as offensive. These advertisers in turn would be threatened with nationwide boycotts if they continued to sponsor questionable programming. (Excerpts from Rev. Wildmon's press statement announcing the formation of CBTV appear as *Exhibit 1*.)

The potential impact of this effort on the advertising budgets for the 1981–1982 season was swiftly recognized. According to one network official: "Though I still believe there are sponsors in control of their advertising destiny, the fuss kicked up by CBTV will be a factor in the pricing of our shows, especially those meriting a clean bill of health and appealing to the family audience."[4]

An agency buyer observed: "The bottom line is that the networks have to make the bucks. With the pressures building on the advertisers, they are going to look for programs with strong

---

2. General Foods spokesperson, quoted in *Marketing and Media Decisions*, art cit., January 1981, Vol. 16, No. 1, p. 107.

3. Ibid.
4. *Advertising Age*, March 30, 1981, p. 1.

moral values and tone down anything considered too offensive."[5]

According to a network buyer: "Let's face it, go into any meeting today, and the Moral Majority is all anyone is talking about. . . . The producers don't really give a damn about Wildmon or the Moral Majority, but once it begins to affect their pocketbooks—well, if it's clean that sells, then that's what they will deliver."[6]

On March 23, 1981, the Moral Majority took out a full-page ad in newspapers across the country explaining its position. The campaign was reported to cost over $100,000, and it had as its central point a defense of the group's role in society: "Moral Majority, Inc., is made up of millions of Americans, including 72,000 ministers, priests, and rabbis, who are deeply concerned about the moral decline of our nation and who are sick and tired of the way many amoral and secular humanists and other liberals are destroying the traditional family and moral values on which our nation was built."[7]

As the potential impact of the organized religious groups became clear, network executives became increasingly nervous. In April 1981 the presidents of the three major networks presented their case at the annual meeting of the American Association of Advertising Agencies. According to NBC's Fred Silverman, threats of boycotts were "the coalition's sneak attack on the foundation of democracy." Gene Jankowski of CBS warned of "the disenfranchisement of the real majority by a determined minority." ABC's Fred Pierce pleaded with the advertisers and their agencies to stand "side by side" with the networks in resistance to the "coercive tactics" of the "self-appointed censors" within the coalition.[8]

The agency people did not appear to respond favorably to these pleas. Their responses included those voiced by executives who felt that the networks were less than consistent in their desire for cooperation with the agencies ("What partnership? Where were these fellows when we were trying to talk to them about . . . rate increases?"). Other responses asserted reluctant sympathy with complaints about programming quality: "I don't want censors like the Moral Majority, Jerry Falwell or any of them. But I don't want 'Three's Company' either—and

that is what I get. The networks program offensive shows, pure trash, and they expect us to defend them."[9]

The network executives, on the other hand, suggested that the mass of viewers be allowed to decide what should be on the air, rather than any special interest groups. As Jankowski observed: "If they (the viewers) are disenchanted with what is offered . . . that fact registers quite clearly. They can be and ought to be trusted to go on doing their own voting with their own dials."[10]

Others disputed this perspective and argued that, in many cases, a program's rating reflected not so much a program's worth as the lack of any superior competition. On this hypothesis, a TV program might have received high ratings because it was the most interesting or appealing of a bad lot in a given time spot—a tribute to the fact that people who are going to watch television will give high ratings to a particular program for want of any meaningful alternative. These same observers also argued that ratings fail to measure a grass roots dissatisfaction with what television is offered. They suggested that the right people were not being polled for their opinions regarding what is on the air. Moral Majority's Thomas observed:

I do a lot of public speaking around the country and in place after place that I go, I take my own polls. I ask for a show of hands of anybody who has *ever* been surveyed by Nielsen or Arbitron, or anybody who has ever been contacted by a pollster with questions about TV programs. I've spoken to tens of thousands of people, and I've never met anyone yet who has ever raised a hand in the affirmative. I don't know who they're polling, but they're polling the wrong people.[11]

A Diverse Set of Stakeholders

It is difficult to estimate the potential impact of a boycott such as the coalition was planning without examining the roles of various stakeholders. Since the response of the advertisers themselves will be considered below, the reader's attention here turns to other parties: agencies, networks, educational leaders, religious leaders, and finally the American public.

5. Ibid., p. 80.
6. Ibid.
7. *New York Times*, March 23, 1981, p. B 11.
8. *Advertising Age*, April 13, 1981, p. 1.

9. Ibid.
10. *Advertising Age*, April 13, 1981, p. 103.
11. *Marketing and Media Decisions*, January 1981, p. 58.

Agencies and Networks

The network leaders failed to find a sympathetic audience among the agency executives. The agency people seemed to be caught between their obligations to procure popular and lucrative time slots for their clients on the one hand, and their reported distaste for potentially objectionable programming on the other. Leo-Arthur Kelmenson, president and CEO of Kenyon and Eckhardts, an advertising agency, deplored the state of television when he wrote: "I don't think I'll get much argument from reasonable people that such [objectionable] program content is damaging to society in general and to impressionable young people in particular."[12]

At the same time, Kelmenson articulated the dilemma faced by the agency executives:

> Only if the decision to forgo rating points for moral principles is mandated in the corporate boardroom—only when the networks rise to the programming challenges they will then face—will agency media buyers feel free to make program credibility one of their evaluative criteria. . . . Given sufficient support at these three levels, perhaps we can hope that . . . [the sex and violence] type of program will stop proliferating. Until then, let society beware.[13]

The networks' financial stakes were substantial. Each Nielsen point advantage was worth $40 million in annual advertising revenue to the individual network. It was feared that programs branded as objectionable by the Moral Majority could have their ad rates fall by as much as 30%.

Throughout the debate, network leaders maintained that they were the targets of unfair, even unconstitutional, tactics. In response to these perceived threats, prominent media, religious, and political leaders joined together to form a group called People for the American Way to battle what it described as a "climate of fear and repression."[14] The groups produced public service announcements with the aid of Norman Lear and featured, among others, Carol Burnett, Goldie Hawn, and Muhammad Ali. Supporters of the group included the Reverend M. William Howard, president of the National Council of Churches, and Barbara Jordan, former Democratic representative of Texas.

One of the central themes of the network response had been summed up by NBC's Fred Silverman in his description of the boycott tactics as an attack on the foundations of democracy. The Rev. Wildmon was quick to respond: "A boycott is as legal and as American as apple pie. Didn't Martin Luther King lead boycotts? . . . I'm not seeking to have a law passed. These are public airwaves and I'm just saying that if an advertiser wants my business, he has to treat me with respect. If there's no public support for our position, the boycott will fail and we'll disappear."[15]

Educational and Religious Leaders

Even moderate voices tended to disagree with the network executives in their protests. Everett Parker, head of the communications office of the United Church of Christ, was a well-known advocate of improved TV programming. Parker, who opposed boycotts as a means to achieve this end, observed: "I think all these speeches they're [network broadcasters] making about censorship are hypocritical. . . . For years they've been putting out all these sleazy programs and thumbing their noses at people who object to them. They've never listened to sensible people, because they knew sensible people wouldn't attack them this way. The coalition has gone for the jugular."[16]

The Reverend Timothy S. Healy, S.J., president of Georgetown University, was another opponent of boycotts and a critic of the Moral Majority. Nonetheless, he recognized the strength of these efforts: "What it [CBTV] is trying to do is as old as American politics and every bit as legal. As long as there is a significant public support behind the pressure it brings, the coalition will be effective." While Healy believed that the boycott threats would ultimately fade because of their excessively negative tone, he observed that CBTV had struck the networks in a weak spot and that it was now in the process of exploiting this weakness: "These are real problems. And because of the problems, elements like the coalition . . . can pressure . . . and hard."[17]

The strongest critique of the Moral Majority and its tactics from the academic community was the assessment of A. Bartlett Giamatti,

---

12. "Vast Wasteland Revisited," *Harvard Business Review*, November–December 1980, p. 29.
13. Ibid.
14. *New York Times*, June 25, 1981, p. C 14.

15. *New York Times*, June 22, 1981, p. A 12.
16. Ibid.
17. *Advertising Age*, August 3, 1981, pp. 33–34.

president of Yale University. In a speech prepared for delivery to Yale's 1981 incoming class, Giamatti painted this picture of Rev. Falwell's group: "Angry at change, rigid in the application of chauvinistic slogans, absolutistic in morality, they threaten through political pressure or public communication whoever dares to disagree with their authoritarian positions. . . . Using television, direct mail, and economic boycott, they would sweep before them anyone who holds a different opinion."[18]

The Moral Majority was quick to respond, accusing Giamatti of an "unprovoked diatribe." A Moral Majority spokesperson contended that the organization "just wants [its] side to be heard and that it became involved in TV programming to seek a better balance than the violence and permissiveness that is broadcast now."[19]

The American People: Would They Boycott?

Another central theme of the network responses was the contention that only a small minority of viewers would actually respond to boycotts:

> A poll commissioned by ABC . . . showed that a maximum of 1.3 percent of the American public would consider supporting a boycott; of that group, only one-half of one percent were Moral Majority members. CBS News found that 30 percent of the groups listed by Wildmon as coalition members said they did not belong to it. An NBC survey concluded that only two programs—"Three's Company" and "Soap"—would be turned off the screen by as many as 3 percent of the public because of sex, profanity or violence they exhibit; twelve would be turned off by one percent or less. In other words, boycott or not, a lot of people would keep tuning in to watch "Dallas" and "The Dukes of Hazzard."[20]

As Kelmenson observed: "The American public . . . does not seem at all repelled by this type of program. A 1977 study by the J. Walter Thompson Company revealed that a mere 1.5 percent of viewers said they had actually boycotted advertisers of violent programs."[21]

During the early months of 1981, NBC had commissioned the Roper Organization to conduct a nationwide survey "to determine the reaction of the adult American public to specific entertainment programs." Though not aimed directly at assessing the likely impact of a boycott, the study clearly had this as an indirect purpose. The results of the study, which network executives interpreted favorably, were eventually shared with both advertisers and ad agencies. Roper summarized the findings:

> Relatively few Americans are critical of any of these shows on sex or violence grounds. Also, there is disagreement on sex and violence: some like the content that others object to. . . . People of strong fundamentalist persuasion are significantly more concerned about sex and profanity than are nonfundamentalists. Yet even this small group watches these shows and is more likely to express favorable than unfavorable opinions of them. . . . NBC concludes from this study that Americans generally like the programs they watch on television and relatively few object to specific network programs on sex and violence grounds. Further, a majority of the very people who are the constituency of the fundamentalist leadership seem to hold attitudes towards programs which are quite similar to those of the general public.

Other studies carried less sanguine messages for advertisers. In Portland, Oregon, a poll taken in the spring of 1981 by the *Oregon Journal* found that 72% of those sampled believed that "the public should boycott the products of those companies sponsoring programs with sex, violence, and profanity."

The *Wall Street Journal* reported on a another study done in early summer 1981 by Warwick, Welsh and Miller, a New York ad agency. Though focused primarily on the content of TV commercials, the survey of 3,440 people concluded that while 40% found TV commercials to be in poor taste, 20% found *programs* to be in poor taste. The report of the survey added that although 55% said they shun products with objectionable advertising, four-fifths of those people said they never complained directly to an advertiser or TV station."[22]

In a somewhat philosophical reflection, Daniel Yankelovich, president of the social research firm Yankelovich, Skelly and White, observed that it was concern for children that gave force

---

18. *New York Times*, September 1, 1981, p. 1.
19. *New York Times*, September 2, 1981, p. A 16.
20. *New York Times*, July 5, 1981, Sect. 4, p. 16.
21. Ibid., p. 29.

22. *Wall Street Journal*, July 23, 1981.

and legitimacy to the television protests. Yankelovich concluded in an article in *Psychology Today* that "we have been neglecting the question, broadly put, of what is best for our children because we have been too busy with the question of what is best for us as adults, assuming—all too comfortably—that the same answer would do for both questions" (see *Exhibit 2*).

Procter & Gamble's Response

Owen B. Butler, chairman of the nation's largest TV advertiser, Procter & Gamble Co., appeared before the Academy of Television Arts and Sciences in Los Angeles on June 15, 1981. Butler announced that P&G, which spent over $480,000,000 on TV advertising in 1980,[23] had "withdrawn sponsorship from over 50 programs, including movies, for reasons of taste" during the year. Butler's presentation went into some depth regarding the reasons for this decision:

> Generations of Americans are being taught far more powerfully about virtues and vices, about morality, about society and individual responsibility by the things they watch on television, the things which you [academy members] create and produce. There is a large, serious and increasingly vocal segment of our population who believe that much of what you are teaching is destructive, that it tears at the character which has enabled this country to become . . . the finest society yet built by mankind.[24]

He expressed concern over the tactics chosen by the CBTV, but concluded that "the coalition may well believe that this was the only way they could ever get very many people to listen." Butler pointed out occasions in the past when P&G had refused to bow to threats of boycott because the company believed in the correctness of sponsoring specific programs. While he also expressed concern over the coalition's data-gathering procedures, he was able to draw the following conclusions:

> Despite this concern about the technique, we think the coalition is expressing some very important and broadly held views

about gratuitous sex, violence and profanity. I can assure you that we are listening very carefully to what they say. . . . For example, while we can't agree with their method of establishing ratings, the fact is that their list of the top ten sex-oriented programs includes seven programs which we had previously decided either to avoid entirely, or schedule only rarely, because of the difficulty of finding episodes which are consistent with our guidelines governing excessive and gratuitous sex. We review every program on which we schedule advertising, and even beyond the coalition's list, we find it necessary to withdraw sponsorships periodically because of offensive program content.

> For sound commercial reasons, we are not going to let our advertising messages appear in an environment which we think many of our potential customers will find distasteful. Beyond that, we are going to be guided by our conscience on the kind of material we sponsor. A corporation is not without personality and character and conscience. A corporation like ours has a character which is the sum of all the tens of thousands of people who have made up that corporation for more than 140 years, and our definition of the kind of media which we would support with our advertising has always involved some moral considerations. . . . It is completely within our character not only to screen out problem programs, but also to actively seek programs of exceptional artistic quality, which are truly inspirational and which challenge the very best in human nature.[25]

The Rev. Jerry Falwell quickly commended P&G's actions, noting that the company would avoid a boycott "if what this speech means is that P&G is in fact pulling away from the most offensive programs."[26]

Advertising executives appeared to be taken by surprise when they learned of the reaction to Butler's remarks. David B. McCall, chairman of McCaffrey and McCall, described the attention that the P&G chairman's speech was receiving as "much ado about nothing." The ad executives claimed that all major advertisers screen programming either directly or through hired agents. Withdrawal of support from programming that was not up to the company's standards was described as routine. "None of

23. *Wall Street Journal*, June 16, 1981, p. 39.
24. "Television Can Show and Tell but Can it Listen?," Speech before the Academy of Television Arts and Sciences, June 15, 1981.

25. Ibid., *Speech.*
26. *Wall Street Journal*, June 16, 1981, p. 39.

us can understand the motivation of the announcement since it is common practice in the business," said J. Walter Thompson's Chairman, Burt Manning. Others were more skeptical. James J. Jordan, chairman of Jordan, Case and McGrath suggested that "Procter & Gamble was trying to focus the attention of the Reverend Jerry Falwell . . . on prime time in order to distract him from daytime programming, where several P&G soap operas are a daily feature." Jordan was also perturbed that Reverend Falwell had "taken it [Butler's speech] out of context [and] was using it for a license to put the Procter & Gamble seal of approval on his entire campaign."[27]

Despite the hesitations of the advertising agency executives, the Procter & Gamble decision seemed to have a ripple effect throughout the business world. Shortly after Butler's speech, Thomas of the Moral Majority observed: "It's like the prime rate. . . . When No. 1 announces, a lot of others follow. The response we've gotten from advertisers since the Procter & Gamble speech has been very gratifying."[28]

The issue had clearly been joined and would not die.

---

27. *New York Times*, June 24, 1981, p. D 18.

28. *New York Times*, June 27, 1981, p. 48.

Exhibit 1
Excerpts from Press Statement by the Reverend Donald E. Wildmon,
Chairman, Coalition for Better Television, February 2, 1981

Tom Shales, noted TV critic for the *Washington Post*, wrote in his column a few weeks ago this item. "An experienced Hollywood screen writer who works occasionally in TV will never forget what a network executive told him when handing back one of the writer's scripts. The executive said, 'Dirty it up a little, will you?'"

Gary Deeb, TV critic for the *Chicago Sun-Times*, wrote a few months back about an interview with Tony Randall. "A CBS executive told my head writer," Mr. Randall is quoted, "to put more t— and a— into the show. . . . These guys would put pornography on television tomorrow if they could get away with it."

Lee Rich, producer of "Dallas," "Knots Landing," "Midland Heights" and several other programs, recently told *TV Guide* his show about teenage sex would be "hot stuff" and laughed, "I'm going to be the porno king of television."

For years concerned citizens have urged, pleaded and even begged the networks to halt the trend toward increasing amounts of sex, violence, and profanity. In reply, they have received answers ranging from a polite "We appreciate your opinion," to a sarcastic "If you don't like what is on, turn it off." The concern of millions of Americans has fallen on deaf ears.

Instead of reason, restraint, and responsibility, the networks have rather displayed an arrogance and indifference rarely matched in the history of corporate America.

We feel that television prides itself on being able to sell products while disclaiming any ability to sell ideas or values.

In the past the networks have attacked those of us who have activated our concern by doing what they are experts at—stereotyping. They have said that we are a small group of religious fanatics whose concerns and cares are to be dismissed and ignored.

If that be true, then we have some good company. People like Erma Bombeck, who wrote in one of her columns: "You told me violence was necessary because it was 'real.' Throwing up is 'real,' but I don't want to see it in color."

And people like Red Skelton. "Then," Mr. Skelton said, "they sell violence. Now they say this doesn't affect your mind in any way whatsoever, but if you can subliminally sell a product in 30 seconds, what does one hour of filth or violence do to your brain?"

To properly do their stereotyping the networks must also include Kathleen Nolan, who, as president of the Screen Actors Guild, said: "The heads of the networks are parasites and tasteless mercenaries. They've trashed up the airwaves almost beyond repair. It's a subhuman situation."

The networks must include in the "religious fanatic" stereotyping Dr. Rose K. Goldsen, professor of sociology at Cornell University. Dr. Goldsen had this to say: "TV is more than just a little fun and entertainment. It's a whole environment and what it does bears an unpleasant resemblance to behavior modification—on a mass scale."

Lucille Ball said: "Television's treatment of sex has gone too far . . . romance has been taken out of sex." Miss Ball's observations were confirmed by Harvard University's Project on Human Sexual Development whose study on television reported that 70% of allusions to intercourse on television occur between unmarried couples or involve a prostitute. "Much of TV's erotic activity involves violence against women," the report stated.

In addition to the networks, the sponsors of TV programs must also share responsibility for the increasing amounts of violence, vulgarity, sex, and profanity. For they have been quick to support these programs with their dollars.

Exhibit 1 (continued)

Because of this situation, we are today announcing the formation of a Coalition for Better Television. As of this morning the coalition includes more than 150 national and regional organizations. We expect that number to continue to grow.

Beginning March 1 the coalition will monitor TV programs for their violent, sexual, and profane content. The monitoring will continue through the months of March, April, and May. At the end of the three-month period the coalition will select one or more advertisers who rank among the top sponsors in the categories mentioned and ask for a one-year voluntary boycott of all their products. In addition, we will select one or more advertisers who support basically quality programs and ask that their products be chosen over their competitors.

It is regrettable and unfortunate that such action is necessary. Most of us who are involved would prefer to be doing something other than dealing with this issue. However, let no one question our resolve.

The networks will respond with the only reply they know—by crying censorship. Censorship, however, is an official act by some official body at some level of government. The clearest expression of the First Amendment is the right of a person to spend his money where he so desires. With our plan of action the networks have the right to spend their money where they desire, the advertisers have the right to spend their money where they desire, and consumers have the right to spend their money where they desire.

Several groups, including those in civil rights and the National Organization of Women, have used economic leverage and, I might add, without the criticism of the networks.

Exhibit 2
The Public Mind, Daniel Yankelovich

STEPCHILDREN OF THE MORAL MAJORITY

Ever since the emergence of the Moral Majority, the takers of the public pulse—politicians, pollsters, network executives, educators, newspeople—have nervously been trying to gauge its political strength and its staying power. Usually these efforts have amounted to one or another kind of survey. Side by side the results present a confusing picture. Last year, 14 months after the Reverend Jerry Falwell founded the organization, the *New York Times* reported its membership at 400,000. Soon after, the Moral Majority claimed that it registered 3 million new voters in the 1980 Presidential election. This year, an ABC-TV survey concluded that 2.9 percent of those interviewed—or a projected 4.6 million Americans—supported the Moral Majority's "attempts to influence [TV] programs to conform to their standards and values" and tentatively projected a membership of 10.6 million. A New York Times/CBS Poll suggested the Moral Majority could be equated with evangelical Christians and thereby implied that the number of people who share the organization's outlook might extend to the stratospheric height of 67 million.

The ludicrously wide range of these estimates, from 400,000 all the way to 67 million, suggests a failure of clear thinking about what is being measured, and why. I suspect that what people want to learn about the Moral Majority is neither how many dues-paying members it has, nor how many voters it recruited in the last election, nor how large is the religious group from whose members some—but not all—moral majoritarians are drawn. What we really want to know is whether the Moral Majority is a passing fad or will take hold in the mainstream of American life.

The key to exploring the potential impact of the Moral Majority is not numbers but issues. What is the basis of the organization's appeal? More specifically, is there a critical social issue that gives it a potential constituency beyond its official membership, whatever that number may be? Once this question is asked, several insights come quickly to light.

We see immediately that the Moral Majority draws its vitality from a concern shared by millions of Americans for whom the Moral Majority is otherwise anathema. The organization's connection with this concern gives the Moral Majority its plausibility and claim to attention as a potentially significant social movement. It leads people who would ordinarily reject its proposals out of hand to say, at least tacitly, "Well, maybe they have a point . . ."

What is this concern? It is that Americans are growing ever more uneasy about the influence of the prevailing moral climate on their children. Let me put the issue first in terms of several imaginary examples. Say I am a parent who believes everyone over the age of consent is entitled to engage in the sexual

---

Concern for children makes the Moral Majority credible for many who would never identify with Jerry Falwell.

Another lamb to the water: the Reverend Jerry Falwell baptizing a child in Lynchburg, Virginia.

Brian Lanker, LIFE Magazine, © 1980 Time, Inc.

Exhibit 2 (continued)

behavior he or she finds most satisfying (short of compelling others to do something against their will). Say I am a parent who believes in freedom of speech. I am sufficiently committed to these beliefs, in fact, to vote against people who, in one way or another, seem to oppose them—which is one reason I oppose the Moral Majority. But still I am not happy about the fact that my 13-year-old son can buy *Hustler* on the newstand. I am not happy, but I am not sure what to do about it.

Say I want to decriminalize marijuana. But I am very concerned already about the easy availability of many kinds of drugs in the high school my 15-year-old daughter attends. Or say that, as a matter of principle, I do not forbid my children to attend any movie or watch any television program or read any book. But the gross violence in many movies they go to see, the deliberately sensational treatment of social problems like urban crime and pregnant teenagers on the television dramas they frequently watch distress me. Must I deny my own principles to do what I, however confusedly, feel is right for my children?

Now I am convinced that many Americans, especially parents, are increasingly uncomfortable with the sweeping permissiveness that their own pursuit of permissiveness has created for young people.

One piece of supporting evidence is provided by the ABC-TV survey I referred to earlier. Not only did it find that 4.6 million Americans supported the Moral Majority's "attempts to influence [TV] programs to conform to their standards and values," it also found that about 33 million (20.5 percent of those interviewed) would support a group using tactics such as organized boycotts to shape TV programming to their moral preferences.

Another item is the finding in a recent nationwide study of the American family conducted by Yankelovich, Skelly, and White that even the most untraditional parents—those who stress self-fulfillment and deemphasize money, work, marriage, and obligations to others—nevertheless raise their children according to traditional moral precepts. These parents (slightly over 40 percent of the sample) are just about as likely as traditionalist parents to teach children that duty comes before pleasure, that sex outside of marriage is wrong, that "my country right or wrong" is the proper attitude.

Are such parents hypocritical? Perhaps. Even if they are, the question is why. I see them as hedging their bets. Uncertain and confused about the full import of their own values, they fall back upon simpler, less individualistic, less *ad hoc* principles—values that exist,

Parents are increasingly uncomfortable with the sweeping permissiveness their own pursuit of new options has created.

as it were, "out there": patriotism, duty, sexual fidelity.

Such parents have not yet made a whole piece of their lives or their principles. Up to now, they have neglected to think through whether the behavior that they consider morally right for themselves as adults—setting personal choices above socially approved ways of life—creates a sound moral world for their children. In their preoccupation with self, they have not devoted the time and energy to wrestle with the question, What kind of social world, what range of individual choices, provides children with healthy security and healthy freedom?

To a member of the Moral Majority, the issue of the moral care and feeding of the young is quite clear. The country is too permissive. This freedom to sin is seen in television programs that sport as their main attraction the exploits of provocatively clothed young women; in legislation that gives women the right to abort fetuses and thus (from this point of view) go through life without accepting responsibility for their sexual conduct; in the willingness of many people to allow homosexuals to teach in schools. To a large portion of the American population, these examples are instances in which people are expressing choices about how to live their lives. But to the Moral Majority, they represent instances in which society unblinkingly allows people to make the wrong choices, even encourages such choices; the very existence of these choices in the public realm creates immorality.

This firm and unquestioned view is integral to the program of the Moral Majority. Briefly, it opposes abortion, busing, the Equal Rights Amendment, homosexuality, pornography, premarital sex, easy divorce; and it supports prayer in the schools, community censorship of textbooks, capital punishment, military superiority over the Soviet Union, a strong and traditional family. All of these varied positions express the core of the Moral Majority's conservatism—an explicit rejection of what it calls "secular humanism," the tradition of modernism that promotes the individual, pluralism, tolerance, and skepticism toward the authority of government and other institutions.

Like all conservative movements, the Moral Majority seeks to strengthen authority, especially the authority of parents over their children. Thus it supports Senator Paul Laxalt's Family Protection Act, which would exclude all forms of corporal punishment from child-

(continued on next page)

Exhibit 2 (continued)

abuse laws, give parents the right to censor textbooks and local school boards the right to prevent boys and girls from participating in sports together. Falwell was quoted in a *New York Times* article on children's rights as follows: "I believe that children should be subservient to their parents. Children have the right to expect their parents to love them and to give them the correct discipline to develop their character. They have the right to be punished properly when they do wrong but never to be abused."

Given all this, how could the majority of parents, people who want their lives to be based on choice and want the same for their children, conceivably find any common ground with the Moral Majority? The answer lies in the intrinsically uneasy tension between the activists in any social movement and its broader constituency. It is in the nature of a social movement that many people can align themselves with it without supporting the full range of its program.

One example is the student movement during the war in Vietnam. Its activists largely held a New Left orientation. But at no time were more than 10 percent of all college students sympathetic to its overall viewpoint, despite the fact that the vast majority of students were against the war. As soon as the war ended, differences surfaced and the movement disappeared.

> **Even highly untraditional parents are likely to raise their children by traditional moral standards.**

The women's movement offers a different example. Among the militant activists have been women who despise the traditional role of women as "mere" wives and mothers. But most women are not opposed in principle to that choice. Their objective is simply to expand their range of choices. The interests of the activists and the general constituency are hardly congruent, they overlap only at the edges; but it is on the basis of this overlap that the women's movement has become one of the most influential of our time.

As with both these movements, so with the Moral Majority. In my view, its program overlaps only to a small degree with the broad social concerns of many of its sympathizers. The resonant issue that forges the link between them is the social climate within which children perforce must grow up. I believe this issue, in a qualified form, also gives credibility to the Moral Majority among many people who shun the idea of identifying with the style of a Jerry Falwell and certainly oppose any efforts to restrict their own freedom.

Whether the Moral Majority goes the way of the New Left after the war in Vietnam or the way of the women's movement depends on two contingencies.

The first is the fate of the economy. If we have a severe and prolonged economic setback, which I do not think will happen, then the Moral Majority will grow stronger. We should remember that there is a deep-rooted American tradition of blaming economic setbacks on failures of moral rectitude. Historian Robert Wiebe recounts the many periods of soul-searching that coincided with recessions in 19th-century America. "Throughout the 19th century a great many looked upon economic downturns as moral judgment, precise punishment for the nation's sins." Not far below the surface of Americans' consciousness there lingers the conviction that today's inflation and other economic ills can be traced to the nation's moral looseness. If, throughout the 1980s, the economy shows moderate health, the Moral Majority will lose one of its least visible but most powerful supports.

The second contingency is what happens to the concern about the moral welfare of young people. If there is polarization at the extremes—total permissiveness versus total restrictiveness—then I believe the restrictive extreme will prevail. When people sense that a situation is out of control, the temptation to fall back on restrictive measures grows overwhelming. If the only voices expressing concern about and offering programs of action to improve the moral climate for children come from the cultural right, those voices will set the agenda. But if a moderate middle ground can be found, the Moral Majority will go the way of the New Left and shrink back to become one of the many minor ideological movements on the fringes of American life.

For such a middle ground we need new thinking about the influences that affect the moral development of children. We need to confront the possibility that adults who now live a life of choice while keeping their own moral center intact are capable of doing so because their upbringing instilled in them a clear sense of right and wrong. We need to recognize that we have been neglecting the question, broadly put, of what is best for our children because we have been too busy with the question of what is best for us as adults, assuming—all too comfortably—that the same answer would do for both questions. It will not. A continuing failure to face this reality will serve to strengthen the Moral Majority.

With this commentary, Daniel Yankelovich, a contributing editor, starts a bimonthly column in *Psychology Today.* Yankelovich is the author of *New Rules* and the president of the social-research firm Yankelovich, Skelly, and White.

H. J. Heinz Company

The Administration of Policy (A)

Richard J. Post, MBA '82, prepared this material from published sources under the supervision of Kenneth E. Goodpaster as the basis for class discussion rather than to illustrate either effective or ineffective handling of an administrative situation. The names of persons have been disguised.

> April is the cruelest month.
>
> *T. S. Eliot*

In April 1979 James Cunningham, H. J. Heinz Company's president and chief operating officer, learned that since 1972 certain Heinz divisions had allegedly engaged in improper income transferal practices. Payments had been made to certain vendors in a particular fiscal year, then repaid or exchanged for services in the succeeding fiscal year.[1]

These allegations came out during the investigation of an unrelated antitrust matter. Apparent improprieties were discovered in the records of the Heinz USA division's relationship with one of its advertising agencies. Joseph Stangerson—senior vice president, secretary, and general counsel for Heinz—asked the advertising agency about the alleged practices. Not only had the agency personnel confirmed the allegation about Heinz USA, it indicated that similar practices had been used by Star-Kist Foods, another Heinz division. The divisions allegedly solicited improper invoices from the advertising agency in fiscal year (FY) 1974 so that they could transfer income to FY 1975. While the invoices were paid in FY 1974, the services described on the invoices were not rendered until some time during FY 1975. Rather than capitalizing the amount as a prepaid expense, the amount was charged as an expense in FY 1974. The result was an understatement of FY 1974 income and an equivalent overstatement of FY 1975 income.

Stangerson reported the problem to John Bailey, vice chairman and chief executive officer; to Robert Kelly, senior vice president–finance and treasurer; and to Cunningham. Bailey, CEO since 1966, had presided over 13 uninterrupted years of earnings growth. He

---

1. H. J. Heinz Company, form 8-K, April 27, 1979, p. 2.

was scheduled to retire as vice chairman and CEO on July 1 and would remain as a member of the board of directors. James Cunningham, who had been president and chief operating officer since 1972, was to become chief executive officer on July 1, 1979.

Subsequent reports indicate that neither the scope of the practice nor the amounts involved were known. There was no apparent reason to believe that the amounts involved would have had a material effect on Heinz's reported earnings during the time period, including earnings for FY 1979 ending May 2. (Heinz reported financial results on the basis of a 52–53 week fiscal year ending on the Wednesday closest to April 30.) Stangerson was not prepared to say whether the alleged practices were legal or illegal. "This thing could be something terrible or it could be merely a department head using conservative accounting practices; we don't know,"[2] one Heinz senior official stated to the press.

Background

Henry J. Heinz, on founding the company in 1869 in Pittsburgh, Pennsylvania, said: "This is my goal—to bring home-cooking standards into canned foods, making them so altogether wholesome and delicious and at the same time so reasonable that people everywhere will enjoy them in abundance."[3] The company's involvement in food products never changed, and in 1979 Heinz operated some 30 companies with products reaching 150 countries. Heinz reported sales of over $2.2 billion and net income of $99.1 million in FY 1978.

After a sluggish period in the early 1960s, a reorganization was undertaken to position Heinz for growth. Under the guidance of John Bailey and James Cunningham, Heinz prospered through a major recession, government price controls, and major currency fluctuations. The 1978 annual report reflected management's pride in Heinz's remarkably consistent growth:

Fiscal 1978 went into the books as the fifteenth consecutive year of record results for Heinz. Earnings rose to another new high. Sales reached more than $2 billion only six years after we had passed the $1 billion mark for the first time in our century-long history. We are determined to maintain the financial integrity of our enterprise and support its future growth toward ever-higher levels. [*Exhibit 1* presents a financial summary of fiscal years 1972–1978.]

Although Heinz was a multinational firm, domestic operations accounted for 62% of sales and 67% of earnings in FY 1978. Five major divisions operated in the United States in 1979.

Throughout the 1970s Heinz's major objective was consistent growth in earnings. While Heinz management did not consider acquisitions to be crucial to continuing growth, it looked favorably on purchase opportunities in areas where Heinz had demonstrated capabilities. Bailey and Cunningham stressed profit increases through the elimination of marginally profitable products. Increased advertising of successful traditional products and new product development efforts also contributed to Heinz's growth. Heinz's commitment to decentralized authority as an organizational principle aided the management of internal growth as well as acquisitions.

Organization

In 1979 Heinz was organized on two primary levels. The corporate world headquarters, located in Pittsburgh, consisted of the principal corporate officers and historically small staffs (management described the world headquarters as lean). World headquarters had the responsibility for "the decentralized coordination and control needed to set overall standards and ensure performance in accordance with them."[4] Some Heinz operating divisions reported directly to the president; others reported through senior vice presidents who were designated area directors (see *Exhibit 2*). World headquarters officers worked with division senior managers in areas such as planning, product and market development, and capital programs.

Heinz's divisions were largely autonomous operating companies. Division managers were directly responsible for the division's products and services, and they operated their own research and development, manufacturing, and marketing facilities. Division staff reported directly to division managers and had neither formal reporting nor dotted-line relationships with corporate staff.

---

2. "Heinz to Probe Prepayments to Suppliers by Using Outside Lawyers, Accountants," *Wall Street Journal*, April 30, 1979, p. 5.
3. H. J. Heinz Company, annual report, 1976.

4. H. J. Heinz Company, form 8-K, May 7, 1980, p. 7.

World headquarters officers monitored division performance through conventional business budgets and financial reports. If reported performance was in line with corporate financial goals, little inquiry into the details of division operation was made. On the other hand, variations from planned performance drew a great deal of attention from world headquarters; then, divisions were pressured to improve results. A review was held near the end of the third fiscal quarter to discuss expected year-end results. If shortfalls were apparent, other divisions were often encouraged to improve their performance. The aim was to meet projected consolidated earnings and goals. Predictability was a watchword and surprises were to be avoided.[5] A consistent growth in earnings attended this management philosophy.

Management Incentive Plan

Designed by a prominent management consulting firm, the management incentive plan (MIP) was regarded as a prime management tool used to achieve corporate goals.[6] MIP comprised roughly 225 employees, including corporate officers, senior world headquarters personnel, and senior personnel of most divisions. Incentive compensation was awarded on the basis of an earned number of MIP points and in some cases reached 40% of total compensation.

MIP points could be earned through the achievement of personal goals. These goals were established at the beginning of each fiscal year in consultation with the participant's immediate supervisor. Points were awarded by the supervisor at the end of the year, based on goal achievement. In practice, personal goal point awards fell out on a curve, with few individuals receiving very high or very low awards.

MIP points were also awarded based on net profit after tax (NPAT) goals. (On occasion, other goals such as increased inventory turnover or improved cash flow were included in MIP goals.) Corporate NPAT goals were set at the beginning of the fiscal year by the management development and compensation committee (MDC) of the board of directors. The chief executive officer, the chief operating officer, the

senior vice president–finance, and the senior vice president–corporate development then set MIP goals for each division, with the aggregate of division goals usually exceeding the corporate goal. Two goals were set—a fair goal, which was consistently higher than the preceding year's NPAT, and a higher outstanding goal. The full number of MIP points was earned by achieving the outstanding goal.

Senior corporate managers were responsible for executing the system. While divisional input was not uncommon, division NPAT goals were set unilaterally and did not necessarily reflect a division's budgeted profits. Once set, goals were seldom changed during the year. The officers who set the goals awarded MIP points at the end of the fiscal year. No points were awarded to personnel in a division that failed to achieve its fair goal, and points were weighted to favor results at or near the outstanding goal. One or more bonus points might be awarded if the outstanding goal was exceeded. Corporate officers also had the authority to make adjustments or award arbitrary points in special circumstances. The basis for these adjustments was not discussed with division personnel.

MIP points for consolidated corporate performance were awarded by the MDC committee of the board. Corporate points were credited to all MIP participants except those in a division that did not achieve its fair goal. The MDC committee could also award company bonus points.

Heinz also had a long-term incentive plan based on a revolving three-year cycle. Participation was limited to senior corporate management and division presidents or managing directors for a total of 19 persons.

Corporate Ethical Policy

Heinz had an explicit corporate ethical policy that was adopted in May 1976.[7] Among other things, it stated that no division should:

1. have any form of unrecorded assets or false entries on its books or records;
2. make or approve any payment with the intention or understanding that any part of such payment was to be used for any purpose other than that described by the documents supporting the payment;
3. make political contributions;

5. Ibid, p. 8.
6. Ibid, pp. 10–12.

7. Ibid, p. 12.

4. make payments or gifts to public officials or customers; or

5. accept gifts or payments of more than a nominal amount.

Each year the president or managing director and the chief financial officer of each division were required to sign a representation letter which, among other things, confirmed compliance with the corporate Code of Ethics.

April 1979

Heinz itself had originated the antitrust proceedings that led to the discovery of the alleged practices. In 1976 Heinz filed a private antitrust suit against the Campbell Soup Company, accusing Campbell of monopolistic practices in the canned soup market. Campbell promptly countersued, charging that Heinz monopolized

the ketchup market.[8] Campbell attorneys, preparing for court action, subpoenaed Heinz documents reflecting its financial relationships with one of its advertising agencies. In April 1979, while taking a deposition from Arthur West, president of the Heinz USA division, Campbell attorneys asked about flows of funds, "certain items which can be called off-book accounts." West refused to answer, claiming Fifth Amendment protection from self-incrimination.[9] Stangerson then spoke with the advertising agency and received confirmation of the invoicing practices.

---

8. "Heinz slow growth behind juggling tactic?" *Advertising Age,* March 24, 1980, p. 88.
9. "Results in Probe of Heinz Income Juggling Expected to be Announced by Early April," *Wall Street Journal,* March 18, 1980, p. 7.

Exhibit 1
Financial Summary, Fiscal Years 1972–1978 ($ thousands except per share data)

	1978	1977	1976	1975	1974	1973	1972
Summary of Operations							
Sales	$2,150,027	$1,868,820	$1,749,691	$1,564,930	$1,349,091	$1,116,551	$1,020,958
Cost of products sold	1,439,249	1,262,260	1,228,229	1,097,093	939,565	772,525	700,530
Interest expense	18,859	16,332	22,909	31,027	21,077	13,813	11,463
Provision for income taxes	69,561	71,119	53,675	49,958	36,730	30,913	30,702
Income from continuing operations	99,171	83,816	73,960	66,567	55,520	50,082	44,679
Loss from discontinued and expropriated operations	–	–	–	–	–	3,530	2,392
Income before extraordinary items	99,171	83,816	73,960	66,567	55,520	46,552	42,287
Extraordinary items	–	–	–	–	8,800	(25,000)	–
Net income	99,171	83,816	73,960	66,567	64,320	21,552	42,287
Per Common Share Amounts							
Income from continuing operations	4.25	3.55	3.21	2.93	2.45	2.21	1.98
Loss from discontinued and expropriated operations	–	–	–	–	–	.16	.11
Income before extraordinary items	4.25	3.55	3.21	2.93	2.45	2.05	1.87
Extraordinary items	–	–	–	–	.39	(1.10)	–
Net income	4.25	3.55	3.21	2.93	2.84	.95	1.87
Other Data							
Dividends paid							
Common, per share	1.42	1.06⅔	.86⅔	.77⅓	.72⅔	.70	.67⅓
Common, total	32,143	24,260	19,671	17,502	16,427	15,814	15,718
Preferred, total	3,147	3,166	1,024	139	146	165	184
Capital expenditures	95,408	53,679	34,682	57,219	44,096	48,322	28,067
Depreciation	31,564	29,697	27,900	25,090	22,535	20,950	20,143
Shareholders' equity	702,736	655,480	598,613	502,796	447,434	399,607	394,519
Total debt	228,002	220,779	219,387	295,051	266,617	249,161	196,309
Average number of common shares outstanding	22,609,613	22,743,233	22,696,484	22,633,115	22,604,720	22,591,287	22,538,309
Book value per common share	28.96	26.27	23.79	22.04	19.61	17.50	17.26
Price range of common stock							
High	40	34⅛	38	34⅜	34⅞	30⅞	31½
Low	28¾	26½	28⅞	18	24⅞	25⅜	25⅞
Sales (%)							
Domestic	62	62	59	58	59	58	57
Foreign	38	38	41	42	41	42	43
Income (%)							
Domestic	67	78	66	71	57	53	54
Foreign	33	22	34	29	43	47	46

Source: Company records

Exhibit 2
Organization Chart, April 1979

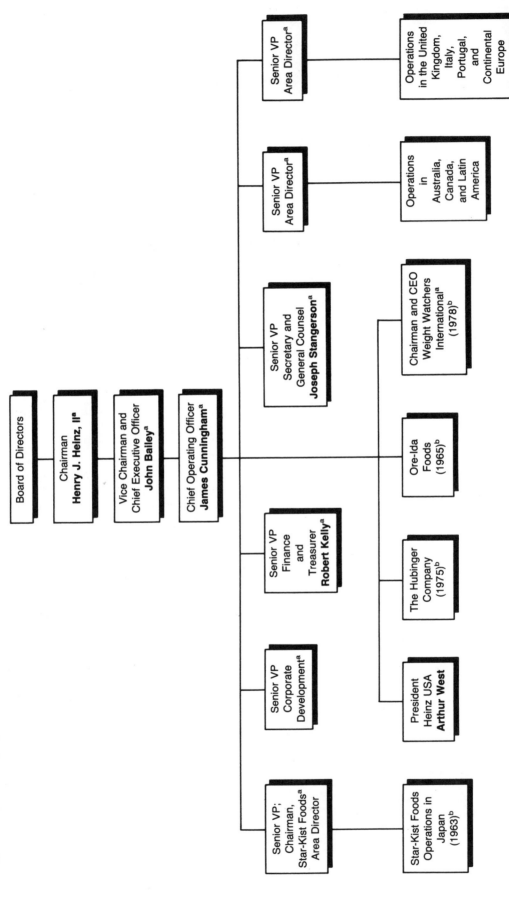

Board of Directors

Chairman
Henry J. Heinz, II[a]

Vice Chairman and
Chief Executive Officer
John Bailey[a]

Chief Operating Officer
James Cunningham[a]

Senior VP;
Chairman,
Star-Kist Foods[a]
Area Director

Senior VP
Corporate
Development[a]

Senior VP
Finance
and
Treasurer
Robert Kelly[a]

Senior VP
Secretary and
General Counsel
Joseph Stangerson[a]

Senior VP[a]
Area Director

Senior VP[a]
Area Director

Star-Kist Foods
Operations in
Japan
(1963)[b]

President
Heinz USA
Arthur West

The Hubinger
Company
(1975)[b]

Ore-Ida
Foods
(1965)[b]

Chairman and CEO
Weight Watchers
International[a]
(1978)[b]

Operations
in
Australia,
Canada,
and Latin
America

Operations
in the United
Kingdom,
Italy,
Portugal, and
Continental
Europe

a. Member of the board of directors
b. Date in parenthesis indicates year acquired.

H. J. Heinz Company

The Administration of Policy (B)

Richard J. Post, MBA '82, prepared this material from published sources under the supervision of Kenneth E. Goodpaster as the basis for class discussion rather than to illustrate either effective or ineffective handling of an administrative situation. The names of persons have been disguised.

In April 1979 Heinz's senior management learned of improper practices concerning the transfer of an undetermined amount of reported income from one fiscal year to the next. At two of the Heinz operating divisions payments had been made to vendors in one fiscal year, then repaid or exchanged for services in the succeeding fiscal year. The scope of the practice and the amounts involved were not then known.

Aware that the practice might have affected the company's reported income over the past seven fiscal years, management consulted an outside legal firm for an opinion on the seriousness of the problem. Based on that opinion, John Bailey, Heinz's chief executive officer, notified the Audit Committee of the board of directors. Composed entirely of outside directors, this committee was responsible for working with internal auditors and financial officers and with the firm's outside auditors, thus preserving the integrity of financial information published by Heinz.

The Audit Committee held a special meeting on April 26, 1979. After hearing from outside counsel and from Joseph Stangerson (Heinz's general counsel) about the practices, the committee adopted a resolution retaining an outside law firm and independent public accountants to assist in a full investigation of the matter.[1]

An attorney from Cravath, Swaine & Moore, the outside law firm, accompanied Stangerson to Washington to advise the Securities and Exchange Commission of the information available and of the investigation then under way. (An excerpt from form 8-K filed with the SEC is attached as *Exhibit 1*.) The two also informed the IRS of possible tax consequences of the practice.

---

1. "Report of the Audit Committee to the Board of Directors: Income Transferal and Other Practices," H. J. Heinz Company, form 8-K, May 7, 1980.

On April 27, 1979, Heinz publicly announced its investigation. "At this stage," the formal statement said, "it isn't possible to determine the scope of the practice or the total amounts involved." It also stated that there "isn't any reason to believe there will be any material effect on the company's reported earnings for any fiscal year including the current fiscal year." While the investigation would cover the period from 1972 to 1979, Heinz would not identify the divisions or vendors involved. Stangerson stated: "We aren't prepared to say whether [the practices] were legal or illegal." He added that the company had informed the SEC and the IRS.[2]

The Investigation

The Audit Committee supervised the conduct of the investigation. Teams composed of lawyers and accountants from the two outside firms interviewed present and former company and vendor personnel about possible improprieties. The investigators focused on the following areas:

1. practices that affected the accuracy of company accounts or the security of company assets;
2. practices in violation of the company's Code of Ethics;
3. illegal political contributions;
4. illegal, improper, or otherwise questionable payments; and
5. factors contributing to the existence, continuance, or nondisclosure of any of the above.

The investigating teams interviewed over 325 Heinz employees, many of them more than once. The teams also interviewed personnel employed by many of Heinz's vendors, including advertising agencies. Accounting records, correspondence, and other files were examined. The board of directors at its regular May meeting asked for the cooperation of all officers and employees.[3]

On May 10, 1979, Heinz announced that a settlement had been reached in its private antitrust suit against the Campbell Soup Company. The settlement resulted in the dismissal of Heinz's action against Campbell, which had been brought in 1976, and of Campbell's counterclaim against Heinz. The court ordered the record of the suit sealed and kept secret.[4]

On June 29, 1979, Heinz disclosed a preliminary figure of $5.5 million of after-tax income associated with the income transferal practices. Stressing that this was a "very soft number," the company indicated that it was delaying release of audited results for FY 1979 (ended May 2, 1979) and that its annual meeting, scheduled for September 12, would be postponed until the investigation (which could continue well into the fall) was completed. The preliminary unaudited figures released by Heinz showed net income of $113.4 million ($4.95 per share) on sales of $2.4 billion, after the $5.5 million deduction. Press reports indicated the investigation was being broadened to include Heinz's foreign units.[5]

On September 13, 1979, it was reported that the preliminary figure had grown to $8.5 million. Heinz's statement, filed with its first quarter FY 1980 earnings report, also stated FY 1979 income as $110.4 million or $4.80 per share. Most of the $3 million growth was attributed to the discovery of improper treatment of sales in addition to the improper treatment of prepaid expenses discovered earlier.[6]

Heinz's 1979 annual report contained audited financial statements for FY 1979 and restated financial statements for FY 1978. The report contained an unqualified opinion from Peat, Marwick, Mitchell & Company, Heinz's auditors, dated November 14, 1979. In Note 2 to the 1979 financial statements, the report also contained a restatement and reconciliation of sales, net income, and earnings per share for the previous eight fiscal years. (The 1979 results are shown in *Exhibit 2*. The restatement of FY 1971–FY 1978 are shown in *Exhibit 3*.) This information was filed with the Securities and Exchange Commission on November 20, 1979.[7]

In February 1980 Heinz reorganized its top management structure (see *Exhibit 4*). Arthur West, formerly president of Heinz USA, was promoted to world headquarters as area director. He assumed responsibility for the Hubinger Company and Weight Watchers Interna-

2. "Results in Probe of Heinz Income Juggling Expected to be Announced by Early April," *Wall Street Journal*, March 18, 1980, p. 7.
3. Audit Committee report, form 8-K, May 7, 1980, p. 4.
4. H. J. Heinz Company, form 8-K, May 10, 1979, p. 2; the *Wall Street Journal*, March 18, 1980, p. 7.
5. "Initial Study of Some Heinz Units Finds $5.5 Million in Profit Juggling Practices," *Wall Street Journal*, July 2, 1979, p. 8.
6. "Heinz Discloses Profit Switching at Units Was Much Broader than First Realized," *Wall Street Journal*, September 13, 1979, p. 15.
7. Audit Committee report, form 8-K, May 7, 1980, p. 2.

Table A
Increase (Decrease) of Consolidated Income before Tax, Net of Recoveries ($ thousands)

FY	*Improper Recognition*		*Other Practices*	*Net Income Before Tax*		*% Effects of Restatement*
	Expenses	*Sales*		*Increase (Decrease)*	*Total After Restatement*	
1972	$(513)	–	–	$(513)	$75,894	(.7)
1973	(1,814)	$(1,968)	–	(3,782)	84,777	(4.5)
1974	(4,250)	(309)	$(1,364)	(5,923)	98,173	(6.0)
1975	2,476	1,527	(615)	3,388	113,137	3.0
1976	(111)	(1,815)	877	(1,049)	128,682	(.8)
1977	(4,139)	(1,294)	268	(5,165)	160,101	(3.2)
1978	734	(2,872)	671	(1,467)	170,198	(.9)
1979	8,888	7,085	396	16,369	183,178	8.9
1980	76	(354)	(233)	(511)	–	–

tional, both of which had previously reported directly to James Cunningham, Heinz's president and new CEO. West was also to be responsible for Heinz's Canadian subsidiary. Heinz USA would now report through Kevin Voight, senior vice president, rather than directly to Cunningham. Unlike other area directors, West would be neither a senior vice president nor a member of the board of directors.[8]

In April 1980 Doyle Dane Bernbach, the only publicly held firm among the advertising and consulting firms included in the Audit Committee's investigation, admitted in an SEC filing that it had participated in the income-juggling practices by prebilling and issuing bills that did not accurately describe the services provided.[9]

On May 7, 1980, the Audit Committee presented its report to the Heinz board of directors. The 80-page report was filed on form 8-K with the SEC on May 9, 1980. (The remainder of this case is derived substantially from the Audit Committee's report.)

The Findings

The Audit Committee reported widespread use of improper billing, accounting, and reporting procedures at Heinz's divisions including Heinz USA, Ore-Ida, and Star-Kist, and a number of Heinz's foreign operations. The two major areas of impropriety were:

---

8. "H. J. Heinz Realigns its Senior Management in Consolidation Move," *Wall Street Journal,* February 19, 1980.
9. "DDB admits Heinz role," *Advertising Age,* April 28, 1980, pp. 1, 88.

1. *Improper recognition of expenses:* These were most often advertising and market research expenses, improperly recorded in the current fiscal period when in fact the services were performed or goods delivered in a later fiscal period. This treatment resulted in an overstatement of expenses (and understatement of income) in one period and a comparable understatement of expenses (and overstatement of income) in a later fiscal period.

2. *Improper recognition of sales:* Sales were recorded in a fiscal period other than that in which those sales should have been recorded under generally accepted accounting principles.

Table A indicates the amounts involved. The accumulated effects of such practices on shareholders' equity and working capital did not exceed 2%.

The Audit Committee indicated that these income transferal practices were designed to adjust the income reported by divisions to corporate headquarters and were motivated primarily by a desire to meet the constantly increasing profit objectives set by world headquarters. While division management supported the publicly announced goal of steadily increasing profits, the committee reported that the management incentive program (MIP) under which the goals were administered created significant pressures. Aside from obvious personal financial considerations, many division-level personnel reportedly viewed the achievement of MIP goals as the key to advancement at Heinz. One manager told the committee that failure to achieve these goals constituted a "mortal sin."

The Heinz principle of decentralized authority extended to financial reporting and internal control procedures. Division financial officers were not responsible to corporate headquarters but to their division president or managing director. The MIP goal pressures provided the incentive, and autonomous control the opportunity, for adopting the improper practices being reported.

One reason for using such reporting techniques was explained to the committee:

> If this fiscal year's goal is, say, $20 million net profit after tax (NPAT), it can be anticipated that next year's goal will be, say, 15% higher, or $23 million NPAT. This year seems to be a good one and it is anticipated that earnings will be $24 million NPAT. But, if that figure is reported to world headquarters, it is likely that next year's goal will be about 15% higher than the $24 million NPAT, or approximately $27 million NPAT. Of course, there is no assurance that there will not be some unforeseen disaster next year. Thus, if it is possible to mislead world headquarters as to the true state of the earnings of the [division] and report only the $20 million NPAT, which is the current fiscal year's goal, and have the additional $4 million NPAT carried forward into next year, the [division] will have a good start toward achieving its expected $23 million NPAT goal next year and will not have to reach $27 million NPAT.

Explanations for accepting these practices at lower levels included job security and the desire to impress superiors.

The committee's report stated: "There is no evidence that any employee of the company sought or obtained any direct personal gain in connection with any of the transactions or practices described in this report. Nor did the investigation find any evidence that any officer or personnel at world headquarters participated in any of the income transferal practices described in this report." The report went on to describe activities at each division in greater detail.

Division Income Transfer Practices

Heinz USA. Income transfer at Heinz USA started late in FY 1974 when world headquarters realized that Heinz USA might report profits in excess of those allowed by the wage and price controls in effect at the time. World headquarters sought to have Heinz USA report lower profits, although no evidence indicates that any world headquarters personnel intended GAAP to be violated. After some commodity transactions lowered expected profits, there was a reluctance in Heinz USA to reduce its expected profits further. Nevertheless, to accomplish the further reduction, $2 million in invoices for services that would not be performed were obtained from an advertising agency and recorded as an expense in FY 1974.

Heinz USA reported FY 1974 NPAT of $4,614,000. NPAT goals for the year were $4.9 million (fair) and $5.5 million (outstanding). In calculating NPAT for MIP purposes, world headquarters allowed an adjustment of $2 million ($1 million after tax) for advertising. This adjustment resulted in Heinz USA achieving its outstanding goal for FY 1974. The division also received a bonus point. The use of improper invoices to manage reported income continued after FY 1974 at Heinz USA, although there was no evidence that world headquarters personnel knew about these transactions.

Beginning in FY 1977, additional income transfer methods were developed. Distribution centers were instructed to stop shipments for the last few days of the fiscal year to allow the recording of sales in the subsequent year. These instructions presented practical difficulties and some of the shipments were not held up. Without the authorization of division senior management, paperwork was apparently altered or misdated to record the sales as desired.

Vendors' credits were often deferred and processed in the subsequent fiscal year to assist the income management program. Detailed schedules were privately maintained that served as the basis for discussions on income management. One employee had the job of maintaining private records to insure the recovery (in subsequent fiscal years) of amounts paid to vendors on improper invoices.

The use of improper invoices spread to the departmental level as well. Individual department managers used either prepaid billing or delayed billing, as required, to insure complete use of their departmental budget without overspending. This practice provided protection against future budget cuts during those periods when the full budget would not otherwise have been spent. Division management actively discouraged these transactions.

Vendor cooperation was not difficult to obtain. One Heinz manager described it as "the price of doing business with us." During the period in question, 10 vendors participated in improper invoicing at Heinz USA, and 8 participated at the department level. Most vendors' fiscal years did not coincide with Heinz's.

In FY 1975 a sugar inventory write-down was used to transfer income. Sugar inventory, valued at an average cost of 37 cents per pound, was written down to 25 cents per pound. This adjustment, which amounted to an increase in FY 1975 expense of $1,390,360, was justified on the basis of an expected decline in price early in the next fiscal year. This would result in lower selling prices in FY 1976 for some division products. The lower NPAT figure that resulted was used for establishing FY 1976 goals, but when FY 1975 performance was evaluated, world headquarters adjusted Heinz USA's income up by the amount of the sugar write-down. The anticipated price decline did not occur.

At other times, inflated accruals, inventory adjustments, commodity transactions, and at least one customer rebate were used to report income other than that required by GAAP.

Ore-Ida. Improper invoices to transfer income were also used at Ore-Ida during that period, and the issue of obtaining these invoices was discussed at meetings of Ore-Ida's management board. Even though the invoices contained descriptions of services that were generic or had no correlation to the actual services to be rendered, members of the management board believed the practice was appropriate because comparable services would have been purchased at some point. During two fiscal years Ore-Ida received interest payments from an advertising agency in connection with the payment of these invoices.

Ore-Ida's management believed that members of world headquarters' management were aware of the income transfer practices, but raised no objections to them. Documents submitted to world headquarters by Ore-Ida contained references to special media billing, pre-bills, year-end media billing, special billing adjustments, and advertising and promotion prebilling. Some documents indicated that these items actually applied to the fiscal year following that of expense recognition. The amount of these expenses was indicated each year to world headquarters' management (in one year, the amount was understated). In FY 1974 corporate management increased Ore-Ida's

income before tax by the amount of the pre-billed advertising expense for MIP award purposes. Ore-Ida's management did not know if world headquarters' management appreciated the fact that this practice did not conform to GAAP.

Star-Kist. Both improper expense recognition and improper sales recognition were used to adjust reported income at Star-Kist. Improper invoices were solicited from vendors to accumulate an advertising savings account. Sales during the last month of a fiscal year were recorded during the first month of the next fiscal year by preventing selected documents from entering the sales accounting system. These practices were apparently present only in Star-Kist's marketing department.

Similar practices were also discovered at some of Heinz's foreign subsidiaries.

Other Improper Practices

Although it focused primarily on income transferal practices, the investigation uncovered a number of other practices. Again, the committee stated that no member of world headquarters' management appeared to have any knowledge of these practices, and no employee sought or obtained any personal financial gain. All of these transactions took place outside the United States. None of the countries in which the transactions took place were identified by the committee.

In one country six questionable payments totaling $80,000 were made during FY 1978 and FY 1979. Two were made to lower-level government employees in connection with alleged violations of import regulations. One was made to a lower-level government employee in connection with the settlement of a labor dispute. Municipal employees received one payment in connection with real estate assessments. Labor union officials received the remaining two payments. In January 1979 three of these payments were reported by division management to world headquarters. A brief investigation ensued and the board of directors reprimanded certain officers of the division.

Star-Kist was involved in several transactions listed in the following section of the report:

1. In one country the payment of interest to nonresidents was prohibited. Star-Kist collected interest on its loans to fishing fleets through the falsification of invoices indicat-

ing the purchase by Star-Kist of supplies for the fleets.

2. In another country Star-Kist acted as a conduit through which funds flowed to facilitate a fish purchase involving two other companies. Letters of credit requiring the approval of the exchange authorities were used.

3. In a third country Star-Kist received checks from a fish supplier and endorsed those checks to a wholly owned U.S. subsidiary of the supplier. These transactions were not recorded in Star-Kist's accounts.

The Heinz operating company in yet another country made payments for goods to individual or designated bank accounts rather than to the supplier involved. These payments were not made through the normal cash disbursement procedure; rather, the division was acting at the supplier's request.

Contributing Factors

The Audit Committee reported that only a small part of the failure to detect these practices could be attributed to weakness in Heinz's internal controls. In most cases, those controls were circumvented by or with the concurrence of division management. With the autonomy enjoyed by division management, it would have been difficult for world headquarters personnel to detect these practices.

The committee attributed part of the problem to a lack of control consciousness throughout the corporation. *Control consciousness* referred to the atmosphere in which accounting controls existed and it reflected senior management attitudes about the importance of such controls. Clearly, control consciousness was not then present in most Heinz divisions. The committee blamed world headquarters' senior management for creating an environment that was seen as endorsing poor control consciousness:

> If world headquarters' senior management had established a satisfactory control consciousness, internal accounting controls that were cost/benefit justified should have been able to survive reasonable pressures to meet or exceed the defined economic goals. In establishing this atmosphere, world headquarters' senior management apparently did not consider the effect on individuals in the [divisions] of the pressures to which they were subjected.

Other factors cited by the committee included:

- corporate internal auditing personnel report to their respective division managers and not to the director–corporate audit;
- the lack of an effective Code of Ethics compliance procedure;
- the lack of standardized accounting and reporting procedures for all Heinz divisions;
- the lack of an effective budget review and monitoring process;
- the lack of enough competent financial personnel at world headquarters and at the divisions; and
- the lack of a world headquarters electronic data processing manager responsible for the control procedures of the divisions' EDP departments.

Conclusions of the Audit Committee

1. The amounts involved in the income transferal practices were not material to the consolidated net income or shareholder's equity of the company in the aggregate during the investigatory period (FY 1972–FY 1978).

2. The income transferal practices were achieved primarily through circumvention of existing internal controls by division personnel who should have exercised responsibility in the enforcement of such controls. Such practices were also assisted by certain inadequacies in the internal control systems of the divisions.

3. Although world headquarters' personnel did not authorize or participate in the income transferal practices, their continuance was facilitated by the company's philosophy of decentralized management and the role played by world headquarters' financial personnel in reviewing the financial reports from divisions.

4. No individual employee obtained any direct financial benefit from the practices uncovered in the investigation.

5. Perceived or de facto pressures for achievement of MIP goals contributed to the divisions' desirability of providing a cushion against future business uncertainties.

6. The income transferal practices did not serve any valid corporate need.

7. The income transferal practices and other questionable practices described in this report [of the Audit Committee] indicate the lack of sufficient control consciousness within the corporate structure; that is, an understanding throughout the company and the divisions that responsible and eth-

ical practices are required in connection with all transactions.

8. The entrepreneurial spirit of the divisions fostered by the philosophy of decentralized autonomy should be continued for the good of the company and its shareholders.

9. World headquarters did not have the number of competent financial personnel needed to fulfill its role.

10. The continuance of the income transferal practices was aided by the independence of division financial personnel from world headquarters.

11. The continuance of the income transferal practices was aided by the reporting relationships of the internal audit staffs within the company.

12. The administration of the MIP and the goal-setting process thereunder did not result in adequate dialogue between senior world headquarters management and managements of the divisions.

13. The board of directors and management of the company have the duty to take all steps practicable to ensure safeguarding the assets of the company and that all transactions are properly recorded on the books, records and accounts of the company.

Exhibit 1
Form 8-K Excerpt, April 27, 1979

Item 5: Other Materially Important Events

On April 27, 1979, the registrant announced that it had become aware that since 1972 in certain of its divisions or subsidiaries payments have been made to certain of its vendors in a particular fiscal year, which were repaid or exchanged for services by such vendors in the succeeding fiscal year.

The registrant stated that at this stage it was not possible to determine the scope of the practice or the total amounts involved, but that there was no reason to believe there would be any material effect on the registrant's reported earnings for any fiscal year including the fiscal year ending May 2, 1979.

The Audit Committee of the registrant's board of directors has retained the law firm of Cravath, Swaine & Moore, independent outside counsel, to conduct a full inquiry of the practice. Cravath, Swaine & Moore will retain independent public accountants to assist in the investigation.

The registrant has heretofore advised the Securities and Exchange Commission and the Internal Revenue Service of the foregoing. At this time the registrant is unable to estimate the extent of any adjustments which may be necessary for tax purposes.

Exhibit 2
Financial Summary, 1979 ($ in thousands except per share data)

	1979	1978[a]	Change
Sales	$2,470,883	$2,159,436	14.4%
Operating income	214,735	187,062	14.8
Net income	110,430	99,946	10.5
Per common share amounts			
Net income	$4.80	$4.28	12.1%
Net income (fully diluted)	4.64	4.17	11.3
Dividends	1.85	1.42	30.3
Book value	32.29	29.33	10.1
Capital expenditures	$118,156	95,408	23.8%
Depreciation expense	38,317	31,564	21.4
Net property	481,688	412,334	16.8
Cash and short-term investments	$122,281	$84,044	45.5%
Working capital	401,169	453,517	(11.5)
Total debt	342,918	228,002	50.4
Shareholders' equity	778,397	711,126	9.5
Average number of common shares outstanding	22,330	22,610	
Current ratio	1.70	2.14	
Debt/invested capital	30.9%	24.7%	
Pretax return on average invested capital	20.7%	20.7%	
Return on average shareholders' equity	14.8%	14.5%	

Source: 1979 annual report

a. As restated

Exhibit 3
Restated Financial Data, 1971–1978

Change in Sales, Net Income and Earnings per Share

In thousands except for per share amounts	1971	1972	1973	1974	1975	1976	1977	1978
Sales as previously reported	$876,451	$1,020,958	$1,116,551	$1,349,091	$1,564,930	$1,749,691	$1,868,820	$2,150,027
Net increase (decrease) resulting from restatement to correct improper treatment of sales	—	—	14,821	(1,777)	(4,747)	4,725	8,480	9,409
Sales as restated	$876,451	$1,020,958	$1,131,372	$1,347,314	$1,560,183	$1,754,416	$1,877,300	$2,159,436
Net income as previously reported	$37,668*	$42,287*	$21,552*	$64,320*	$66,567	$73,960	$83,816	$99,171
Net increase (decrease) in income before income taxes resulting from restatement: Correct improper treatment of sales, net of related costs	—	—	1,968	309	(1,527)	1,815	1,294	2,872
Correct improper recognition of income/expense	1,290	512	1,813	5,615	(1,861)	(684)	3,822	(1,417)
	1,290	512	3,781	5,924	(3,388)	1,131	5,116	1,455
Income tax effect	(671)	(263)	(1,566)	(2,698)	1,254	(604)	(2,203)	(680)
Net adjustments	619	249	2,215	3,226	(2,134)	527	2,913	775
Net income as restated	$38,287	$42,536	$23,767	$67,546	$64,433	$74,487	$86,729	$99,946
Income per common share amounts: Income from continuing operations as previously reported	$1.71	$1.98	$2.21	$2.45	$2.93	$3.21	$3.55	$4.25
Net increase (decrease) from restatement	.02	.01	.09	.14	(.09)	.03	.12	.03
Income from continuing operations as restated	1.73	1.99	2.30	2.59	2.84	3.24	3.67	4.28
Loss from discontinued and expropriated operations	.02	.11	.16	—	—	—	—	—
Income before extraordinary items	1.71	1.88	2.14	2.59	2.84	3.24	3.67	4.28
Extraordinary items	—	—	(1.10)	.39	—	—	—	—
Net income	$1.71	$1.88	$1.04	$2.98	$2.84	$3.24	$3.67	$4.28

*Net income as previously reported above includes losses from discontinued and expropriated operations and extraordinary items as shown.

In thousands	Income from continuing operations	Loss from discontinued and expropriated operations	Extraordinary items	Net income as previously reported
1971	$38,171	$ (503)	$ —	$37,668
1972	44,679	(2,392)	—	42,287
1973	50,082	(3,530)	(25,000)	21,552
1974	55,520	—	8,800	64,320

The following table presents the as-reported and as-restated interim results, which are unaudited, for 1978 and 1979.

In thousands except per share amounts	Sales As Reported	Sales As Restated	Gross Profit As Reported	Gross Profit As Restated	Net Income As Reported	Net Income As Restated	Earnings Per Share As Reported	Earnings Per Share As Restated
1978								
First Quarter	$ 491,469	$ 472,955	$156,538	$152,639	$19,645	$ 17,621	$ .83	$ .74
Second Quarter	520,051	525,440	169,476	170,348	23,613	22,676	1.00	.96
Third Quarter	523,640	517,738	170,621	169,001	19,901	20,208	.85	.86
Fourth Quarter	614,867	643,303	214,143	221,992	36,012	39,441	1.57	1.72
Total	$2,150,027	$2,159,436	$710,778	$713,980	$99,171	$ 99,946	$4.25	$4.28
1979								
First Quarter	$ 555,558	$ 536,301	$178,250	$171,330	$21,161	$ 16,783	$ .91	$ .72
Second Quarter	620,230	619,627	203,708	203,964	28,204	26,026	1.23	1.13
Third Quarter	575,410	566,747	202,171	199,497	23,301	21,192	1.01	.91
Fourth Quarter	—	748,208*	—	267,584*	—	46,429*	—	2.04*
Total	$ —	$2,470,883*	$ —	$842,375*	$ —	$110,430*	$ —	$4.80*

*Not previously reported.

Source: 1979 annual report

Exhibit 4
Organization Chart, February 1980

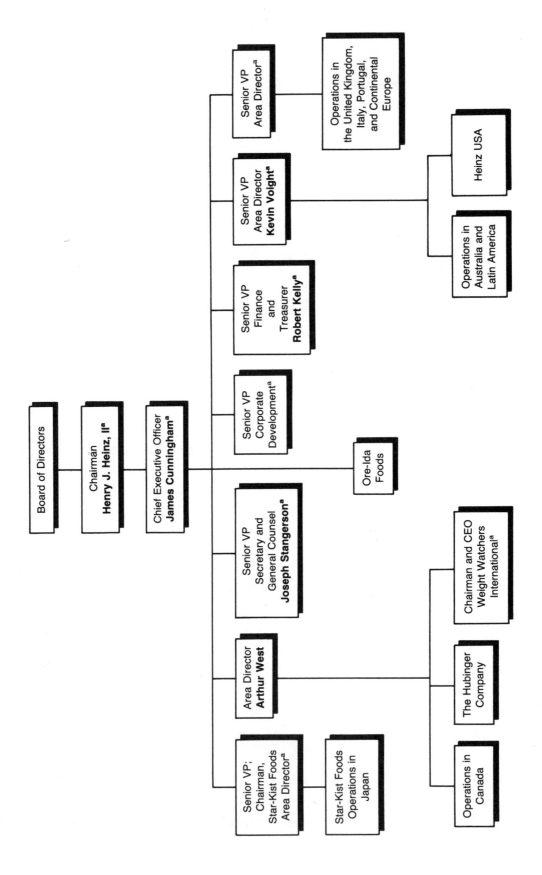

a. Member of the board of directors

Duke Power Company

Affirmative Action (A)

David E. Whiteside, research associate, prepared this case under the supervision of Kenneth E. Goodpaster as the basis for class discussion rather than to illustrate either effective or ineffective handling of an administrative situation.

In the mid-1970s, for the first time in its history, the financial condition of Duke Power Company required layoffs. The board of directors had decided to make major cutbacks in construction that would require dismissing about 1,500 of its 4,646 construction workers.

Bill Lee, senior vice president–engineering and construction, was not sure how he should handle the layoffs. In the past individuals had been discharged only on the basis of performance. He was bothered, however, by the amount of subjectivity involved in using performance as the criterion. If he used last hired, first fired as a standard, the company would undo much of the progress it had made in increasing the number of its minority employees. Going by inverse seniority, he estimated that everyone with less than three years' experience would be discharged, including most of the black construction workers. The alternative of protecting minority workers from being laid off would require firing white construction workers with up to seven years' seniority. This might provoke considerable resentment and lead to demands for a union. Bill Lee also did not want to compromise the company's high standards for quality of construction. Maintaining that standard required a skilled and experienced work force.

A prompt decision was necessary. Lee arranged a meeting with his superior, B. B. Parker, for 8:00 A.M. the next day, August 22, 1974, to tell him what he wanted to do. He talked with Bob Dick, vice president–construction, to find out how many employees in each trade were needed for the projects scheduled for completion. Bill Grigg, senior vice president–legal and finance, told him that the law allowed him to do what he chose in this situation (see *Figure A* for organization chart). That night Lee prayed long and hard; by morning, he knew what he would do.

Figure A
Organization Chart, August 1974

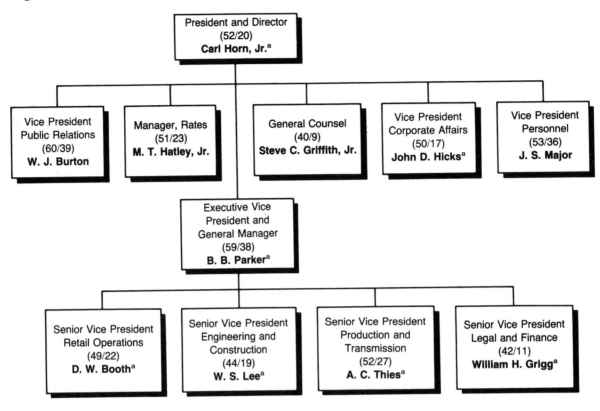

Note: Figures in parentheses denote age and length of service.
a. Director and member of executive committee.

Company Background

Duke Power Company was an electric utility engaged in the generation, transmission, and distribution of electric power to the general public and industry in North and South Carolina. The company was originally incorporated in New Jersey in 1917 as the Wateree Electric Company. The name was changed to Duke Power Company in 1924, and in June 1964 incorporation was shifted to North Carolina.

In 1974 Duke Power was the sixth largest investor-owned utility in the United States. It served approximately 1,100,000 customers, and its service area encompassed some 20,000 square miles throughout the industrial Piedmont of the two states. Generating capability at the start of 1974 was 8.5 million kilowatts (kw). This consisted of 5.9 million kw from fossil-fueled steam stations, 0.8 million kw from nuclear-fueled steam stations, 1.1 million kw from hydroelectric stations, 0.4 million kw from

combustion turbines, and purchased power of 0.3 million kw. Duke Power's home office was in Charlotte, North Carolina, with retail customers served locally through 98 district and branch offices. In 1974 there were 13,063 employees. (*Figure B* shows the company's service area, its facilities, and work in progress.)

Duke Power owned three subsidiaries. The Crescent Land and Timber Corporation was formed in 1963 to manage the company's nonutility lands. The Eastover Mining Company and Eastover Land Company were organized in 1970 to purchase and develop coal properties in Virginia and eastern Kentucky. The Mill Power Supply was chartered in 1910 and was an authorized distributor for many of the largest electrical equipment manufacturers in the country. In addition to selling items to Duke Power and others as a wholesale distributor, Mill Power Supply purchased virtually all supplies, equipment, and fuel required by the parent company.

Figure B
Duke Power Service Area

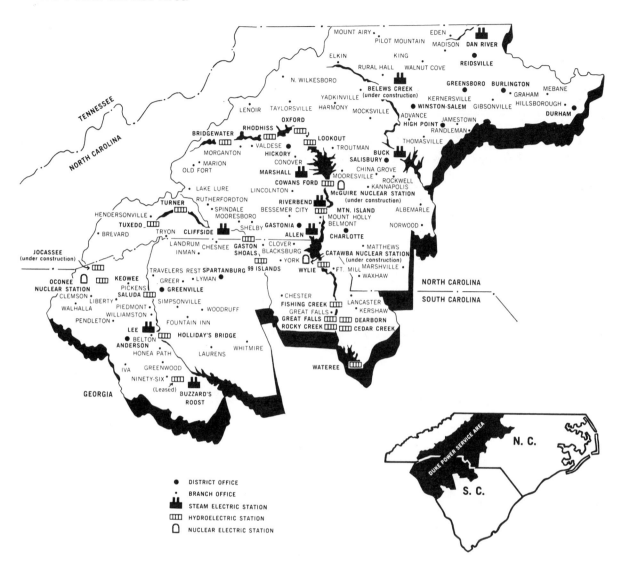

● DISTRICT OFFICE
• BRANCH OFFICE
▮ STEAM ELECTRIC STATION
▥ HYDROELECTRIC STATION
▢ NUCLEAR ELECTRIC STATION

The company was the only major U.S. utility to design and construct its own power plants. In 1974 it undertook new construction at the rate of over $3 million every working day. If ranked by output, its construction department would have been in the top dozen construction companies in the country. It had an excellent reputation for efficient construction and operation of generating facilities. The Marshall Steam Station had been acclaimed as the most efficient coal-burning plant in the nation for the past seven years; for the past two years, the steam-electric generating system had been rated #1 by the Federal Power Commission (FPC).

Rates were set by the FPC for wholesale customers and by the North Carolina Utilities Com-mission (NCUC) and the Public Service Commission of South Carolina (PSCSC) for retail customers. Economies of scale and new technology made the utility industry a declining costs industry up to 1969. Combined with Duke Power's efficiency, this had resulted in six major rate reductions for Duke Power's customers in the 1960s. In 1969 its retail prices were 18% below the national average.

Organizational culture at Duke Power was similar to a family-run business, especially prior to the company's rapid expansion in 1969. Things were done informally with few written policies or procedures. Even multimillion dollar contracts had often been finalized by a hand-shake. Heads of departments had considerable autonomy. Those who had problems in their departments were expected to make recommendations and, if approved, to take responsibility for implementing them. There was also a norm for rapid decision making and implementation.

Minority Employees

In November 1966 the 13 black workers at Duke Power's Dan River plant filed suit against the company. They claimed that the educational and testing requirements used by Duke Power were discriminatory and invalid, and that prior to the Civil Rights Act of 1964, blacks had been relegated to the lowest-paying department. The plaintiffs also argued that centuries of cultural and educational discrimination had placed them at a disadvantage when competing with whites for positions allocated by education or performance on standardized tests.

Griggs v. Duke Power, as the case was known, was heard by the Federal District Court and the Fourth Circuit Court of Appeals with mixed results before the Supreme Court agreed to review the case. The Federal District Court ruled that Duke Power had followed a policy of overt racial discrimination prior to the Civil Rights Act, but it acknowledged that such conduct had since ceased. In 1970, the Supreme Court ruled 8 to 0 that although it was not Duke Power's intent to discriminate against blacks, the educational and testing requirements used by the company were not related to job performance and thus were illegal. It was also stated that these requirements would operate to "freeze the status quo of prior discriminatory employment practices." Closely followed by the press, the decision was a landmark in labor relations and heralded as a victory for blacks.

In 1973 the company hired Dewitt Reid as director of equal employment opportunity (EEO). Reid, age 46, was a native of Charlotte, had been a teacher for 20 years and had worked in personnel at another company for 7 years. He reported through the manager of employee relations to Joseph Major, vice president–personnel.

Reid's formal job responsibilities were to help Duke Power reach its affirmative action goals and monitor its compliance with EEO guidelines. He also made himself available as a consultant to managers on minority issues. Because of his position and his personality, black employees often voiced their concerns to him.

Reid himself was particularly interested not only in the company's long-range goal of having the same proportion of blacks working at Duke Power as there was in Duke's service area, but also in having blacks receive their fair share of management positions. (In 1970 about 23% of the population of Charlotte was black.) In January 1974 there were 19 black managers among the company's 1,229 managers and officers.

In 1974 top management believed that there had been more affirmative action progress in the past three years than in all the company's history. Special attention had been paid to increasing the number of minorities and making Duke Power a more attractive place for minorities to work. The company was especially concerned with increasing the number of minorities in the construction department where the percentage of blacks was among the lowest. In 1970 the department had started an employee-orientation program for minorities to make working at Duke Power easier. It also had a learner's progressive skills (LPS) program in which workers were taught trades other than those they already knew. The company, and especially Reid, had encouraged blacks to use this program as a means of gaining the opportunity to move out of utility, or common laborer, positions. Most blacks in construction were unskilled and worked as cement finishers. Although desirous of adding blacks to the payroll as engineers or highly skilled workers, management found it difficult to locate qualified people. The department's search to hire its own director of minority affairs in the early 1970s was unsuccessful because it could not find a suitable person.

Duke Power did not keep statistics on minority employment before 1966, and because of inconsistent counting methods the company had no reliable figures before 1970. In that year a computerized and standardized system was established. *Table A* presents the number of Duke construction workers and the minority percentages from 1970 to 1974. During that time the percentage of minorities companywide changed from 7.6% to 10.3%.

Labor Relations in the Construction Department

Duke Power's labor practices not only enabled the company to have the lowest construction costs per unit of output of any utility in the nation, but also provided an unusual degree of job security for its skilled construction workers.

Table A
Minorities in Construction at Duke Power

	Construction Total	Minorities No.	%
1970	2,853	204	7.2
1971	3,407	256	7.5
1972	4,290	327	7.6
1973	4,894	379	7.7
1974	4,646	360	7.7

Source: Data compiled by Duke Power Company from EEO-1 reports

When one project was completed the company would transfer its skilled workers to another project and pay their relocation expenses. The LPS program also enabled the company to shift employees from one trade to another, as needed. This would not have been possible if the work force had been unionized.

Although there had been several attempts at labor organization, in 1974 there were no unions in the construction department. In 1968 the Buildings and Trades Council union was defeated 7 to 1 in a vote at the Oconee Nuclear Station. In 1972 the ironworkers union was defeated in its vote at the McGuire nuclear plant. In 1972 the International Brotherhood of Electrical Workers was also defeated in a construction department election. In addition, there had been several occasions in the early 1970s when unions had withdrawn petitions on the day before an election because they believed they would be defeated.

From 1970 to 1973 coal miners at the Brookside mine in Harlan County, Kentucky, were represented by the Southern Labor Union (SLU). Brookside was operated by Duke Power's subsidiary, the Eastover Mining Company. In July 1973 miners at Brookside voted to have the United Mine Workers (UMW) represent them. The company would not agree to some of the terms of the UMW contract and the miners went on strike. The UMW took out full-page ads in newspapers in Duke Power's service area urging Duke's customers to oppose the company's rate increase requests. It also launched an ad campaign in the *Wall Street Journal* to discourage potential investors in Duke Power securities. Eventually the company agreed to the union's major demands.

In the spring of 1974 Bob Dick was concerned

that the personnel function had been particularly slow to develop in the construction department. There were no written statements of policy for promotions, discipline, transfers, or termination, for example. Such decisions were based almost exclusively on the recommendations of supervisors as to employees' work quality. Dick felt that in too many cases this resulted in discharge or discipline because the supervisor "didn't like the way the man parted his hair." He wanted to change this way of operating, although he knew that both supervisors and foremen liked the tradition of hiring and firing based on performance.

The Ecstasy

Business was booming for Duke Power in 1969. Earnings per share were a record $2.05 and return on common equity was 13%. Common stock had reached a record market high of $43.50 with a book value of $16.62. The company's bond rating was AAA.

In the 1960s, peak load growth for most utilities had averaged about 7% a year. (*Peak load* refers to the greatest demand on the company's generating system during a particular time period.) Projections for the next several years indicated an annual growth rate of over 9% for the company's service area. The 1969 annual report pointed out that "every company record involving the sale of electricity for residential purposes was smashed." Duke Power had aggressively promoted "total electric living" and was proud of the fact that it led the country in the number of total electric units added each year and that average use per customer was 40% higher than the national average. Industrial, commercial, and agricultural uses were projected to show similar increases.

Duke Power's peak loads had increased from 2.48 million kw in 1959 to 5.61 million kw in 1969. Throughout the early 1960s peak loads had consistently exceeded forecasts. Reserve generating capacity declined from 22% in 1959 to 3% in 1969, although the company had firm purchases of an additional 8% to meet unexpected demand that year. It was generally held in the industry that a minimum of 20% reserve capacity was safe.

Based on its projections and experience, the company embarked in 1969 on the most ambitious expansion and modernization program in its history. Utilities across the nation were doing the same.

Expansion plans included nuclear, coal, and hydroelectric facilities. The planned construction and the work in progress would double Duke Power's generating capacity by 1977. In 1969 investment in new power generation, transmission, distribution, and other plant facilities was a record $283 million, more than $43 million above the previous high in 1968. Projected capital expenditures from 1969 through 1971 totaled $1.04 billion. During these boom years, Bob Dick had said that the company was "beating the bushes" to find and hire enough qualified construction workers.

The Agony

After 1969 a gradual downward spiral began. The single most damaging event was the unexpected increase in the cost of coal. In 1969 coal was priced at $7.80 per ton. The next year the price jumped to $11.00 per ton and cost the company an unexpected $49 million. In 1974, a year after the Arab oil embargo, coal soared to $27.64 per ton. From 1969 to 1974 investment and operating costs also increased due to inflation, delays in construction, and the installation of air pollution equipment.

Top management responded in a variety of ways to increase revenues and lower operating expenses. The company began applying for unprecedented rate increases as early as 1969, but it had a difficult time obtaining adequate increases due to regulatory lag. The utility commissions set rates by examining the company's performance over a test period in its recent past. Based on what was considered a reasonable rate of return on equity, they would then establish rates. Throughout the 1960s the commissions had allowed Duke Power a return on equity of 12%–13%. Since requests usually took six months to a year to be acted on, the increases no longer covered actual operating costs by the time they were approved.

From April 1970 to August 1974 the company filed over 16 applications for increases. About 75% of the requested amounts were granted. Although none of the company's revenues came from rate increases in 1969, in 1973 24% of total revenues were from rate increases. Despite these increases, the company was not able to maintain its customary return on equity. As requests were approved, prices to residential customers increased 50% from 1970 to 1974. Protests from these customers made it even more difficult to obtain further increases.

Duke Power was also hampered by not having a fuel-adjustment clause that would allow it to pass on to its customers the increased costs of fuel. Although it applied for such a clause in April 1969, it was not until April 1973 that the FPC approved a coal-adjustment clause for wholesale customers. And only in January 1974 was the company given the initial approval by the state utility commissions for residential customers.

Although the company's financial condition had declined, projections for high energy demands caused Duke Power to announce plans in 1973 to build an additional eight nuclear plants and another hydroelectric facility. Construction work in progress in that year totaled $866 million.

Earnings per share dropped from $2.05 in 1969 to $1.57 in 1973 and by 1974 were still only $1.74. By 1974 return on equity was down to 8.8%. The company's fixed charges coverage dropped from 6:1 in 1965 to 2:1 in 1969. Its bond rating dropped from AAA to A.

The deterioration in Duke Power's fixed charges coverage had forced the company on four occasions since 1971 to meet its expenses by obtaining short-term loans at rates substantially above what would have been required if conventional sources of capital had been available. On three of these occasions short-term borrowing exceeded available lines of credit. By 1974 cost increases outstripped revenue increases. (*Figure C* shows changes in revenues, earnings, and costs from 1969.)

In 1969 the company had 23.2 million shares of common stock outstanding and by the beginning of 1974 had sold an additional 15.3 million shares. As the market value of its stock dropped below book value, each offering of common stock diluted its value. In April 1974 additional shares of common stock were sold at 75% of book value.

In mid-July 1974 the company was faced with $200 million cash shortage. Although Bill Grigg worked feverishly for several weeks, he was only able to raise $2 million. In a desperation move, the company sold $100,000,000 of unsecured five-year notes at 13%, the highest rate of interest ever paid by an electric utility.

Emergency Measures

On August 20, 1974, the board of directors authorized significant cutbacks in construction. "Duke has thoroughly investigated all available

Figure C
Percent Change in Revenues, Major Costs, and Earnings
1969–1974

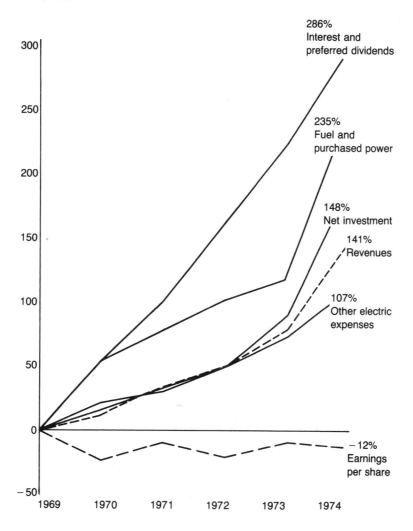

Source: Duke Power Company

means of financing and is convinced it is impossible to raise the huge sums needed to maintain the former construction schedule," announced Carl Horn, Jr., CEO, in a statement to the press. The cutbacks would reduce capital expenditures $150 million through 1975 and would total $1.5 billion through 1979. Under the new construction schedule, completion of nuclear stations then in progress would be delayed up to two years. Despite a decrease of 2.5 million kw in the company's peak load projection, there would be a reserve capacity in 1980 of only 12%. Citing the national energy supply situation and the need to insure that the cutbacks would not curtail the company's ability

to provide electricity, Horn also announced that a load management program would be developed to reduce total system load and peak loads.

Bill Lee

"He's been a dynamic leader in anything he's undertaken. He just doesn't know the word 'failure.' It isn't in his vocabulary," was the way one of Bill Lee's peers described him.

Lee was the grandson of the company's first chief engineer. He joined Duke Power in 1955 as a junior designer. Named vice president–engineering in 1965, he was promoted to senior vice president–engineering and construction in

1971. The Marshall Steam Station and the Keowee-Toxaway project, both of which won national awards for engineering excellence, had been largely designed by him. In 1972 he won the American Society of Mechanical Engineers' George Westinghouse gold medal award for engineering.

Bill Lee was also highly regarded as a manager. His associates felt that he brought out the best in the people who worked for him and that he had a genuine personal concern for Duke Power's employees. He took pleasure in the fact that before the company expanded rapidly in the late 1960s, he knew many of the construction workers by their first names. Reflecting on his job, he had said: "We won't be remembered for our power plants, but for what kind of people we leave to design and manage them."

Lee was known as a thorough but fast decision maker. In October 1969 he left a meeting in which he learned that completion of the Oconee plant would be delayed and went immediately to a pay telephone. He asked his boss for approval to begin construction at once on another power plant. From that phone booth, in the next 45 minutes, he ordered $40 million worth of equipment.

Bill Lee also had a reputation for being fair and trying to use the Golden Rule as a guide for running the construction department. Besides being an Elder in the Presbyterian church, he was active in numerous community service organizations. Lee was particularly pleased about the relationships he had cultivated with the black community. He had promoted Duke Power as a work place for minorities by speaking at local black colleges and at meetings of black business leaders.

Braniff International

The Ethics of Bankruptcy (A)

David E. Whiteside, research associate, prepared this case under the supervision of Kenneth E. Goodpaster as the basis for classroom discussion rather than to illustrate either effective or ineffective handling of an administrative situation.

On Friday, May 7, 1982, Howard Putnam, chief executive officer of Braniff International (BI), walked to his car after another long week. The day before he had spoken at the annual stockholders' meeting and then chaired a board meeting. The company had been on the verge of bankruptcy since he took charge on September 22, 1981. For the next seven months, he and Phil Guthrie, his chief financial officer (CFO), had lived constantly on razor's edge trying to get through the next cash crisis. At that point BI owed $439 million to 39 senior-secured creditors. Despite a cash infusion from a deal in which Eastern Airlines had leased BI's South American routes, Putnam did not know if Braniff would have enough cash to meet its payroll on Thursday, May 13.

Suggestions were made that BI have another 2-for-1 sale like the highly successful one held in February 1982, when passengers received one free ticket for every one purchased. But Putnam was concerned about whether or not the public would view it as a last-ditch attempt to raise cash. He and Guthrie had also been invited to make a BI presentation to institutional investors on Wall Street but had declined the offer. With Braniff's future uncertain, they believed the timing was inappropriate. Too much talk about bankruptcy could be a self-fulfilling prophecy. If bankruptcy was under consideration, however, didn't people have a right to know ahead of time? The ultimate question was when to file; if BI had to file, then Putnam wanted to file under Chapter XI to preserve Braniff's assets and reorganize. There was always the danger—especially with rumors of impending bankruptcy—that BI would be placed in involuntary bankruptcy by a creditor and thus be forced to liquidate all of its assets.

If You've Got It, Flaunt It

BI was founded in 1928 by Tom Braniff in Tulsa, Oklahoma. In 1942 the airline moved to Dallas and served the Midwest until 1946, when it began flights to Latin America. In 1965 Harding Lawrence, who had been in charge of daily operations at Continental Airlines, became CEO and president of BI. Under Lawrence, Braniff gained a reputation for innovation. Shortly after his arrival, he announced his dream for a new airline, including an all-jet fleet. With the encouragement of advertising executive Mary Wells, whom Lawrence later married, he declared the end of "the plain plane," had BI's fleet painted in bright colors, and adopted the slogan "If you've got it, flaunt it." He paid artist Alexander Calder $100,000 for his design ideas and had the stewardesses wear Pucci-designed uniforms.

From 1965 to 1977 BI grew rapidly and enjoyed strong returns. In 1973, for example, the company earned $17 million on revenues of $372 million, a 99% increase in earnings over 1972. In November 1977 the airline began construction of its lavish $70 million world headquarters at the Dallas–Ft. Worth (DFW) airport.

In October 1978 the Airline Deregulation Act was passed. Lawrence seized the opportunity to expand aggressively, fearing that Congress might soon reverse its decision. Within six months BI had obtained the authority to serve—if it desired—437 of the 1,300 new routes offered by the Civil Aeronautics Board (CAB). In this time span the company opened new routes to Europe, Asia, and the Middle East. In a single day—December 15, 1978—BI began flying to 16 new cities. By comparison, United Airlines, the largest carrier in the industry, added only one new route.

Braniff increased capacity to service its new routes. It bought 41 new Boeing planes over a three-year period, including three 747s, and it took options on 44 other aircraft for a total cost of $925 million. From 1978 to 1979 BI increased its available seat miles by 32%, and its break-even load factor changed from 50.2% to 59.9%.[1]

---

1. Because costs in the airline industry were more directly related to the number of seats flown over a given distance than to the number of passengers, the unit of production was the *available seat mile*, or one passenger seat flown one mile. The product of the number of passengers carried and how far they flew gave *revenue passenger miles* (RPMs). *Load factor* was a measure of how full an airline's planes were, expressed as the ratio of revenue passenger miles to available seat miles.

The gods of the airline industry, however, did not smile upon Lawrence's hubris. In 1979 the economy entered a severe recession and passenger traffic plummeted; at the same time, the cost of fuel doubled. With rate setting by the CAB eliminated, airlines began competing by offering discount fares that reduced yields per revenue mile (the amount passengers paid per mile of flight). A $45 million net income in 1978 turned into a $44 million loss in 1979 and a $131 million loss in 1980. (*Exhibits 1* and *2* document the dramatic change in BI's financial fortunes.) In December 1980 Lawrence resigned under pressure, it was reported, from BI's lenders and board of directors.

Lawrence was replaced by John J. Casey, who had been Braniff's vice chairman. Casey started a major turnaround effort that included streamlining management, dropping unprofitable routes, selling unneeded aircraft, and gaining salary and productivity concessions from employees. In February 1981, nonetheless, the company's creditors refused to grant BI additional credit, thus putting it on a cash-in-advance basis for such major operating expenses as fuel. In March 1981 Casey was successful in persuading BI's employees to accept an across-the-board 10% paycut. In July of that year Casey negotiated a postponement of the interest and principal due on BI's $653 million debt until February 1, 1982. By then, Braniff was supposed to have a financial restructuring plan acceptable to all 39 major lenders; if not, all of its debt would be declared in default and therefore immediately due in full.

BI was not alone in these dire straits. In 1980 there was a net operating loss for U.S. airlines of $225 million, with losses for 1981 expected to be even greater because of the sluggish economy. The firing of air traffic controllers on August 3, 1981, caused an even further decline in traffic for the entire industry. It was estimated that 15,000 domestic airline employees had been laid off in 1981 before the controllers' strike and that another 15,000 would be laid off by the end of that year.

Leaving Profits for Problems

When Putnam was in his early forties, he asked his son to join him in parachuting from a small plane at 3,000 feet. His son replied, "Why on earth would anyone want to jump out of a perfectly good airplane?" Yet, for Putnam, who had soloed at 16 from a pasture near the family farm in Iowa, it was something he had always wanted to do. Accompanied by his daughter as he prepared to jump, Putnam thought, "This is the scariest thing I've ever done." Although he acknowledged that it was fun, he did not think he would do it again, "but sometimes in life, there are challenges you must attempt."

When Putnam was asked by Casey to become Braniff's president, he had been CEO at Southwest Airlines from 1978-1981. Southwest was the most profitable airline in the industry, and Putnam and Guthrie, his CFO there, were credited with much of its success. During their term Southwest had nearly tripled its revenues, earnings, and route size. Putnam insisted on bringing Guthrie with him to BI.

Industry experts lauded the choice of Putnam to try to turn Braniff around. One airline analyst said: "He obviously looked over Braniff's books. And a man of Mr. Putnam's caliber would not take the position if he didn't think there was hope to turn Braniff around." Putnam was also known for his interest in people and had built a reputation for working with employees, characterizing himself at one time as the "head cheerleader" for Southwest's employees.

To avoid any conflict of interest, Putnam and Guthrie restricted themselves to learning about BI's financial condition from published sources and information generally available from its management. In discussing the possibility of bankruptcy with BI's executive committee, he said: "If you are expecting me to go for a government bailout, I am not your guy. I will not do that. If we can make it live on its own, fine, and if we can't, it will die." No one dissented.

On arriving at BI, Putnam and Guthrie found an airline that had no free assets—all had been pledged; in addition, it had no borrowing capability and had a negative net worth. Although the company was marginally cash positive, advance bookings were decreasing dramatically. There was no coherent marketing strategy. According to one observer, the atmosphere was one of a continuing cash crisis. Because BI's employees had frequently been told that BI was in trouble, crisis comments were "starting to run off everybody's back like water off your raincoat."

Within a week after Putnam started, he learned that both Lawrence and Casey had discussed retaining bankruptcy counsel with the board of directors. He was also shocked to learn that there was only enough cash on hand to cover 10 days of operations. This was particularly alarming because every Thursday BI had to pay $7 million in cash for the next week's fuel, and every other Thursday there was a $12 million payroll due. What was more, Guthrie told Putnam that there would be a severe cash crunch from February to April, 1982. Putnam also learned that BI's top management believed American Airlines was competing unfairly; he was advised not to talk with American's executives without clearance from counsel.

On September 30 BI reported a third quarter net loss of $20.3 million, bringing its losses through September to $85 million. Load factors had dropped from 62% for the third quarter of 1980 to just under 58% for the third quarter of 1981.

Shortly after his arrival Putnam sent out questionnaires to employees to find out what was on their minds. The first page began, "Dear Mr. Putnam, Braniff can be improved by . . ." with the rest of the page blank and an option for the person's signature. Putnam had stated that he would personally respond to every questionnaire received, and although it took several months, he did handwrite a note to each of the 3,000 or so respondents. Putnam later stated, "That effort by employees and management opened up communications and improved productivity immediately."

Putnam and other senior officers began having three or four meetings with employees per week to field questions and get suggestions. Putnam once showed up unannounced and dressed in coveralls to load bags for a morning to find out what was on the minds of the employees. He commonly found several employees outside his door at 5:00 P.M. waiting to talk. Sometimes he went to DFW on Saturday mornings and spent about an hour going from gate to gate talking with employees. When he was asked if Braniff was going to make it, his answer was a contingent one: "Folks, our future rests on the following points." He then would summarize what was happening, what the risks were, what he wanted to happen, and what the unions and employees could do to help.

Fourth Quarter, 1981

Putnam quickly announced a turnaround plan that he hoped to have in place by Christmas 1981. First, he wanted to restructure BI's $591 million debt. Second, he wanted to find a niche in the marketplace. "There may not be one. If not, we have to find a way to create one," he said. Third, he wanted to increase the productivity of BI's employees, although he did not plan to ask for another pay cut. Putnam also wanted to reshape the organization from top to bottom with an emphasis on achieving efficiency through simplicity. Finally, he planned to reduce costs as soon as possible. On October 22, BI offered to sublet all or part of its headquarters building, which cost about $500,000 in monthly payments.

As part of its new marketing strategy, BI announced on November 4 the start of "Texas Class" beginning November 24. BI had previously offered 582 different fares, but in a move described by Putnam as going "back to basics," the airline would now have only 15 fares nationwide. Prices were also lowered 45–55% from the previous full fare levels. Braniff's one-way full fare between Dallas and Los Angeles, for example, was lowered from $248 to $135. In addition, all first-class seats were replaced by coach seating with extra leg room, thus expanding capacity on most planes from 134 to 146. Putnam explained: "Texas Class had several purposes. It simplified fares and employee work load, increasing productivity. It meant a higher quality of service, all the same class. Since 80% of all airline passengers were already traveling on discounted fares, the overall yield dilution was only 10–12%. It was also an excellent marketing tool to show fare comparisons to the old, full fares."

As Putnam expected, BI's new fares were immediately matched by American, which competed with Braniff on almost all of its domestic routes. An American spokesperson said: "There will be no route on which Braniff and American compete where there will be a fare offered lower than American's." Delta Airlines soon lowered its fares in the "cutthroat madness," as it was called by Wall Street. The Atlanta-based airline said that its planes would have to fly 105% full for it to break even in the Dallas market.

Although the new fares caused BI's break-even load factor to rise from 59% to mid-60%, Putnam was optimistic that the increase in traffic would more than offset the low fares. He also reasoned that because operating costs were rapidly being trimmed, the new fare structure would be profitable in the long run.

BI's creditors had given the airline until February 1, 1982, to restructure its debt. A second deadline was March 31, when the plan had to be presented in writing. Putnam and Guthrie immediately began meeting with the 39 senior-secured creditors to work out a plan, but were hampered because every issue and covenant had to be unanimously approved.

They usually met with a committee that represented the principal banks and insurance companies. Small meetings had 30–40 people and the larger ones up to 150. Within the secured creditor committee there were specialty committees that looked at such things as asset values and aircraft maintenance. Some of the large creditor institutions had full-time staff members whose only job was to monitor how well Braniff was doing and to look after the creditor's interests. Starting in October, there were large formal meetings at least twice a month, more frequent meetings of smaller groups, and daily telephone contacts with at least 10 of the major lenders. Aside from the 39 senior-secured creditors, there were about 3,000 bondholders and 40,000 small, unsecured creditors—principally employees and ticket-holders.

In plotting the flow of cash receipts for an airline, the results would not be a smooth line but a series of spikes representing three major points for settling receipts. Cash from the sale of tickets by travel agents came through the Area Settlement Plan (ASP) and occurred weekly or monthly depending on the travel agency's size. Each agency reported its ticket sales and sent a check to the area settlement bank which then broke out the portion owed each airline and sent it a draft for that amount. Thus, an airline would not know until it received this draft how much it would get from the ASP. A monthly receipt of cash also came through the Airline Clearing House (ACH). Carriers would send tickets that they had written, but which included travel on other carriers, to the ACH for collection or payment. The ACH would take all of these tickets and derive a total for each airline. The third important receipt was the settlement of credit card travel, which usually occurred on a weekly basis. The uncertainty about the amounts of these receipts meant that if one overlaid the flow of receipts on disbursements, BI was vulnerable to cash shortages.

Putnam found negotiating with the creditors and unions frustrating. Typically, one group would say that it was in favor of what he was proposing, but that it would not cooperate until another group conceded something as well. Some of the creditors told him that they would agree to certain proposals only if the unions made concessions. But the unions did not take seriously the creditors' statements that they would neither provide additional cash nor continue to defer debt repayment.

There were five unions at BI: The International Association of Machinists (IAM), the Association of Flight Attendants (AFA), the Airline Pilots Association (ALPA), the Teamsters, and a dispatchers' union. In November Putnam was negotiating with the IAM for productivity increases in return for profit sharing when L. T. Faircloth, the union's representative, told him, "I would rather see Braniff go under than give you anything."

In a move to halt big cash "bleeders," BI stopped serving Canada on November 1; this move saved half a million dollars a month. Although BI had already reduced its work force by 1,100 after the air traffic controllers strike, the suspension of service to Canada resulted in the additional furlough of 132 pilots and 88 flight attendants.

On December 5 it was announced that ALPA had ratified a two-year contract with BI, increasing each pilot's maximum flying time from 75 hours to 85 hours per month. Putnam stated, "Our pilots have given us the opportunity to increase our aircraft utilization up to 16% over current levels without incurring additional pilot expense. We are delighted with the agreement and the constructive attitude demonstrated by our pilots." He also said that because of this new contract BI would begin 21 new flights from DFW to 11 cities.

January 1982

By the beginning of January, the results of Texas Class were starting to come in. For the month of December, Braniff's load factor of 60.7% was the highest in the industry. Advanced bookings had also risen sharply.

This infusion of cash enabled Putnam and Guthrie to negotiate a financial restructuring from a stronger position. This was finally accomplished on January 22. As part of the restructuring, BI was forgiven interest and principal payments until October 1, 1982. Summertime was typically a period of high traffic for airlines, thus the new deadline would enable BI to improve its financial position from the hoped-for good season. Not having a restructuring in place until only eight days before the deadline, however, had sparked numerous rumors of bankruptcy and had adversely affected bookings.

On January 26, BI's board named Putnam CEO and president. Casey retained the title of chairman and, according to one source, would be "spending a lot of time in employee communications."

Despite the initial success of Texas Class, BI showed a negative cash flow for the first time in January and Putnam and Guthrie agreed that the only prudent thing to do was to retain bankruptcy counsel. The board also agreed that if it did not bring in bankruptcy counsel at this point, it would not be doing the right thing.

February 1982

Braniff chose the law firm of Levin and Weintraub and Crames in New York, and the president, Michael Crames, agreed to take on the case himself. Putnam invited him to the February 4 board meeting to begin educating all of them about the bankruptcy process. At that meeting Crames reviewed the bankruptcy law and the mechanics of filing. He emphasized that if they planned to file under Chapter XI of the bankruptcy law and attempt to reorganize, they had to protect their assets (see *Exhibit 3*). He stressed that the only way that this could be accomplished was through surprise. BI should not reveal that it was considering filing because assets might be impounded and not available for reorganization. Advance notice could also cause a creditor to file for involuntary bankruptcy and result in a liquidation. In addition, who would want to fly on an airline that might go bankrupt? From this point on, there was almost daily telephone contact between Crames and either Putnam or Guthrie.

Considering the concrete details of bankruptcy was difficult for Putnam. He had grown up in a small town in Iowa with only *one* bankrupt person. His father had told him, "Son, when you get out in the real world, watch out for that bankrupt guy. That's bad. You want to pay your bills."

On February 11, BI announced that for every ticket purchased at full fare during a 48-hour period, it would sell a second ticket of equal or lesser value for $1. Within hours American matched the offer without the $1 charge; Delta followed suit the next day. Ticket sales skyrocketed. One BI sales office that usually sold

700 tickets per day by mail sold more than 6,000 by noon the next day. Some people stayed up all night in long lines to make sure they got a ticket.

Denying that BI had initiated the 2-for-1 sale out of financial desperation, Sam Coats, vice president in charge of public relations, stated, "We didn't have a two-day sale to save the airline. It was intended to boost sagging traffic levels during a slow period." Remarking on how the sale enabled many people to visit places they would not ordinarily have gone to, Coats mentioned that BI was trying to promote goodwill with the sale. Putnam also stated that the overall intent of the sale was "to generate cash and yet to try to retain public confidence."

That same week Putnam and Guthrie went to a New York meeting with major creditors. When they asked for the right to proceed with accounts receivable financing, they were refused. One lender said the employees should make more concessions and proposed a 50% pay cut for six months. On that visit, Putnam and Guthrie tried to sell the airline's accounts receivable to commercial credit lenders. This had never been done before in the airline industry, and the proposal was turned down every place they tried.

On February 20 BI furloughed an additional 825 employees and announced that more layoffs would be made in 90 days. It also stated that it had sold 21 airplanes during the past three months, thereby reducing its fleet to 75 planes, down from 116 at the end of 1979.

At the end of February Braniff reported a record $160.6 million loss for 1981. It was expected that Braniff's accountants would once again include in the annual report, as they had in 1980, the statement: "There are conditions which indicate that the company may be unable to continue as a going concern."

March 1982

"Braniff Move Called Last Resort" was the headline on a March 3 article in the *Dallas Morning News*, reporting the airline's decision to defer for a week 50% of that week's payroll. The article reported that BI told its employees they would receive half their paycheck that week and the remainder the next week; subsequent paychecks would be postponed a week. It was estimated that this would free up about $8 million in short-term cash. Guthrie said, "I wouldn't characterize this action as desperate.

This should not be looked on as a last-ditch effort. We are in an obvious cash flow slump." Commenting on the pay deferral, Marvin Schlenke, president of Teamster's Local 19, said, "It was get paid 50% or nothing at all. We don't want to see 10,000 people without jobs. I don't think anyone likes it. But nothing can be done."

On March 4 the headline on the front page of the *Dallas Morning News* read, "Braniff Chief Uncertain if Firm Can Survive." Putnam was quoted in an interview: "A woman called on the phone today and asked if her ticket to Honolulu would be good in May. I told her I didn't know. She probably went right out and traded the ticket in for one on another airline." He continued, "I can't just name a date and say I know we have enough cash to operate until then. It's not that easy. We certainly have no current plans to cease operations, but I can't guarantee we won't."

At that point Putnam began to suspect that travel agents were diverting traffic from BI because bookings from agents were down considerably. When individual agents were asked, however, they denied it. One Dallas travel agency did state that "increasing numbers of potential Braniff passengers are requesting other airlines." It was learned that BI's load factor for February was 51.9%, down from last February's 57.6%, and well below the break-even load factor of 65%. BI announced another 2-for-1 sale on March 5, but it was limited to flights in Texas and Oklahoma. American again immediately matched the offer.

On March 6 the CAB approved a plan that provided for other airlines honoring tickets on any airline that went bankrupt, including tickets issued by travel agencies. When he returned from the CAB meeting in Washington, Putnam was met at the airport by several hundred cheering Braniff employees. He told them the airline had a "more than 50% chance" of survival.

It became apparent at this time that there was no White House support for a rescue if BI failed. David Kirstein, general counsel for the CAB, said, "The view is that it's tough out there and there are some people who are not going to make it." Drew Lewis, secretary of transportation, stated, "We would like for it [Braniff] to survive. It would be in the best interest of the nation. But we will not provide any subsidy. We won't provide a bailout of the type Chrysler received."

Around mid-March Putnam received a letter from Lanny Rogers, president of District 146 of the IAM, citing the union's labor contract. He said: "We have seen the contract openly and flagrantly violated almost daily and almost always with the excuse from management that 'We can't help it. We must save the airline.'" The letter went on to accuse BI of using "fear and scare tactics"; it stated: "The most flagrant example of this is the company's garnishment of one-half of the employee's pay. This must be regarded as one of the most cavalier acts I have ever witnessed by any chief executive." Rogers ended by asking Putnam to restore normal paydays, to cease labor contract violations, and to negotiate with the union. Commenting on the letter, Putnam said that it was "obvious that Rogers had not recognized the seriousness of the situation."

On March 16 John Casey resigned and accepted a position in operations at Pan American World Airways (Pan Am). One New York analyst said: "I don't blame John for taking the job. He had been stripped of one job after another at Braniff. He is a strong, capable operations man. And I can't say I am surprised that he accepted the Pan Am offer."

Although no airline had ever leased its routes before, Putnam began negotiating in March with Ed Acker, chairman of Pan Am, to lease its South American routes on which it had lost $15 million the previous year. Putnam's plan was to lease the routes for a few years and then get them back when BI was healthy. A major reason for leasing the routes was that BI's South American fleet had to be replaced shortly because of new federal noise regulations, and BI could not purchase or lease new aircraft. Furthermore, Putnam sought to lease the South American routes because BI was the designated carrier for the State Department and Department of Defense, and he wanted to make sure these services would not be interrupted if BI filed for bankruptcy.

Putnam and Acker arranged a deal in which Pan Am paid BI $7 million in cash immediately, would pay another $13 million later in the spring, and a final $10 million in 1983. BI's petition to the CAB to approve the agreement asked that a decision be made by April 13. If approved, Pan Am would have a monopoly on service to South America and BI would lay off 1,100 domestic employees. On March 27 Putnam and Guthrie flew to Miami, where most of BI's South American flights originated, and ex-

plained to a group of 200 somber and hostile Miami employees why they would be losing their jobs if the CAB approved the Pan Am venture.

April 1982

During the first week of April, Braniff reported that its 2-for-1 ticket sale had boosted traffic for the month of March. Traffic for what was normally a slow month increased 7.6%, and load factor increased by .7% to 60.3%. On domestic routes, passenger traffic was up 19.4% and load factor was up to 61.8% from 57.2% in March 1981. On South American flights, the company reported a 20.8% decline in revenue passenger miles, and a drop in load factor from 66.2% to 55.5%.

Rumors traveled quickly in the airline industry. Sometimes a rumor would work its way to London after being killed in the United States, and then after being killed there, would resurface in New York, only to have the cycle begin again. Conventional wisdom was that if a company was going to file for bankruptcy, it would be done on a Friday. From mid-February on, a Friday did not pass without inquiries from the press or creditors as to whether or not BI would be filing that day. To cope with the rumor mill, Putnam began to send out daily messages to employees briefing them on what was happening. He had decided that only he, Guthrie, and Coats could speak for the corporation. He also made himself accessible to the press, granting numerous interviews.

During the first part of April, Putnam and Acker made the rounds in Washington to drum up support for the proposal to lease BI's South American routes to Pan Am. Both Texas senators and 10 of its congressional representatives wrote the CAB to support the plan. The Department of Transportation also publicly supported it, and the State Department said that the South American routes were an important foreign policy concern and asked that the CAB act quickly.

Citing "broad competitive reasons," the CAB turned down BI's request on April 15 to lease its South American routes to Pan Am. The board invited Braniff to find another carrier as a partner in the venture.

A few days later, a local comedy club hosted a roast for Putnam. The capacity crowd gave Putnam a standing ovation and booed loudly whenever American was mentioned. Putnam was introduced as "a man who took a shaky, financially troubled airline and turned it into a shaky, financially troubled airline dependent on Pan American." Some of the other jokes were: "If God had intended us to fly, He would not have invented Braniff Airlines" and "Braniff is so poor, the meals are catered by Goodwill."

During this time the Justice Department began inquiries into allegations that American was illegally trying to force BI out of business, including the following charges: (1) dumping tickets on the industry clearing house to create a cash shortage for Braniff; (2) encouraging ticket agents to urge customers to fly American instead of Braniff; (3) holding meetings to discuss ways to hurt Braniff; (4) American pilots causing unnecessary delays on runways; and (5) fabricating technical problems on its own planes, thus causing BI to make costly preparations to accommodate displaced passengers that never showed up. Denying these allegations, American's president Robert Crandall said, "American's ethical standards are as high as its service standards. The company has done nothing and will do nothing to compromise those standards."

On April 23, Braniff filed an emergency request with the CAB asking it to reconsider its Pan Am proposal. President Reagan, the State Department, and the Department of Transportation sent letters to the CAB asking it to decide quickly. That night Frank Borman, chairman of Eastern, called and said he was interested in the South American routes. Putnam and Guthrie flew to New York and met Borman and his staff Sunday night, and working until 3:00 A.M. they put together a deal. On April 26 the CAB kept its office open later than usual to receive Braniff's documents; at about 11:00 P.M. that night Putnam was called by Dan McKinnon, CAB chairman, and told that the leases to Eastern were approved. Under the arrangement, Eastern would immediately pay Braniff $11 million, another $7 million when the relevant South American countries approved the venture, and a final $12 million in monthly payments to begin in 1983. Eastern agreed to take about 1,200 of BI's South American personnel, but BI would still lay off about 1,100 of its domestic employees. Braniff used the cash, obtained on Wednesday, to meet its Thursday payroll. Putnam was hopeful that the Eastern agreement would help with the next restructuring of the company's debt.

Pan Am's Acker was furious when Putnam called to say he was sorry. It was part of the original agreement that the $7 million paid by Pan Am to Braniff was unreturnable, although BI had guaranteed the transaction with collateral of five of its gates at Houston's Intercontinental Airport. Acker sued Braniff for $107 million—$100 million for damages and the rest was to get back what Pan Am had already paid. Putnam said he was flattered that Pan Am thought Braniff had even close to $100 million.

May 1982

On May 1 Braniff announced it lost $41.4 million during the first quarter of 1982; other airlines were reporting similar losses. Putnam said, "We believe the appeal of Texas Class service to the traveling public and the increased productivity that we are receiving from our physical and personnel resources have postured Braniff in a unique position to reap the benefits that an upturn in the economy will have on airline passenger traffic." Putnam also mentioned that he was pleased with the size and cost reductions the airline had made. BI's cost per available seat mile was 7.24 cents in March, down from 8.6 cents in the first quarter of 1981. Its yield per revenue mile was only 10.10 cents, however, far below the industry rule of thumb that yield had to be double unit cost to have a profitable airline. Braniff would have 7,900 employees after the layoffs from the Eastern deal, and it hoped to be down to 6,800 by the summer. Load factors in April had declined, at times being in the low 30s. Domestic travel agency sales were down 40–50% from the previous year.

On May 3 Braniff began a 3-for-2 sale. This "Great Escape Sale" allowed customers over a nine-day period to purchase two full-fare tickets to any of eight destinations to be used that summer and receive a free roundtrip anywhere in the continental United States for use in the off-season that fall. American immediately made a similar offer with fewer restrictions. In contrast to the 2-for-1 sale, there was little response this time. A disappointed Putnam said, "We gave a party and nobody came."

At the stockholders' meeting on May 6 Putnam reviewed the financial condition of BI when he had started, and the changes he had made; he then stated:

> We have proven to ourselves, to the industry, and to our lenders that on the operating cost side, we have a viable entity. We now have to generate revenue to make this

airline successful for the long term. The shadow of doubt that hangs over our future creates a "chicken-and-egg" dilemma as we approach financial restructuring. We need to remove the cloud to get results. The lenders want to see results before they remove the cloud.

The company continues to evaluate all possible alternatives including, but not limited to, continuing new marketing innovations, pricing promotions, new infusions of capital from outside investors, potential combinations with other entities, operating agreements with other airlines and, as a last resort, seeking protection under the federal bankruptcy statutes. This last alternative is obviously a last resort after all other alternatives have been exhausted.

Putnam concluded by praising the support of Braniff's employees and the community but added, "All the moral support in the world will not replace the monetary support needed to keep your company and your investment alive." When Putnam finished, a stockholder stood up and said, "Let's have a hip, hip, hooray for management," and the crowd cheered and applauded. He was amazed that his remarks about bankruptcy had such little impact and told his secretary, "They didn't even listen."

Putnam then met with the board. First, he and Guthrie reviewed the cash flow. Because load factors were running in the low 30s and advanced bookings were very low, it was clear that the hoped-for increase in summer traffic

would not happen. The settlement of the ACH and travel card receipts on May 11 would be critical. Putnam also told the board that he would be in New York the following week to testify in a suit brought by ALPA over the dismissal of pilots as a result of the Eastern deal. Although previous company attempts and those of its investment banker, Lazard Freres, had not uncovered any parties that might be interested in a merger or joint marketing venture, Putnam received permission to contact other airline presidents to explore such arrangements.

In the next few days, Putnam explored these possibilities with several airlines and financiers but had no success. He asked Bill Huskins, executive vice president of operations, to put together a plan over the weekend to see how small an airline they could possibly run under Chapter XI, even though no airline had ever continued flying while under Chapter XI.

Driving home exhausted late that night from an interminably long day of appointments, anxious faces, and ringing telephones, Putnam relaxed in the darkness of his car with the lights from the dashboard softly glowing like a cockpit. He thought of all the people whose lives depended on his decisions—employees, families, pensioners, creditors, stockholders, travelers, travel agents, and still others. He wondered who would be harmed the most if the company went under and if there was a right and a wrong way to go bankrupt. Perhaps the only remaining option was to file for Chapter XI.

Exhibit 1
Five-Year Review of Selected Financial Data, 1977–1981
($ thousands except per share amounts)

	1981	1980	1979	1978	1977
OPERATING REVENUES					
Airline:					
Passenger	$1,097,232	$1,305,305	$1,200,329	$845,353	$678,177
Revision of prior years' revenue estimates	(25,200)	—	—	—	—
Other transport revenues	80,422	104,893	107,824	95,161	84,062
Transport related	28,510	31,595	28,213	24,789	21,795
Nonairline subsidiaries	8,011	10,337	9,909	6,805	7,123
Total operating revenues	1,188,975	1,452,130	1,346,275	972,108	791,157
OPERATING EXPENSES					
Airline flying, maintenance and ground operations	974,943	1,215,171	1,106,167	682,013	543,925
Nonairline subsidiaries	5,066	2,488	3,271	2,992	2,965
Sales and advertising	172,785	198,906	158,659	108,737	83,416
Depreciation and amortization	83,551	89,296	75,343	60,980	55,593
General and administrative	47,430	53,762	41,273	37,227	36,230
Total operating expenses	1,283,775	1,559,623	1,384,713	891,949	722,129
OPERATING INCOME (LOSS)	(94,800)	(107,493)	(38,438)	80,159	69,028
NONOPERATING EXPENSES (INCOME)					
Interest expense	62,396	92,101	55,919	34,201	28,275
Interest capitalized	(6)	(3,398)	(6,265)	(4,992)	(2,278)
Other nonoperating income — net	(691)	(60,613)	(6,362)	(4,285)	(6,428)
Total nonoperating expenses	61,699	28,090	43,292	24,924	19,569
INCOME (LOSS) BEFORE INCOME TAXES AND PREFERRED DIVIDENDS	(156,499)	(135,583)	(81,730)	55,235	49,459
PROVISION (CREDIT) FOR INCOME TAXES	—	(7,072)	(37,400)	10,005	12,767
INCOME (LOSS) BEFORE PREFERRED DIVIDENDS OF SUBSIDIARY	(156,499)	(128,511)	(44,330)	45,230	36,692
PREFERRED DIVIDENDS OF SUBSIDIARY	4,112	2,925	—	—	—
NET INCOME (LOSS)	$ (160,611)	$ (131,436)	$ (44,330)	$ 45,230	$ 36,692
NET INCOME (LOSS) PER COMMON SHARE	$ (8.02)	$ (6.57)	$ (2.21)	$ 2.26	$ 1.83
WEIGHTED AVERAGE NUMBER OF COMMON SHARES OUTSTANDING	20,019	20,019	20,019	20,016	20,008
CASH DIVIDENDS DECLARED PER COMMON SHARE	$ —	$ .05	$ .36	$ .345	$ .285
SELECTED BALANCE SHEET ITEMS					
Current assets	$ 200,237	$ 197,790	$ 211,041	$156,519	$134,028
Current liabilities	405,077	341,032	276,330	170,543	124,008
Working capital (deficiency)	$ (204,840)	$ (143,242)	$ (65,289)	$(14,024)	$ 10,020
Property and equipment — net	$ 777,471	$ 868,443	$ 863,429	$612,189	$493,319
Total assets	$1,008,297	$1,107,368	$1,157,901	$870,165	$699,523
Senior debt	$ 438,980	$ 488,600	$ 507,912	$320,985	$235,312
Subordinated debt	80,250	95,002	70,286	27,692	37,307
Noncurrent liabilities under capital leases	71,782	69,473	87,047	49,393	47,988
Total long-term obligations, less current maturities	$ 591,012	$ 653,075	$ 665,245	$398,070	$320,607
Redeemable preferred stock of subsidiary	$ 39,455	$ 35,343	$ —	$ —	$ —
Common stock and paid-in capital	$ 56,795	$ 56,795	$ 56,795	$ 56,792	$ 56,732
Retained earnings (deficit)	(151,226)	9,385	141,822	193,359	155,035
Total common shareholders' equity (deficiency)	$ (94,431)	$ 66,180	$ 198,617	$250,151	$211,767

Source: Braniff International annual report, 1981.

Exhibit 2
Five-Year Statistical Review, 1977–1981

	1981	1980	1979	1978	1977
REVENUE PASSENGER MILES (in thousands)					
Continental U.S.	5,612,863	6,597,957	8,216,145	6,402,163	5,399,563
Hawaii	643,680	738,442	1,272,529	771,207	557,283
Mexico	336,470	354,390	367,882	332,858	247,620
South America	1,781,707	1,950,520	1,888,128	1,535,289	1,307,053
Atlantic	463,152	1,731,072	1,445,106	562,908	—
Pacific	—	527,586	230,549	—	—
Total scheduled	8,837,872	11,899,967	13,420,339	9,604,425	7,511,519
Charter	52,521	98,344	266,265	395,562	353,948
Total	8,890,393	11,998,311	13,686,604	9,999,987	7,865,467
AVAILABLE SEAT MILES (in thousands)					
Continental U.S.	10,112,406	12,002,065	15,486,324	12,477,921	10,877,174
Hawaii	1,089,998	1,075,519	1,759,381	1,192,125	975,527
Mexico	570,596	549,555	572,613	565,124	550,096
South America	2,912,705	3,079,151	2,991,437	2,652,514	2,392,957
Atlantic	839,127	2,724,932	2,523,879	951,144	—
Pacific	—	929,533	511,822	—	—
Total scheduled	15,524,832	20,360,755	23,845,456	17,838,828	14,795,754
Charter	74,595	136,774	339,801	491,557	452,642
Total	15,599,427	20,497,529	24,185,257	18,330,385	15,248,396
REVENUE PASSENGERS ENPLANED (in thousands)					
Scheduled	10,453	12,153	14,354	11,550	9,814
Charter	42	71	154	194	169
Total	10,495	12,224	14,508	11,744	9,983
SYSTEM SCHEDULED PASSENGER LOAD FACTOR (%)	56.9	58.4	56.3	53.8	50.8
BREAKEVEN PASSENGER LOAD FACTOR BEFORE INCOME TAX (%)	63.6	64.5	59.9	50.2	46.8
REVENUE PLANE MILES (in thousands)					
Scheduled	103,737	132,422	161,803	131,014	114,259
Charter	488	947	2,306	3,366	3,058
Total	104,225	133,369	164,109	134,380	117,317
REVENUE BLOCK HOURS FLOWN	279,063	349,518	435,621	362,154	316,779
AVERAGE SEGMENT LENGTH IN SCHEDULED SERVICE (MILES)	637	665	648	583	554
AVERAGE DAILY AIRCRAFT UTILIZATION (BLOCK HOURS)	8:07	8:23	10:42	10:16	9:45
YIELD PER REVENUE PASSENGER MILE	12.42c	10.97c	8.94c	8.80c	9.03c
OPERATING JET FLEET (at December 31)					
Owned Aircraft:					
Boeing 747-200	1	1	1	—	—
Boeing 747SP	1	2	1	—	—
Boeing 727-100*	3	10	14	15	17
Boeing 727-200	58**	58**	66	59	49
Douglas DC-8-62	8	8	8	7	1
Douglas DC-8-51	—	—	4	4	4
Total Owned	71	79	94	85	71
Leased Aircraft:					
Boeing 747-100	1	2	3	3	1
Boeing 747-200	1	2	2	—	—
Boeing 727-100*	6	7	8	6	6
Boeing 727-200	4	5	5	5	5
Douglas DC-8-62	—	2	2	2	7
Douglas DC-8-51	—	—	2	2	2
Total Leased	12	18	22	18	21
Total	83	97	116	103	92

*B727-100 aircraft were removed from operating fleet in January 1982.
**Includes seven aircraft owned by Braniff Realty Company which are leased to Braniff Airways.

Source: Braniff International annual report, 1981.

Exhibit 3
Chapter VII and Chapter XI, Bankruptcy Reform Act, 1978

Bankruptcy legislation served, first, to effect an equitable distribution of the debtor's property among his creditors and, second, to discharge the debtor from his debts and enable him to rehabilitate himself and start afresh.

Chapter VII of the Bankruptcy Reform Act of 1978 provided for the liquidation and termination of the business of the debtor, distribution of his assets, and usually a discharge of all dischargeable debts. Under Chapter VII there could be either a voluntary or an involuntary petition. In a voluntary bankruptcy, the debtor filed a petition with the courts asking to be declared a bankrupt. In the involuntary case, the debtor is forced into bankruptcy by creditors who file a petition requesting that the debtor be judged a bankrupt.

After secured creditor claims were satisfied, proceeds from the liquidation of assets were distributed according to a priority of claims: (1) expenses of administering the estate, (2) unsecured claims incurred after the filing of the petition and before either the appointment of a trustee to administer the estate or the judge's ruling, (3) wage, salary, and commission claims up to $2,000 earned within 90 days before the filing or the cessation of the debtor's business, (4) claims for contributions to employee benefit plans for services rendered 180 days before filing or the cessation of business and up to $2,000 per employee, (5) unsecured claims up to $900 for monies deposited in connection with the purchase, lease or rental of property or the purchase of services, for personal, family, or household use, (6) specified taxes owed to governmental units for certain income, property, employment, or excise taxes. Remaining unsecured creditors shared proportionately in any remaining assets.

Chapter XI had as its goal the rehabilitation of debtors by allowing them to reorganize and restructure their debt while assets were protected from creditors' claims. To be confirmed by the courts and be binding upon all parties, several conditions had to be met, including *feasibility*. This meant that the reorganized debtor must have adequate working capital, sufficient earning power to meet fixed lien charges, reasonably good credit prospects, ability to retire or refund its proposed debt over the period of extended maturity, must be soundly capitalized with no disproportionate ratio of debt to total value of assets, and have assurance of competent management. Before confirmation, it also had to be established that each holder of a claim or interest either accepted the plan or would receive as much under the reorganization plan as would be received in liquidation proceedings. For secured creditors, this meant that they would receive the value of their security either by payment or by delivery of the property. After a plan was confirmed, the reorganized entity began life anew with only those obligations imposed on it by the plan.

Note: Adapted from L. Y. Smith et al, *Business Law*, 5th ed. (St. Paul, Minn.: West Publishing Co., 1982), p. 792. On June 28, 1982, the U.S. Supreme Court ruled that provisions of the Bankruptcy Reform Act of 1978 concerning the jurisdiction of judges were unconstitutional and gave Congress until October 4, 1982, to make appropriate changes. As of June 1984, this had not been done, leaving the status of the Act itself in limbo. See *Northern Pipeline Construction Co.* v. *Marathon Pipe Line Co. and United States*, 458 U.S. 50 (1982).

Note on Product Safety

Dekkers L. Davidson,
research associate, prepared this
note under the supervision of
Kenneth E. Goodpaster *as a*
basis for class discussion.

General managers readily admit today that we have entered an era of increased emphasis on safety in the design, production, and distribution of products. The problem of business's responsibility for its products and services is large in scope. According to government statistics, 20 million Americans are injured annually as a consequence of incidents involving consumer products, with 30 thousand of those killed. In addition, each year 5 million Americans are injured and 30 thousand killed as a result of automobile accidents. One safety engineer concluded: "The odds against escaping an injury at home, at work, or at the steering wheel are thus surprisingly low for the average American family of four—an injury every four years or so."[1]

Since the birth of the Industrial Revolution, a product-oriented philosophy has dictated that principles of efficiency should guide the design of industrial and consumer goods. This efficiency was reflected in lower operating expenses and lower per unit costs for finished goods. Obvious safety problems—ones impinging directly on the bottom line—were faced and many were solved. As the revolution matured, this product orientation gave way to a market orientation that "literally bombarded twentieth-century man with delights that an earlier age would have considered both miraculous and beyond the economic grasp of common people."[2] Consumers quickly grew accustomed to an economy that delivered innovative

---

1. John Kolb and Steven S. Ross, *Product Safety and Liability* (New York: McGraw-Hill Book Company, 1980), p. 4.
2. Ibid., p. 1.

products capable of improving the buyer's lifestyle. Eventually, a conditioned public began to insist on infallibility in its products as well as availability.

The emphasis on product safety has been growing since World War II. Consumerism—a social movement that sought to augment the rights and powers of buyers in relation to sellers—was born of a paradoxical market situation.[3] Although business had tried to pay full attention to the needs, wants, and satisfactions of its market, consumers began to raise their voices, exclaiming that business did not *care* about them. The problem in part for the general manager is philosophical: what constitutes a safe society, and what is a *safe* product for that society? While answers to such questions can be elusive, ignoring the spirit of such questions can lead to severe consequences not only for consumers but also for business and its managers.

Managing product safety requires that general management consider its economic, legal, and ethical responsibilities. As *Figure A* illustrates, these responsibilities are not mutually exclusive, nor are they intended to portray a continuum with economic concerns on one end and social concerns on the other. Rather, they are nested domains—the economic within the legal and both of these within the ethical.

Economic Responsibilities

Business is expected to deliver desired goods and services at a profit. Although consumers usually accept some degree of risk with products they find necessary, most buyers assume that companies will be prudent in the design, production, and distribution of their products. While business can employ specialists (risk managers, insurers, lawyers) to weigh product risks against rewards (consumer benefit), it is the general manager who is held accountable. But the competitive dynamics of the "invisible hand" can often create tensions for general managers in the area of product safety.

Legal Responsibilities

Society expects business to operate within the laws and regulations society has laid down. Courts have moved toward a doctrine of strict liability, holding manufacturers responsible for any product defects that result in injury. Plain-

Figure A
General Management's Responsibilities

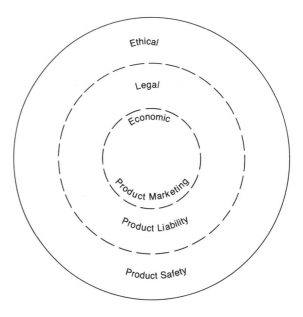

tiffs no longer need to prove manufacturer negligence to win a personal injury case. Increasingly, the courts and the regulatory agencies are placing the blame for corporate lawbreaking on the top manager, who is being held personally responsible and even jailed. The doctrine of "vicarious liability" holds that it is irrelevant whether the executive was directly involved in the illegal activity or whether he or she was simply informed of such activity. A "responsible manager" cannot always count on a corporate shield of protection. Nevertheless, this sue syndrome and the increasing frequency and size of court-ordered awards results in skyrocketing premiums for product liability insurance. *Caveat venditor* (let the seller beware) is replacing the old adage *caveat emptor* (let the buyer beware) as a watchword for business. Public policy, through the promulgation of numerous regulations, codifies many of management's responsibilities for product safety. In a world of rapidly emerging technologies, however, the "hand of government" does not always provide relevant guidance to the general manager.

Ethical Responsibilities

Society has expectations of business that transcend economic and legal requirements. Ethical responsibilities are difficult to define and consequently difficult for business to deal with. When the economic and political systems fail to

---

3. Philip Kotler, "What Consumerism Means for Marketers," *Harvard Business Review*, (May-June 1972) p. 49.

provide guidance on product safety, however, the "hand of management" must fill the void.

Corporations have increasingly recognized the importance of social issues to their performance and success. At the same time, awareness of management's multidimensional responsibilities has not always been translated into meaningful action. A first step for managers who must deal with product safety controversies is to develop a philosophy to guide their future actions. As *Figure B* illustrates, companies that have been involved in product safety controversies can pass through several phases of social response.

Lacking adequate information and time for a complete analysis of the situation, managers must rapidly formulate some kind of public *reaction* in response to allegations that one of its products is not safe. If both the company and its critics believe there is time to discuss the safety controversy, a more thorough resolution is likely. This is seldom the case, however, especially when the public perceives a clear and present danger. When overwhelmed by public scrutiny and media attention, many business organizations—believing they have been unfairly attacked—will recoil in *defense*. The product safety crisis still remains in the public eye, however, thus further tarnishing the company's reputation. The *insight range* represents the most agonizing moment in the controversy. At this point, the company's stakes can be enormous and may involve its very survival. Management must remodel the situation in light of pressing external forces. *Accommodation* might consist of two different options: the company, still believing in its product, should refute the charges, if it can, that its product is not safe; otherwise, it must postpone its defense and withdraw the product to ameliorate public anxiety. *Agency* will involve actively researching the causes of the safety problem and then an education program to comfort or warn the public about the safety of the product in question.

A comprehensive understanding of the behavior of companies entangled in product safety controversies can help other general managers assess their own responsibilities and options. A company's social response strategy, if properly selected, can help it anticipate and confront difficult situations. Its reputation and future prosperity may hinge on its ability to gain insight into, and deal with, such crises.

The practical and philosophical issues raised in product safety controversies are profound. From a practical viewpoint, the management student is challenged to evaluate and compare specific responses to each product safety controversy. From a philosophical viewpoint, it is worth noting that the challenges involve more than product and safety considerations. In many ways, these issues cut to the core of the relationship between organizations and society. Goods and services of all kinds affect the physical and mental health of people both inside and outside the corporation. Safety is an issue that has both highly visible and subtle influences on the well-being of the community. The relationship among economic, legal, and ethical reasoning in the mind of an agent (either an individual or an organization) can become stressful as a particular controversy unfolds. Understanding how each crisis is handled sheds light on the values and beliefs that guide individuals and organizations involved in business activity. Although risk is inevitable in a society that considers innovation its economic bread and butter, the educated executive will be pressed to carefully balance the rewards of technology with the responsibilities of general management.

Figure B
Corporate Social Response Phases

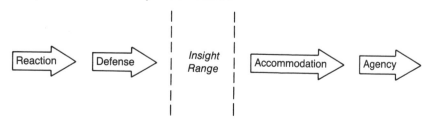

Source: Adapted from Archie B. Carroll, "A Three-Dimensional Conceptual Model of Corporate Performance," *Academy of Management Review* (1977, Vol. 4, No. 4), p. 502.

Managing Product Safety:
The Ford Pinto

*Dekkers L. Davidson,
research associate, prepared this
case under the supervision of
Kenneth E. Goodpaster as a
basis for class discussion rather
than to illustrate either effective
or ineffective handling of an
administrative situation. This
case was developed from public
source material.*

On Tuesday August 9, 1977, Herbert L. Misch, vice president of environmental and safety engineering at Ford Motor Company, picked up a copy of the magazine *Mother Jones* featuring an article entitled "Pinto Madness." This exclusive story would surely stir up a public controversy over the safety of the company's successful subcompact car, the Ford Pinto.

This self-styled radical magazine had cited Ford "secret documents" which, according to the author, proved the company had known for eight years that the Pinto was a "firetrap." The article claimed that preproduction rear-end crash tests had revealed the dangerous nature of the design and placement of the car's fuel tank. According to the author's investigation, Ford was so anxious to get the car on the market that it decided design changes would not be made—they would "take too much time and cost too much money." The article went on to charge that Ford had used "some blatant lies" to delay enactment of a government safety standard that would have forced the company to change the Pinto's "fire-prone" gas tank. The article concluded: "By conservative estimates, Pinto crashes have caused 500 burn deaths to people who would not have been seriously injured if the car had not burst into flames."[1]

Nothing in Ford's records supported the contentions made in the article. Nevertheless, Misch knew that the overall effect of this *Mother Jones* article—one that relied heavily on the testimony of a former Ford engineer—could be highly damaging to the company. It would sharpen consumer criticism of the U.S. auto industry in general and Ford in particular. Misch and his associates at Ford were angered by the allegations and were ready to denounce the article as "unfair and distorted."[2] They knew, however, that it

1. Mark Dowie, "Pinto Madness," *Mother Jones*, September/October 1977, p. 18.
2. "Ford is Recalling Some 1.5 Million Pintos, Bobcats," *Wall Street Journal*, June 12, 1978, p. 2.

would not be an easy task to counter such sensational charges with their own statistical analyses of accident reports.

Ford's management believed that the source of this trouble, like so much of the criticism leveled at the auto industry, was external to its operation. The development of a large consumer movement, along with the enactment of the National Traffic and Motor Vehicle Safety Act of 1966, had revolutionized the car business. In the view of *Mother Jones*, the industry had been considered the "last great unregulated business" in the United States.[3] The industry now had to answer to many more people than just auto buyers. The multitude of often conflicting regulations had, according to auto executives, placed unreasonable burdens on domestic automakers. An exasperated company chairman, Henry Ford, II, lamented, "It's the mess in which we live."[4]

The company had dealt with all of the major federal regulatory agencies in earlier controversies, some of which had involved the beleaguered Pinto. The National Highway Traffic Safety Administration (NHTSA)—a regulatory agency in the Department of Transportation—was considered the industry's chief antagonist. NHTSA investigations had led to previous Pinto recalls because of problems with engine fires and fuel-line hose construction. The appointment of Joan Claybrook—a Ralph Nader lobbyist—as NHTSA administrator had been strongly, but unsuccessfully, opposed by the auto industry. Claybrook was expected to press hard for increased safety and miles-per-gallon (MPG) features.

The Environmental Protection Agency (EPA)—a regulatory agency reporting directly to the U.S. president—had pressed the industry to reduce auto emissions in an effort to clean up air pollution. In 1973, after an internal audit, Ford volunteered it had withheld information from the EPA concerning unauthorized maintenance performed on emission test cars. The agency subsequently levied a $7 million fine on Ford. In one incident, a small number of Pintos had been recalled because of a flaw in the car's air pollution control equipment. The Federal Trade Commission (FTC)—a regulatory agency reporting directly to the U.S. Congress—had

decided to become more involved in oversight activities in the industry. The FTC was mostly concerned that product performance features be candidly disclosed. It had charged that gas mileage claims made by Ford's Lincoln-Mercury division were inaccurate and exaggerated.

While relations between the government and the auto industry were often adversarial, each side realized that self-interest lay in maintaining a workable peace. Auto companies would often settle disputes by agreeing to a recall without admitting fault and without a flurry of negative publicity. The government preferred such voluntary actions because court battles were usually time consuming and rarely resulted in an efficient resolution of a product controversy.

Another group that served as an industry watchdog was the Center for Auto Safety, a privately funded consumer advocate organization founded by Ralph Nader in 1970. The center had noticed in its records a larger-than-expected number of accident reports involving burn deaths in the Ford Pinto. In this, as in other cases, it forwarded the information to NHTSA in an effort to force the agency's hand in confronting the automobile companies. The center's director, Clarence M. Ditlow, who often pressed for auto recalls, had claimed that "the number of recalls and the [number of] cars involved would be high for several more years."[5] In the minds of some industry observers, the center had targeted the Pinto for special attention.

Ford was determined to fight hard for the Pinto. Since it was put into production in 1970, the subcompact had become one of the company's best-selling cars and had allowed Ford to fight off some of the foreign competition. Furthermore, company executives knew that its next-generation small car would not be ready for introduction until 1980.

Competitive Environment

The American automobile industry's fortune had historically been tied to the pattern of the nation's economic cycle. Three or four good years were inexorably followed by one or two poor years. There had been a shakeout of the weakest companies over the years, leaving four major U.S. automakers. In 1977 General Motors (46.4% market share), Ford (22.3%), Chrysler

---

3. Dowie, "Pinto Madness," p. 23.
4. Walter Guzzardi, Jr., "Ford: The Road Ahead," *Fortune*, September 11, 1978, p. 39.

5. "Detroit Stunned by Recall Blitz," *New York Times*, March 12, 1978, Sec. 3, p. 1.

(11.1%), and American Motors (1.8%) shared the $100-plus billion U.S. auto market. Imports, consisting mostly of subcompact cars, had captured 18.4% of this market. Car sales were made primarily through manufacturers' franchised dealers located across the country.[6]

Competition among the four U.S. firms was intense. Pricing, performance features, consumer financing, and advertising had always been important competitive weapons. With the arrival of stiffer foreign competition, however, pricing became an even more critical selling feature. Moreover, in the aftermath of the Arab oil embargo, good fuel economy became especially important, a trend that had favored foreign producers because they had adapted to high fuel costs in their home markets.

For domestic car companies profit margins on all vehicles had declined in the early 1970s, mostly reflecting poor recovery from inflation-related cost increases. Pricing was limited first by price controls, then by the 1974–1975 recession. According to industry experts, domestic labor costs had served significantly to disadvantage American automakers. Small-car margins continued to decline after the recession as a result of reduced demand for small cars in general, heightened competition from imports, and cost increases to achieve safety, damageability, and emission requirements. Large cars, still in demand, fared much better.

Though auto companies were very secretive about new car designs and technologies, there were otherwise very few secrets in the car business. Auto company engineers could, and often would, tear apart a competitor's new car to glean details about a new design or production technique. If one firm changed its price structure or its financing rate, the competition would be able to adjust its strategy quickly. Because of its dominance in the American market, General Motors was considered the market leader and usually dictated the sales strategies for its smaller rivals.

Ford Motor Company was founded in 1903 and had been a family-owned and family-managed business until stock was first sold publicly in 1956. Family members still retained 40% of the voting power in the company, which ranked third (in sales) on the 1977 *Fortune* 500 list of the largest U.S. industrial corporations.

Much like its principal competitor, GM, Ford produced a complete range of cars and trucks. The company had scored some notable successes, however, in cultivating market segments ill-served by General Motors. Ford gained an early edge on its rival by producing the first American-made compact car, the Falcon, in 1960. Its luxury cars, the Thunderbird and Cougar, were also considered attractive by the American car buyer. The Mustang, designed and introduced in 1964 by Lee Iacocca (who later became Ford's president), gained wide favor as the "sports car for the masses."[7]

Despite the successes of these specialty cars, Ford did not gain any ground on General Motors during the 1960s. Furthermore, some Ford executives believed that imports were posing a threat to Ford's traditionally strong position in the small-car market. Though the company was ready with new compact cars (the Maverick was introduced in 1969), it still did not have a subcompact to counter effectively the import challenge.

In June 1967 Ford management became embroiled in a protracted internal debate over the company's position on subcompacts. When it was over, Lee Iacocca had become Ford's president and the Pinto was born. Iacocca directed that the Pinto was to be in showrooms with 1971 models. Formal planning started immediately and the journey to production took less time than the prevailing industry average. In September 1970 the Pinto was introduced as a "carefree little American car," and it gained quick acceptance by the market.[8] After six years of production over 2 million Pintos had been sold, making it one of the company's all-time best-selling automobiles.

Between 1970 and 1977, the Pinto helped stabilize Ford's market position. The 1973–1974 Arab oil embargo hit Ford's major competitors (GM and Chrysler) particularly hard because neither had a large offering of small cars. The following year, Congress set mandatory fuel economy targets that encouraged automakers to sell smaller cars. GM quickly responded with a massive downsizing program that helped it become more small-car oriented. Chrysler, in bleak financial straits, belatedly followed with

6. "You're Damned If You Do . . . ," *Forbes*, January 9, 1978, p. 35.

7. Mark B. Fuller and Malcolm S. Salter, "Ford Motor Company (A)," Case No. 382-161 (Boston, Massachusetts: Harvard Business School, 1982), p. 4.

8. Lee Patrick Strobel, *Reckless Homicide?* (South Bend, Indiana: and books, 1980), p. 82.

its own small-car program. Ford undertook a program to convert its Wayne, Michigan, assembly plant from production of full-size cars to compact cars, completing this transition in only 51 days. By 1975 subcompact and compact cars glutted the market, however, as consumers shunned small cars. Burdened with high inventory levels, the industry began to offer rebates on most small cars. The Pinto, however, continued to outsell most competitive offerings in its size category. Consequently, Ford management decided to focus its new product development on a replacement for the compact-sized Maverick which had been introduced two years before the Pinto. The Pinto would have to hold the consumer's interest until the company was ready to make the investment in the next-generation subcompact.

By mid-1977 the outlook for the auto industry was uncertain in the opinion of most industry analysts. While some predicted the coming year would bring record sales, others worried that shrinking consumer credit would reduce car buying. Apart from sales volume, several industry observers believed Detroit's profits would be hurt by declining margins and a "less rich" sales mix that included more small cars. Each company was scrambling to insure that its fleet averaged the legally mandated 18 miles per gallon in 1978. This meant selling more models that were smaller and fuel efficient but were also less profitable. Faced with intensified competition, most automakers were placing a premium on innovative design and engineering.

Product Safety Controversy, 1970–1977

To meet the competition from imported subcompacts, Ford accelerated the Pinto planning process. In June 1967 Ford commenced the design and development process; production of the Pinto began on August 10, 1970. Ford achieved this 38-month development time, 5 months under the average time of 43 months, by assembling a special team of engineers who directed their efforts entirely to the Pinto. Unlike the development cycles for most new car lines, Pinto start-up planning was simplified and included only a two-door sedan (hatchbacks and station wagons were added in later years). Pinto engineers were constrained by Iacocca's goal, known as "the limits of 2000"—the Pinto was not to weigh an ounce over 2,000

pounds and not to cost a cent over $2,000.[9] These limits, according to former Ford engineers, were strictly enforced. Even at this price and weight, the Pinto would still cost and weigh more than some imported subcompacts.

An early question during the car's design stage was where to safely put the gas tank. Although engineers were familiar with ways to move the gas tank away from the rear of the car—Ford had a patent for a saddle-type tank that could fit above and mostly forward of the car's rear axle—they opted for a strap-on tank arrangement located under the rear floorpan and behind the rear axle. At that time almost every American-made car had the fuel tank located in the same place. Late in the design process, however, an engineering study determined that "the safest place for a fuel tank is directly above the rear axle."[10] It was later determined by senior company engineers that such a design, while moving the tank farther away from a rear-end collision, actually increased the threat of ignition in the passenger compartment. The over-the-axle location of the fuel tank would also require a circuitous filler pipe more likely to be dislodged in an accident. Raising the height of the fuel tank by putting it above the axle would also raise the car's center of gravity, thereby diminishing its handling capabilities. In the opinion of Ford's senior engineers, this would undermine the car's general safety. Practical considerations also dictated the traditional location. The fuel tank could not be placed over the axle, for example, if a station wagon or a hatchback option was going to be offered. The over-axle location would also greatly reduce storage space and would make servicing more difficult.

When the Pinto was in the blueprint stage, the federal government had no standards concerning how safe a car must be from gas leakage in rear-end crashes. In January 1969, NHTSA proposed its first rear-end fuel system integrity standard, called Standard 301. The original standard required that a stationary vehicle should leak less than one ounce of fuel per minute after being hit by a 4,000 pound barrier moving at 20 mph. Ford supported such a stan-

---

9. "Ford Ignored Pinto Fire Peril, Secret Memos Show," *Chicago Tribune*, October 13, 1979, Sec. 2, p. 12.
10. Strobel, *Reckless Homicide?*, p. 80.

dard in writing and voluntarily adopted the 20-mph standard as an internal design objective for its entire line of cars. In mid-1969 the company began a series of crash tests with preproduction Pinto prototypes, as well as with other car lines, in an attempt to meet this objective. Four tests were conducted on vehicles modified to simulate the Pinto's rear-end design. In three of these tests, the leakage slightly exceeded the one-ounce-per-minute standard. In the other test, massive fuel leakage occurred because an improperly welded fuel tank split at the seams.[11] After these tests Ford altered the Pinto's fuel tank design and was able to incorporate these changes before production began. The first Pinto rolled off the assembly line on August 10, 1970. A month later the subcompact was introduced to the American consumer, boasting a price tag of $1,919—about $170 less than GM's subcompact and within $80 of the best-selling Volkswagen Beetle.[12]

The 20-mph *moving-barrier* standard proposed by the government was never adopted. Just days after the manufacture of the first Pinto, NHTSA announced a proposal requiring all vehicles to meet a 20-mph *fixed-barrier* standard within 18 months. In a fixed-barrier test, the vehicle is towed backwards into a fixed barrier at the specified speed. NHTSA also indicated that its long-term objective for rear-end crashes included a 30-mph fixed-barrier standard. This new proposal caught automakers by surprise and provoked universal industry opposition. Ford estimated that a 20-mph fixed-barrier test could, because of the laws of kinetic energy, be nearly twice as severe as a 20-mph moving-barrier test. Many auto engineers were quick to point out the unrealistic nature of fixed-barrier tests: in the real world, vehicles are not driven backwards into walls. Moreover, data available to Ford indicated that 85% of rear-end collisions occurred at speeds equivalent to or less than a 20-mph moving-barrier standard.[13] In addition, the available information indicated

that only .45% of injury-producing accidents involved fire.[14] Preventing injuries from fires caused by rear-end impacts at very high speeds was beyond practical technology, according to many auto executives. Protection against fire at such high speeds would be of little benefit, it was argued, since the force of impact alone was likely to be fatal.

Ford considered it unlikely that the government would adopt fixed-barrier standards. Nevertheless, the company began to test its vehicles against this proposed requirement to determine what would have to be done to meet NHTSA's proposals. Subsequent fixed-barrier tests conducted with standard Pintos at 20 and 30 mph resulted in excessive leakage. To meet the more stringent fixed-barrier standards, a major tear-up of all cars would be required to modify vehicle design. Because of the significant costs involved and doubts about the viability of the fixed-barrier standard, Ford management decided to continue with its own internal 20-mph moving-barrier standard. Engineering work on developing ways to meet a 30-mph moving-barrier standard—which Ford believed NHTSA would eventually adopt—continued.

In early 1971 a junior company engineer began to explore various ways to make the company's smaller cars capable of meeting the 30-mph moving-barrier standard. A 30-page study, called the "Pricor Report," listed several specific recommendations for how to make the car substantially safer from fuel leakage and fire in rear-end crashes. An over-the-axle gas tank, a repositioned spare tire, installation of body rails, a redesigned filler pipe, and an "inner-tank" rubber bladder were among major options for improving the Pinto's overall performance.[15] The first four suggestions were ruled out on the grounds that they would require extensive vehicle design changes. The rubber bladder—a tank liner with an estimated variable cost of $5.80—was seriously considered. On the basis of a crash test in which a bladder was hand placed inside a Pinto tank, a company engineer concluded that the bladder tank "provided a substantial improvement in crash-wor-

---

11. Ford Motor Company Crash Tests 1137, 1138, 1214; memorandum, H.P. Freers to T.J. Feaheny, January 31, 1969.

12. Strobel, *Reckless Homicide?*, p. 82.

13. Fuel System Integrity Program, Percent of Rear Accidents Occurring at/or Below Equivalent Fixed (Movable) Barrier Speeds, Car Product Planning, March 14, 1971. (Accident data file from Accident Crash Injury Research [ACIR] Project at Cornell Aeronautical Laboratory.)

14. "Observations on Fire in Automobile Accidents," Cornell Aeronautical Laboratory, Inc., February 1965.

15. A. J. Pricor, "197X Mustang/Maverick Program: Fuel Tank Integrity," Ford Motor Company.

thiness."[16] In cold weather, however, the bladders became stiff, making gas filling very difficult. And in very hot climates, the bladders failed under test conditions.

In August 1973, NHTSA announced a proposal for a 30-mph *moving-barrier*, rear-end fuel system integrity standard, effective September 1976 for all 1977 models. A prolonged debate ensued between government officials and industry executives over the appropriate test technique. NHTSA was a proponent of car-to-car testing, arguing that this was a closer approximation to actual accident situations. Auto representatives maintained that a standard moving barrier (which was towed along a track to the point of impact) was much more appropriate because it was repeatable and, therefore, a more reliable measurement of crashworthiness.

At the same time that NHTSA proposed the rear-end crash standard, it also adopted a fuel system integrity standard applicable to rollover accidents. Although Ford did not oppose the rear-end standard, it vigorously fought the rollover standard. Under provisions of the rollover test, minimal gasoline leakage would be permitted when a car was turned upside down in an accident. This presented automakers with obvious problems, since leakage would occur from the carburetor, fuel vents, and the gas cap air hole when a car was upside down; yet, each of these openings was necessary for the normal functioning of the fuel intake. After extensive study Ford determined that the rollover requirement might be met by installing an $11 valve on each of its 12.5 million cars and trucks then on the road. Among the materials submitted was a cost-benefit analysis prepared according to NHTSA criteria and using government figures ($200,000 per death, $67,000 per injury). The values reflected only the economic loss to society resulting from injuries and deaths, because the government had no estimate to place on human pain and suffering. The analysis, done by Ford personnel with no design responsibilities, presented the case that the $137 million in cost far outweighed the dollar values assigned for the 180 burn deaths, 180 serious burn injuries, and 2,100 burned vehi-

cles.[17] The rollover standard was eventually adopted with some minor modifications. The cost-benefit analysis on rollover accidents became the basis for countless media claims that Ford delayed *rear-end* fuel system integrity standards because "its internal cost-benefit analysis, which places a dollar value on human life, said it wasn't profitable to make the changes sooner."

The first notable public criticism of the Pinto's fuel tank design came in late 1973. Byron Bloch, an independent consultant in automobile safety design, warned a Department of Transportation conference that the Pinto's fuel system design was "very vulnerable . . . to even minor damage."[18] On a national television program, Bloch held up a model of a Pinto and pointed out what he saw as its fuel system hazards. When Ford announced it was recalling the Pinto for minor repairs, Bloch urged the government to require a recall that would improve the car's resistance to fire in rear-end crashes. Early in 1974 the Center for Auto Safety pressed NHTSA to investigate the fuel system integrity of the Ford Pinto and the Chevrolet Vega. The center cited concerns expressed by attorneys engaged in liability lawsuits, as well as its own research findings, in calling for a defect investigation. NHTSA reviewed these complaints and determined that there was no demonstrable safety problem.

NHTSA, still a relatively new federal agency in the mid-1970s, was seriously hampered in most of its investigatory work by a lack of relevant and meaningful statistical information. In early 1975 a study commissioned by the Insurance Institute for Highway Safety concluded that the number of fire-related incidents involving vehicles was growing more rapidly than the number of other incidents of fire. The study noted a striking difference between Ford's 20% national representation among domestic passenger cars and its 35% frequency in surveyed collision-ruptured fuel tanks.[19] The study's author cautioned, however, that it was not possible to draw definitive conclusions about causal

---

16. "Ford 157 Report-Bladder Fuel Tank Test," Ford Motor Company.

17. "Fatalities Associated with Crash Induced Fuel Leakage and Fires," E.S. Grush and C.S. Saundby, Ford Motor Company, September 19, 1973.
18. Strobel, *Reckless Homicide?*, p. 145.
19. Eugene M. Trisko, "Results of the 1973 National Survey of Motor Vehicle Fires," *Fire Journal* (March 1975), p. 23.

relationships; nor was it possible to identify differences between car models. This study, and others like it, came at a time of growing public concern over motor vehicle fires. Between 1974 and 1976 consumer groups and Congress exerted considerable political pressure on NHTSA to finally implement all provisions of the fuel system integrity standard. In 1977 Standard 301 was fully enacted.

On August 10, 1977, the allegations contained in the *Mother Jones* article were first made public at a news conference in Washington, D.C. The charges against Ford appeared to have been based on quotes attributed to either past or present company engineers, along with a digest of confidential company memoranda. Ford executives took a dim view of the magazine, but they knew its editors had obtained some key sensitive documents that could easily be misinterpreted by the public. As far as the company knew, no government investigation was being conducted that concerned the Pinto's fuel system.

Postscript

On September 26, 1977, Ford officials publicly responded to the *Mother Jones* article—which had appeared seven weeks earlier—by issuing a news release aimed at refuting the magazine's allegations. The news release claimed: "There is no serious fire hazard in the fuel system of the Ford Pinto, nor are any Pinto models exceptionally vulnerable to rear-impact collision fires. [NHTSA] statistics establish that Ford Pinto is involved in fewer fire-associated collisions than might be expected considering the total number of Pintos in operation." Ford cited government figures for the period 1975–1976 for which comprehensive information was available. These figures showed that Pintos were involved in about 1.9% of fire-accompanied passenger car fatalities in 1975–1976, years in which Pintos made up an average of about 1.9% of passenger cars. Ford explained that early experiments with its rubber bladder gas tank were conducted to see if the company could meet its own ambitious performance requirements. "The truth is that in every model year the Pinto has been tested and met or surpassed the federal fuel system integrity standards applicable to it."[20]

The company acknowledged that later-model Pintos had an improved fuel system design, but argued that "it simply is unreasonable and unfair to contend that a car is somehow unsafe if it does not meet standards proposed for future years or embody the technological improvements that are introduced in later model years." The company denied that it had purposely delayed Standard 301 and said it had only "opposed . . . certain excessive testing requirements."[21]

In September 1977, NHTSA opened an investigation into the Pinto's fuel tank system and ran an engineering analysis of the pre-1977 Pinto. As reported by the *Wall Street Journal*, the agency found that "the fuel tank's location and the structural parts around it permitted easy crushing or puncturing of the tank in a crash. Officials also found that the short fuel tank filler pipe could easily pull away from the tank." There was "a real potential for trouble," said one government official.[22]

Ford's management was angered by NHTSA's inquiry and believed the basis for its examination to be unfounded. In a 1974 investigation of complaints, NHTSA had determined that no action concerning Pinto fuel system integrity was necessary. Indeed, by NHTSA's own admission, its action was in response to the enormous flood of mail demanding that it do something about the Pinto. Company management was further incensed when the agency acknowledged that its accident statistics were "notoriously incomplete." NHTSA had only begun to develop a comprehensive accident reporting system.

By early 1978 the Pinto controversy began to attract national attention. The Center for Auto Safety had called for a national campaign to force Ford to recall the country's 2-million-odd Pintos and retrofit a safety bladder into the gas tank of *all* Pintos. The car's image was further tarnished by recalls due to piston scuffing and steering failures.

In February 1978 a California jury handed down a verdict that assessed $125 million in punitive damages against Ford in a case involving the rupture and explosion of the fuel tank

20. Ford Motor Company news release (Dearborn, Michigan: Ford Motor Company, September 26, 1977), p. 1.

21. Ibid, p. 1.
22. "Car Trouble: Government Pressure Propels Auto Recalls Toward A New High," *Wall Street Journal*, August 16, 1978, p. 1.

on a 1972 Pinto. One person had died in the fiery Pinto crash, and the surviving passenger had undergone 60 different operations in the six years since the accident. It was testimony by Harley Copp, a former Ford senior engineer, that apparently convinced the court the Pinto was, in the words of one juror, "a lousy and unsafe product."[23] The massive amount of money awarded by the jury, easily the highest for such a suit in American history, led to heightened media interest in the Pinto issue. A judge later reduced punitive damages to $3.5 million.

During the same month as the California verdict, NHTSA conducted experimental crash tests of the Pinto as part of its ongoing investigation. A total of 11 rear-end crash tests of 1971–1976 Pintos were staged at speeds between 30 and 35 mph. Two cars tested at 35 mph caught fire, and the other tests at 30 mph resulted in "significant leakage."[24] When NHTSA similarly tested GM's Chevrolet Vega, a larger and slightly heavier vehicle than the Pinto, minimal gasoline leakage was reported. Ford management believed these tests were unfair and inappropriate. Some of the tests were more severe than the government required even for later-model vehicles, and this was apparently the first time the agency had ever used car-to-car crash tests to determine if there was a safety defect.

In March 1978 Pinto owners in Alabama and California filed class action suits, demanding that Ford recall all Pintos built from 1971 through 1976 and modify their fuel systems. The California civil complaint alleged that Ford "persistently and willfully failed and refused to remedy the design defect in the fuel tank." Around this time the head of the American Trial Lawyers Association, in an unprecedented step, had appealed to the company to "recall all of the cars in question."[25] Later that same month, NHTSA notified Ford that its 1976 Pintos had not passed a 30-mph *front-end* barrier test. This test result, which revealed occasional fuel leakage in the engine compartment, led to a recall of 300,000 Pintos.

On May 9, 1978, NHTSA announced that it had made an "initial determination" that a safety defect existed in the fuel systems of Ford Pintos for the 1971 through 1976 model years. This finding had been reached after eight months of analysis, testing, and review of pertinent company records. The government claimed that it was aware of 38 cases in which rear-end collisions of Pintos had resulted in fuel tank damage, leakage, and/or ensuing fires. Of those 38 cases, it said, there were 27 fatalities among occupants and 24 instances in which individuals suffered nonfatal burns. In its four-paragraph letter to Ford's President Iacocca, NHTSA informed the company that it could respond to the initial findings at a public hearing scheduled for mid-June.[26] During late May and early June, Ford officials met with NHTSA to discuss privately the government's findings and to consider possible remedies. A few days before the hearing date, the decision was made to recall the cars.

On June 9, 1978, after years of vigorously defending the safety of the Pinto's fuel system, Ford management announced the recall of 1.5 million of its subcompacts. In a press release issued on the day of the recall announcement, Ford management insisted "that it does not agree with the agency's initial determination . . . that an unreasonable risk to safety is involved in the design of [the Pinto], and that it believes it can be demonstrated that the actual performance of the vehicles is comparable to that of other subcompact and compact cars manufactured during the same periods." The company did concede that "NHTSA had identified areas in which the risk of fuel leakage could be reduced significantly on a practical basis." Accordingly, Ford decided to offer the modifications to "end public concern that had resulted from criticism of the fuel system in these vehicles."[27] The company agreed to notify all Pinto owners that it was ready to replace the fuel filler pipe and install a polyethylene shield across the front of the fuel tank. Ford estimated this offer could cost the company as much as $20 million after taxes. During the previous

23. "Why the Pinto Jury Felt Ford Deserved $125 Million Penalty," *Wall Street Journal*, February 14, 1978, p. 1.
24. National Highway Traffic Safety Administration, *Report of Defects Investigation* (Washington, D.C., NHTSA, May 1978), p. 11.
25. "Class Action Suit Seeks Recall of 1971–76 Pintos," *Wall Street Journal*, March 7, 1978, p. 34.

26. "U.S. Agency Suggests Ford Pintos Have a Fuel System Safety Defect," *New York Times*, May 9, 1978, p. 22.
27. "Ford Orders Recall of 1.5 Million Pintos for Safety Changes," *New York Times*, June 10, 1978, p. 1.

year Ford had earned a total of $1.5 billion after taxes.[28]

NHTSA administrator Joan Claybrook said the government wanted to work out a voluntary agreement with Ford to avoid a long drawn-out court battle. In response to Ford's recall, the government closed its investigation without making a final determination.

In Detroit, Michigan, Ford Chairman Henry Ford, II, said: "The lawyers would shoot me for saying this, but I think there's some cause for concern about the [Pinto]. I don't even listen to the cost figures—we've got to fix it."[29]

28. "Ford is Recalling Some 1.5 Million Pintos, Bobcats," *Wall Street Journal*, June 12, 1978, p. 2.

29. Guzzardi, "Ford: The Road Ahead," p. 42.

Note on the Export of Pesticides from the United States to Developing Countries

*David E. Whiteside, research associate, prepared this note under the supervision of **Kenneth E. Goodpaster**.*

The sale or distribution of any pesticide within the United States was prohibited by law unless it was registered with the Environmental Protection Agency (EPA). Registration required the submission of toxicity data showing that intended use of the pesticide posed no unreasonable risk to people or the environment. Each year, however, U.S. companies exported to developing countries millions of pounds of unregistered pesticides and pesticides whose registration had been canceled or restricted. In 1976, for example, 25% of U.S. exports, or 140 million pounds, were unregistered and another 31 million pounds were pesticides whose registrations had been canceled.[1] This practice was legal as long as these pesticides were manufactured only for export.

As concern about the environment increased in the 1970s, the morality of this practice, what to do about it, and who was responsible for changing it became widely debated. In *Circle of Poison*, David Weir and Mark Schapiro claimed that the export of these pesticides resulted in tens of thousands of poisonings and scores of fatalities in developing countries each year. Referring to the practice as an international scandal, they blamed the pesticide industry for dumping these pesticides in developing countries and argued that Americans were also harmed because imports treated with these pesticides contained toxic residues. The *Christian Science Monitor* called the situation morally indefensible and urged government intervention.[2] A main charge of critics was that the practice was based on a double standard—the lives of people in developing countries were less valuable than the lives of Americans. Phillip Leakey, assistant minister of the environment in Kenya, asserted:

1. *Better Regulation of Pesticide Exports and Pesticide Residues in Imported Foods is Essential* (Washington, DC: General Accounting Office, 1979), p. 3.
2. "Exporting Poisons," *Christian Science Monitor*, February 13, 1980, p. 12.

Key to Acronyms

ADI	acceptable daily intake
AID	Agency for International Development
Amvac	American Vanguard Corporation
EPA	Environmental Protection Agency
FAO	Food and Agricultural Organization
FDA	Food and Drug Administration
FFDCA	Federal Food, Drug, and Cosmetic Act
FIFRA	Federal Insecticide, Fungicide, and Rodenticide Act
GAO	General Accounting Office
GIFAP	Groupement International des Associations Nationales de Fabricants de Produit Agrochimiques
IPM	Integrated pest management
NACA	National Agricultural Chemicals Association
OSHA	Occupational Safety and Health Administration
OXFAM	Oxford Committee for the Relief of Famine
WHO	World Health Organization

"There is no question that the industrial nations and the companies which are manufacturing these things are guilty of promoting and sponsoring dangerous chemicals in countries where they think people don't care."[3] "What is at stake here is the integrity of the label *Made in U.S.A.*," argued Rep. Michael D. Barnes (D–Md.), who introduced legislation in 1980 to limit the export of dangerous pesticides abroad.[4]

The U.S. pesticide industry was opposed to more government regulation and countered that it, too, was concerned about the harm done by pesticides, but that this was largely a result of misuse. Spokespeople for the industry argued that they were making significant attempts on their own to reduce harm through education and by developing safer promotional and advertising methods. A principal argument of the industry was that each country had the right to make up its own mind about the risks and benefits of using a particular pesticide. Dr. Jack Early, president of the National Agricultural Chemicals Association (NACA), accused critics of elitism and asked: "Should we tell other countries on the basis of our affluent standards where the appropriate balance of benefits and risks should lie for them? What does the EPA know—or care, for that matter—about the strength of Brazil's desire to obtain a particular pesticide that has some undesirable ecological effect?"[5]

Some Examples of Manufacturers and Pesticides

Velsicol and Phosvel

In 1971 Velsicol Chemical Company of Chicago began U.S. production of Phosvel, its trade name for the pesticide leptophos. The WHO classified leptophos as extremely hazardous due to its delayed neurotoxic effects — it could cause paralysis for some time after exposure. Phosvel was not approved for sale in the United States by the EPA, although it was granted a temporary registration. Velsicol, however, sold it to developing countries where there were no restrictions on its importation.

Reports circulated in 1971 that Phosvel was involved in the deaths of water buffalo in Egypt.[6] Citing the report of the U.S. Pesticide Tolerance Commission, Velsicol contended that a conclusive determination of Phosvel's role in the incident could not be made because of incomplete facts. In 1973 and 1974 there were additional accounts of poisonings of animals and people.[7]

In 1976 OSHA revealed that workers at Velsicol's Bayport, Texas, plant which manufactured Phosvel had developed serious disorders of the nervous system. They vomited, complained of impotence, were fatigued and disoriented, and became paralyzed. Workers sued Velsicol, the EPA sued for pollution violations, and OSHA leveled fines. The company then withdrew its application for registration of Phosvel and closed its Bayport plant.

From 1971 to 1976, when Velsicol stopped manufacturing Phosvel, estimates were made that it exported between $10–18 million worth of Phosvel to developing countries. After the Bayport incident, several countries banned the import of Phosvel. Claiming that Phosvel was safe when used properly, Velsicol tried to sell

3. "Kenya tries to put cap on imports of hazardous chemicals," *Christian Science Monitor*, May 3, 1983, p. 13.
4. "Hazards for Export," *Newsday*, December 1981, reprint, p. 14R.

5. Ibid., p. 13R.
6. Cited by Jacob Scherr, *Proceedings of the U.S. Strategy Conference on Pesticide Management* (Silver Springs, Maryland: Teknekron Research, Inc., 1979), p. 33.
7. David Bull, *A Growing Problem* (Oxford, England: OXFAM, 1982), p. 40.

its remaining stocks of Phosvel in developing countries.[8]

In 1978 Velsicol began reforms to change its environmental image. Responding to criticisms of the company, Richard Blewitt, vice president of corporate affairs, stated: "I'm sorry to say we don't have control over worldwide inventories of Phosvel. Velsicol has made an attempt . . . to secure at our cost those inventories and make sure they are properly disposed of . . . which far exceeds our obligation."[9] He observed, however, that some distributors were resisting efforts to buy back Phosvel inventories.

As of 1984, Velsicol also sold heptachlor, chlordane, and endrin to developing countries. Use of these pesticides had been canceled or restricted in the United States because they were suspected of being carcinogenic or mutagenic. Velsicol claimed there was no medical evidence that exposure to these chemicals had caused any case of cancer or birth defects in humans.

Amvac and DBCP

After workers at an Occidental plant in California were found to be sterile in 1977, the state canceled the use of another pesticide, DBCP. At that time Dow, Occidental, and Shell stopped producing it. In 1979 the EPA canceled all uses of DBCP except for use on Hawaiian pineapples because it was suspected of being carcinogenic.

After the ban the American Vanguard Corporation (Amvac) could no longer sell DBCP directly to American companies, but it did continue exporting it. The company's 1979 10-K report stated: "Management believes that because of the extensive publicity and notoriety that has arisen over the sterility of workers and the suspected mutagenic and carcinogenic nature of DBCP, the principal manufacturers and distributors of the product (Dow, Occidental, and Shell Chemical) have, temporarily at least, decided to remove themselves from the domestic marketplace and possibly from the world marketplace." The report continued: "Notwithstanding all the publicity and notoriety surrounding DBCP it was [our] opinion that a vacuum existed in the marketplace that [we] could temporarily occupy. [We] further believed that

with the addition of DBCP, sales might be sufficient to reach a profitable level." According to Weir and Schapiro, a former executive had stated: "Quite frankly, without DBCP, Amvac would go bankrupt."[10]

Dow Chemical and 2,4-D and 2,4,5-T

2,4-D and 2,4,5-T were herbicides that often contained dioxin as a contaminant. These herbicides were probably best known as components of Agent Orange, one of the herbicides used as a defoliant by the United States during the war in Vietnam. A study done by Dr. Marco Micolta, director of the San Antonio Central Hospital in rural Colombia, claimed that 2,4-D and 2,4,5-T were responsible for the many miscarriages and birth defects—usually harelip and cleft palate or both—that occurred in the region.[11] In the United States 2,4-D and 2,4,5-T were manufactured and sold abroad by several companies, including Dow Chemical Company. All uses of these pesticides containing dioxin were illegal in the United States, and use of them without dioxin was restricted.

"Dioxin Reportedly Worst Cancer Causer" read the headline of an article in the *Boston Globe*. The article summarized a report by scientists for the EPA which concluded that dioxin was "the most potent cancer causing substance they have ever studied." It was further stated that dioxin probably caused cancer in humans and presented an unacceptable cancer risk when found in water in parts per quintillion. A trillionth of a gram of dioxin in a cubic meter of air would produce about nine additional cases of cancer for each 100,000 people, it was reported. The article pointed out that the conclusions in the report contrasted sharply with industry claims that "the most serious health effect caused by exposure to dioxin is a serious skin rash called chloracne."[12]

In testimony to Congress, a Dow vice president and toxicologist, Perry Gehring, stated that dioxin had "only mild effects on humans." Consistent with its policy of maintaining that 2,4-D and 2,4,5-T were safe when properly used, Dow had been lobbying to have restrictions of these pesticides eased. Robert Lundeen, chairman, said that Dow was trying to reverse the 1979 suspension of 2,4,5-T because "it was patently unsound and had no scientific merit.

---

8. David Weir and Mark Schapiro, *Circle of Poison* (San Francisco, CA: Institute for Food and Development Policy, 1981), p. 23.
9. *Newsday*, p. 11R.

10. Weir and Schapiro, p. 22.
11. *Newsday*, p. 11R.
12. The *Boston Globe*, July 24, 1983, p. 19.

If we caved in on this one, we might lose the next one, when it was important." One study of the herbicide followed 121 workers in a Monsanto plant that produced 2,4,5-T. They had been accidentally exposed to dioxin in 1949 and developed chloracne and other temporary symptoms. After 30 years of observation, the University of Cincinnati's Institute of Environmental Health reported that their death rate was below average and rates of cancer and other chronic disease was at or below normal.[13]

What Is a Pesticide?

Most pesticides were synthetic organic chemicals that were able to kill pests, including insects, weeds, fungi, rodents, and worms. (Clearly, people had different ideas as to what counted as a pest. One survey in the Philippines found that the farmers studied believed that any insect found in their fields should be killed by insecticides.) Pesticides were classified either by use or by chemical makeup. The three major kinds of pesticides by use were herbicides, insecticides, and fungicides. Classification by chemical makeup produced four major categories: organochlorines, organophosphates, carbamates, and pyrethroids. In addition to the generic names of the active ingredients (e.g., paraquat), pesticides also had been given brand names by the companies that produced them (e.g., Gramoxone).

In assessing the risks or hazards of using a pesticide, it was common to distinguish between the intrinsic properties of the chemical and aspects of risk that were under human control. Toxicity, persistence, and fat solubility were important innate characteristics to consider. Toxicity was measured in terms of the lethal dose (LD_{50}) required to kill 50% of the test animals—usually rats. Acute toxic effects included nausea, dizziness, sweating, salivation, shortness of breath, unconsciousness, and possibly death. Some commonly used pesticides, like parathion, could cause death by swallowing only a few drops or by skin contact with a teaspoon of the chemical. Chronic toxicity was produced by long-term, low-level exposure and was evidenced by infertility, nervous disorders, tumors, blood disorders, or abnormal offspring.

A pesticide was considered persistent if it did not break down easily. Since persistent chemicals remained in the environment longer, they were more likely to affect organisms other than the target pest. The persistence of a chemical varied according to its interaction with the environment. For example, DDT had a half-life of 20 years in temperate climates but was reported in some studies to have a half-life of less than a year in the tropics as a result of increased sunlight, warmth, and moisture.[14] If a pesticide was fat soluble, it could bioaccumulate in the body and remain there. This accumulation might result in long-term harm. Although not acutely toxic, DDT was considered hazardous because of its persistence and fat solubility.

Controllable risk factors included the precautions taken in the manufacture, storage, and transport of a pesticide; the nature of the formulation of the active ingredients; the manner of application; the place used; and the amount of chemical applied.

The Pesticide Industry

The first step in producing a pesticide was synthesizing or creating thousands of chemicals and testing them for useful biological activity—in this instance, the ability to kill pests. If the chemical passed this initial screen (and only 1% did in the first stage of development) then laboratory tests for acute toxicity began, along with a patent application. In the second stage of development, laboratory and greenhouse tests continued. The chemical was tested for specificity of action—did it kill only a few pests or a wide variety? An experimental permit was also applied for. In the final stage testing continued, full registration was applied for, and final preparations for manufacturing and marketing began. (*Figure A* shows the process in more detail.) In 1981 it took six to seven years from the time of discovery of a chemical with biological efficacy to final registration with the EPA. A company might have screened 12,000–30,000 chemicals before it brought one to market. It was estimated that the research and development costs for a single pesticide averaged $20 million.

---

13. "Dow vs. the Dioxin Monster," *Fortune*, May 30, 1983, pp. 84–85.

14. Ram S. Hamsagar, "Petrochemicals and the Environment." Paper published by *Groupement International des Associations Nationales de Fabricants de Produit Agrochimiques* (GIFAP), September 23, 1983, p. 4.

Figure A
Pesticide R&D Process: Activities and Timing

Years	1	2	3	4	5	6	7

Lead Compound Bioefficacy Confirmed

Acute Tox.

Export Registration Application

Chronic Toxicology

Metabolism and Residue Studies

Registration Application

Commercialization of Product

Greenhouse Small Field

Full Scale Efficacy

Field Tests Continue

Interim Facilities

Process Evaluation

New Plant

Process Development and Design

Design Constr.

Make Prod.

Increase Capacity

Small Lot Manufacturing

Scope Book and Construction

Commercial Production

Chemical Analogs

Patent Coverage

Source: Data gathered by casewriter

Table A
Top 10 Producers of Pesticides, 1980

Company	Value ($ mil.)	Production (mil. lb.)	% Market Share by Value	% Cumulative Market Share
Monsanto	$552–580	169–173	20%	20%
Ciba-Geigy	354–358	142–147	13	33
Stauffer	330	150–117	12	45
Eli Lilly	285–300	72– 82	10	55
DuPont	220	75– 99	8	63
Cyanamid	220	82	8	71
Union Carbide	150–160	57– 63	6	77
Shell	132–155	40– 55	5	82
FMC	135–140	55	5	87
Mobay	125–135	40– 45	5	92

Source: *U.S. Pesticides Market* (New York: Frost and Sullivan, Inc., 1981), p. 126.

Major pesticide companies synthesized active ingredients and formulated them, or combined the active ingredients with inert substances to make them ready for application. U.S. production moved from the pesticide manufacturer to distributor to dealer to the farmer. Production in developing countries was similar, except that dealers in the United States were often trained by pesticide companies and were knowledgeable about pesticide use, whereas in developing countries the user often bought pesticides from a small shopkeeper who was not well informed about pesticide use and toxicity. In addition, some large companies had established plants in developing countries that formulated the basic toxicants, which were then imported by the parent company. This enabled companies to decrease production costs due to lower labor costs and less government regulation. They also were able to take advantage of tax incentives offered to foreign investors in these countries. (*Table A* lists the top 10 producers of pesticides in 1980.)

From the 1940s to the late 1970s the pesticide industry, driven by the frequent introduction of new products, experienced rapid growth. Investment in R&D was high to sustain innovation and cheaper manufacturing processes. In 1981 R&D budgets were 8% of sales. The industry also required high capital investment because of the rapid obsolescence of plant and equipment; thus, capital expenditures were 7.2% of sales. These high technology costs, as well as high regulation and marketing costs, posed significant barriers to entry.

Sales of U.S. producers steadily increased from $1.2 billion dollars in 1972 to $5.4 billion in 1982. (*Figure B* shows the increase in sales and exports of pesticides from 1960 to 1980.) Exports steadily rose from $220 million in 1970 to about $1.2 billion in 1980. Production of pesticides in the U.S. rose from 675 million pounds in 1960 to a peak of 1.7 billion pounds in 1975 and declined to 1.3 billion pounds in 1980.

Figure B
U.S. Sales of Pesticides, 1960–1980

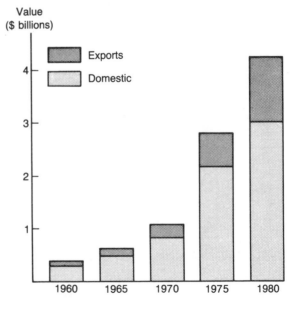

Source: Data gathered by casewriter

Prices and profits for pesticides depended largely on whether or not patents were involved. Pretax profit margins on proprietary products that had a market niche were about 48%. Older products, like DDT and 2,4-D, functioned more like commodities and returned considerably less on investment. Even though a product was patented, competing companies often developed similar products not covered by the original patent. Prices of pesticides tripled between 1970 and 1980; in 1981 herbicides had the highest price and accounted for 60% of sales.

The pesticide industry was a mature industry and U.S. markets had become saturated. As demand in the U.S. slowed, exports increased. In 1978 exports were 621 million pounds and were 36% of total shipments. In 1990, it was predicted, exports would be 855 million pounds and would be 43% of total pesticide shipments. Dollar volume of U.S. exports was projected to reach $2.6 billion by 1990.[15]

Industry analysts agreed that exports would provide the fastest growth for U.S. producers, since the U.S. markets were saturated. Farmers were also using fewer pesticides because of increased costs, declining acreage under cultivation, a slowing of growth in farm income, and increased use of integrated pest management (IPM) techniques which relied more on cultural and biological controls and less on pesticides.

There were 35 producers of pesticides worldwide with sales of more than $100 million per year. In 1982 total worldwide sales were $13.3 billion, up from $2.8 billion in 1972. Six countries—United States, West Germany, France, Brazil, the USSR, and Japan—accounted for 63% of worldwide sales. All of the developing countries combined accounted for 15% of the worldwide market in dollar volume. A report by the U.S. General Accounting Office (GAO) estimated that pesticide requirements in dollar value for these countries were expected to increase fivefold from 1979 to 1985.[16]

The Benefits of Pesticides

The pesticide industry and many agricultural scientists defended the sale of pesticides to de-

veloping countries, declaring that pesticides were necessary to feed an ever-increasing world population, most of it poor, and that pesticides were of great value in fighting diseases which primarily affected the poor. They also argued that there were important secondary benefits.

In 1979 the world population reached approximately 4.4 billion people. Using a minimum-intake level for survival, with no allowance for physical activity, the Food and Agricultural Organization (FAO) of the United Nations estimated that there were 450 million chronically malnourished people in the world. Using a higher standard, the International Food Policy Research Institute put the figure at 1.3 billion.[17]

World population doubled from 1 A.D. to 1650 A.D.; a second doubling occurred after 200 years; the next took 80 years; and the last doubling took place in 1975, requiring only 45 years. Given the 1980 worldwide average birthrate of 2.05%, according to Norman Borlaug the next doubling would occur in 2015, when world population would total 8 billion. At that birthrate, 172 people would be born every minute, resulting in an additional 90 million people each year. David Hopper of the World Bank stated that developing countries accounted for 90% of this increase.[18]

In 1977, Borlaug noted, world food production totaled 3.5 billion tons, 98% of which came directly or indirectly from plants. Based on rates of population growth and projected income elasticities for food, Hopper emphasized the necessity for an increase in food availability of about 3% per year, requiring a doubling of world food production to 6.6 billion tons by 2015. Increasing demand for food by developing countries was reflected in the fact that imports of grains to these countries rose from 10 million tons in 1961 to 52 million tons in 1977, according to Maurice Williams, and food shortages were projected to reach 145 million tons by 1990, of which 80 million tons would be for the low-income countries of Asia and Africa.[19]

A major cause of these shortages was that

15. "Pesticides: $6 Billion by 1990," *Chemical Week*, May 7, 1980, p. 45.
16. *Better Regulation*, p. 1.

17. Maurice J. Williams, "The Nature of the World Food and Population Problem," in *Future Dimensions of World Food and Population*, ed. by R. G. Woods (Boulder, Colorado: Westview Press, 1981), p. 20.
18. Norman Borlaug, "Using Plants to Meet World Food Needs," *Future Dimensions*, p. 180; David Hopper, "Recent Trends in World Food and Population," *Future Dimensions*, p. 37.
19. Borlaug, pp. 118, 128; Hopper, p. 39; and Williams, p. 11.

food production in developing countries had not kept pace with the increased demand for food. While per capita production of food for developed countries had steadily increased since 1970, per capita production in developing countries *decreased* by an average of 50%, with the economies of Africa and Latin America showing the greatest drop.

Although experts agreed that it was important to attack the world food problem by lessening demand, they also concurred that deliberate efforts to slow population growth would not produce any significant decline in demand for food for the next decade or so. It was argued, then, that ameliorating the world food problem depended on increasing the food supply. Norman Borlaug, recipient of the 1971 Nobel Peace Prize for the development of the high-yield seeds that were the basis for the Green Revolution, argued that developed countries would not make significant additional increases in yields per acre and that developing countries had to increase their per capita food production. Due to the scarcity of easily developed new land, Borlaug concluded that increases in world food supply could only come from increased yields per acre in these countries, and that this required the widespread use of pesticides.[20]

There was little argument, even from critics, that pesticides increased food production. The technology of the Green Revolution, which depended on pesticides, had enabled scientists in the tropics to obtain yields of 440 bushels of corn per acre versus an average yield of 30 bushels per acre by traditional methods.[21] The International Rice Research Institute in the Philippines had shown that rice plots protected by insecticides yielded an average of 2.7 tons per hectare (2.47 acres) more than unprotected plots, an increase of almost 100%. They also found that the use of rodenticides resulted in rice yields up to three times higher than those of untreated plots.[22] (*Only* producing more food would not end world hunger. What kinds of foods people eat and the quantity are correlated with income. Thus, many experts maintain that economic development is equally important in eliminating world hunger.)

Even with the use of pesticides, worldwide crop losses because of pests before harvest averaged about 25% in developed countries and around 40% in undeveloped countries. In 1982, GIFAP estimated that total crop losses due to pests for rice, corn, wheat, sugar cane, and cotton were about $204 billion. Most experts (quoted in Ennis et al) estimated an additional loss of 20–25% of food crops if pesticides were not used.[23]

Pesticides also contributed to reducing losses after harvesting. A National Academy of Sciences study identified most postharvest loss resulting from pests and observed that "conservative estimates indicate that a minimum of 107 million tons of food were lost in 1976; the amounts lost in cereal grains and legumes alone could produce more than the annual minimum caloric requirements of 168 million people." Postharvest losses of crops and perishables through pests were estimated to range from 10% to 40%. Insects were a major problem, especially in the tropics, because environmental conditions produced rapid breeding. The National Academy of Sciences noted that "50 insects at harvest could multiply to become more than 312 million after four months." In India, in 1963 and 1964, insects and rodents attacked grain in the field and in storage and caused losses of 13 million tons. According to Ennis et al, this amount of wheat would have supplied 77 million families with one loaf of bread per day for a year.[24]

Many developing countries also relied on the sale of agricultural products for foreign exchange that they needed for development or to buy the commodities they could not produce. Cotton, for example, was an important cash crop for many of these countries. Several experimental studies in the United States had shown that untreated plots produced about 10 pounds of seed cotton per acre, but over 1,000 pounds were produced when insecticides were used.[25] It was estimated that 50% of the cotton produced by developing countries would be destroyed if pesticides were not used.

It was also argued that major indirect benefits

---

20. Borlaug, p. 114 and pp. 129–134.
21. Hopper, p. 49.
22. Bull, p. 5.

---

23. *GIFAP Directory* 1982–1983, p. 10; W. B. Ennis, W. M. Dowler, W. Klassen, "Crop Protection to Increase Food Supplies," in *Food: Politics, Economics, Nutrition, and Research*, ed. P. Abelson (Washington, DC: American Association for the Advancement of Science, 1975), p. 113.
24. E. R. Pariser, et al., *Post-Harvest Food Losses in Developing Countries* (Washington, DC: National Academy of Sciences, 1978), pp. 7, 53; Ennis, p. 110.
25. William Hollis, "The Realism of Integrated Pest Management as a Concept and in Practice—with Social Overtures," paper presented at Annual Meeting of Entomological Society of America, in Washington, DC, December 1, 1977, p. 7.

resulted from the use of an agricultural technology that had pesticide use as an essential component. This "package" was more efficient not only because it increased yields per acre, but also because it decreased the amount of land and labor needed for food production. In 1970 American food production, for example, required 281 million acres. At 1940 yields per acre, which were generally less than half of 1970 yields, it would have taken 573 million acres to produce the 1970 crop. This was a savings of 292 million acres through increased crop yields.[26] The estimated 300% increase in per capita agricultural production from 1960 to 1980 also meant that labor resources could be used for other activities. Other experts estimated that without the use of pesticides in the United States, the price of farm products would probably increase by at least 50% and we would be forced to spend 25% or more of our income on food.[27] It was held that many of these same secondary benefits would accrue to developing countries through the use of pesticides.

Pesticides also contributed both directly and indirectly to combating disease; because of this, their use in developing countries had increased. Pesticides had been highly effective in reducing such diseases as malaria, yellow fever, elephantiasis, dengue, and filariasis. Malaria was a good example. In 1955, WHO initiated a global malaria eradication campaign based on the spraying of DDT. This effort greatly reduced the incidence of malaria. For example, in India there were approximately 75 million cases in the early 1950s. But in 1961 there were only 49,000 cases. David Bull estimated that by 1970 the campaign had prevented 2 billion cases and had saved 15 million lives. In 1979 Freed estimated that one-sixth of the world's population had some type of pest-borne disease.[28]

Risks to Humans

Reliable estimates of the number of pesticide poisonings worldwide were difficult to obtain because many countries did not gather such statistics. Using figures from WHO, Bull of the Oxford Committee for the Relief of Famine (OXFAM) calculated that in 1981 there were 750,000 cases of pesticide poisoning and about 14,000

deaths worldwide, with over half of the fatalities being children. OXFAM estimated that in developing countries there were 375,000 cases of poisoning with 10,000 deaths a year. Thus, developing countries, with 15% of pesticide consumption, suffered half of the accidental poisonings and three-fourths of the deaths. Another survey by Davies et al estimated that in 1977, the annual worldwide mortality rate was over 20,000.[29]

Experts agreed that these estimates contained large margins for error, and they believed that the actual number of cases was substantially higher. Many countries did not collect statistics on pesticide poisonings. In addition, pesticides were often used in remote areas that lacked easy access to clinics or had physicians who were not trained to recognize the symptoms of pesticide poisoning.

Causes of Pesticide Poisoning in Developing Countries

Pesticide poisoning resulted from many causes in developing countries. Workers would remain in the fields when planes were spraying crops; they may not have left for fear that they would lose their jobs, or they may not have understood the risk. Much of the spray drifted through the area to cover homes, utensils, clothes hanging on lines, children playing, irrigation ditches, and animals. Sometimes workers too quickly entered a newly sprayed field; the pesticide, then still moist on the plant, rubbed off on their skin and clothing. Later, when they washed, they did so with what was available—the pesticide-contaminated water in the irrigation ditches. This may also have been the source of their drinking water. Reports also surfaced of pilots dumping excess pesticide into lakes or rivers that were often vital food and water sources.

Another cause of pesticide misuse was the lack of education—many of the people who used pesticides in developing countries were illiterate. In addition, they knew little or nothing about the dangers of pesticides and how they interacted with the environment. Developing countries did not have the elaborate agricultural extension services that existed in industrialized countries, especially in the United

---

26. Borlaug, p. 106.
27. Ennis, p. 113.
28. Bull, p. 30; Virgil Freed, *Proceedings*, p. 21.

29. Bull, p. 38; John Davies, et al., *An Agromedical Approach to Pesticide Management* (Miami, FL: University of Miami, 1982), p. 9.

States. The farmers and laborers often did not know safe or effective methods for transporting, mixing, applying, storing, and disposing of pesticides.

Consider the example of one village on the shore of Lake Volta in Ghana. The fishermen began using Gammalin 20 (lindane) to catch fish. They would pour the pesticide into the lake and wait for the poisoned fish to float to the surface. The village depended on the lake for its food, income, drinking water, and water for cooking and washing. Soon the people around the lake complained of blurred vision, dizziness, and vomiting—all symptoms of lindane poisoning. The number of fish in the lake declined 10–20% a year. The villagers initially did not connect their symptoms with the declining fish population. They believed that both were due to natural causes. When they did become aware that the fish were poisoned, they believed the poison remained in the fish's head and that cutting off the head made the fish safe to eat.[30]

Sometimes poisoning resulted because proper safety precautions were not taken when chemicals were mixed and applied. Often workers mixed the pesticides with their hands, or, if in granular form, they sprinkled pesticides on the plants with their hands. The director of the National Biological Control Research Center in Thailand reported: "When mixing the formulation for spraying, the farmer may dip his finger into the mix and taste it by dabbing his finger to his tongue. If it gets numb it indicates the right concentration." Frequently, workers were not supplied with protective clothing, could not afford it, or chose not to wear it because of the heat. They also often had faulty equipment. If sprayers were carried on their backs, leaky valves allowed the pesticide to run down their shoulders. One survey done in the Philippines indicated that none of the farmers studied knew that a leaky valve could be fatal. Another survey in Gujarat, India, showed that none of the farm workers had face masks, only 50% covered their noses and mouths with a cloth, and 20% did not wash after spraying.[31]

Distribution methods in developing countries also caused problems. Pesticides were shipped in bulk containers and were then repackaged in smaller containers. Local merchants customarily sold the products in unlabeled bottles and kept them on shelves with other foodstuffs. Farmers relied on the local shop owner, often untrained, to advise them about what pesticide to use and how. For example, paraquat, which was dark in color, caused numerous poisonings because it was mistaken for coke, wine, or coffee.

The large drums in which pesticides were shipped were frequently used to hold drinking water and store food. Few understood that the residues of the pesticide on the walls of the drum might still be toxic. In one case 124 people were poisoned, eight fatally, after eating food prepared in recycled pesticide drums.[32]

Critics contended that labels often failed to give the detailed information necessary for safety precautions and were sometimes not written in the language of the area in which they were to be distributed. Even when they were, however, many of the users could not read them because they were illiterate. According to Dr. Fred Whittemore, pest management specialist for AID, a check in Mexico found that 50% of the pesticides sold were incorrectly labeled. Labels usually did not state first-aid recommendations or contained recommendations that were unrealistic. In a remote part of India one pesticide label specified calling a physician and using atropine and 2 PAM as an antidote; however, the local clinic was hours away and, when checked, had never heard of 2 PAM.[33]

Critics charged that through promotion and advertising, companies encouraged farmers to view pesticides as panaceas. They emphasized that frequently the advertisements failed to mention the dangers of pesticides and created the impression that pesticides were safe to use. Critics also argued that companies occasionally encouraged overuse by advocating calendar spraying rather than spraying on the basis of the number of pests attacking a crop. They pointed out that many in developing countries trusted the goodwill of American companies. As Dr. Harold Alvo Nunez, former Colombian Minister of Health, put it: "You know, the label 'Made in U.S.A.' is very powerful here."[34]

30. Ruth Norris, ed., *Pills, Pesticides and Profits* (Croton-on-Hudson, NY: North River Press, 1982), p. 13.
31. Bull, p. 49.
32. Davies, p. 88.
33. Bull, p. 89.
34. *Newsday*, p. 11R.

Risks to the Environment

Problems with pesticide overuse were particularly severe in developing countries. For example, Weir and Schapiro estimated that pesticide use was 40% higher in Central America than necessary to achieve optimal production. In 1975 El Salvador, with a population of 4.5 million people, was using 20% of the world production of parathion. This averaged out to 2,940 pounds per square mile, according to Wolterding.[35]

In *A Growing Problem*, David Bull described the process by which farmers became hooked on using greater and greater quantities and more and more varieties of pesticides. He called this the *pesticide treadmill*. When an insecticide was used, for example, not only did it kill the targeted insect but also other insects that were its natural enemies. These natural controls also kept in check other insects that potentially could become pests. Once the natural controls were killed, not only could there be an increase in the original target pests but also an increase in these secondary pests. Faced with an unexpected increase in pests, the farmer's typical response was to spray even more. Another result of repeated pesticide use was that pests developed a genetic resistance to them. Once this happened, the usual response again was to spray in larger quantities and then to try another kind of pesticide. An additional reason for overuse was that formulation and methods of application for many chemicals had been developed for use in temperate climates. The more rapid breakdown of chemicals in tropical climates, however, required more frequent and larger applications.

The cultivation of cotton in Central America illustrated the pesticide treadmill at work. At the turn of the century, Central American farmers began growing cotton, which was native to the region, on a commercial scale. At that time, the boll weevil was cotton's only major pest and it was controlled by natural enemies and by hand removal from the cotton plants.

In the 1950s, as the amount of acreage under cultivation increased, mechanization and intensive use of pesticides began. Initially, insecticides were applied about eight times a year and resulted in improved yields. By the mid-1950s,

three new pests were attacking cotton. During the 1960s insecticide use increased; as many as 50 different pesticides became available for a single pest. The number of applications increased to 28 per season. By 1970 there were eight pests causing serious damage to cotton. As new pests appeared the old ones became more resistant, and farmers applied more and more pesticides. By 1974, Central American growers were spraying up to 40 times a season. An average of 3,380 pounds of pesticide was being applied for every square mile.[36]

Food crops as well as cash crops were affected. Rice was the staple crop for hundreds of millions of people in Southeast Asia. One study reported that 8 rice pests were resistant to at least one insecticide in 1965; 14 pests were resistant to pesticides by 1975.[37]

Pests worldwide have rapidly developed resistances to pesticides. In 1951 there were 6 species of pests of either medical or agricultural importance that were resistant. By 1961 Davies estimated that the number was 137 and in 1980 resistant pests increased to 414 species. An exacerbating factor was that sometimes pests developed multiple resistance to a whole group of chemicals in the same class. An example was the diamondback moth, which attacked cabbage in one region of the Malay peninsula. The moths had become so resistant that farmers now sprayed three times a week, often using a "cocktail" made up of several insecticides. The diamondback moth, in turn, developed some degree of resistance to at least 11 insecticides. Bull estimated that in 1978 insecticides accounted for one-third of the production costs of cabbages. It was believed that soon it would no longer be profitable to grow cabbage in the region.[38]

In the 1970s a resurgence occurred in the incidence of malaria. For example, in India, although the number of cases dropped from 75 million in the 1950s to 49,000 in 1961; the figure rose to 6.5 million in 1976. In Haiti there were 2,500 cases in 1968 but 26,000 in 1972. Worldwide the number of cases increased by over 230% between 1972 and 1976.[39] This increase was attributed to the disease-carrying mosquito's resistance to pesticides. (As *Figure C* indi-

---

35. Weir and Schapiro, p. 6; Martin Wolterding, "The Poisoning of Central America," *Sierra*, September–October 1981, p. 64.

36. Wolterding, p. 64.
37. Bull, p. 13.
38. Davies, p. 65; Bull, p. 18.
39. Bull, p. 30.

**Figure C
Resistant Species of Arthropods and
New Insecticides, 1938–1980**

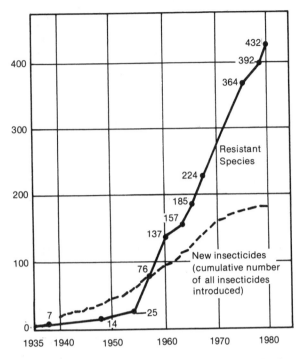

Source: David Bull, *A Growing Problem* (Oxford, England: OXFAM, 1982), p. 24. Reprinted by permission.

cates, the rate of introduction of new pesticides had not kept up with the rate at which pests were developing resistance.)

Industry Response

The pesticide industry argued that each country had the right to set its own policy based on its individual estimate of the risk/benefit ratio of using a particular pesticide, and that the risk/benefit ratio for developing countries varied with economic and social conditions. A country with widespread malnutrition or insect-borne disease might be more willing to risk using a pesticide whose use had been canceled or restricted in the United States. Dr. William Upholt, consultant to the U.S. National Committee for Man and the Biosphere, stated: "Less industrial countries may consider a few cases of cancer in older people a small price to pay for increased yield of food crops. So it is reasonable to conclude that all nations do not need the same pesticide. There is an old saying that one

man's food is another man's poison, and I guess that could be reversed."[40]

DDT was cited as an example of a pesticide whose registration had been canceled for use on food crops, but which was still produced in India and used by several developing countries. Robert Oldford, president of Union Carbide's Agricultural Products Division, said:

How do some of the developing countries consider chemicals that have been banned or restricted here? Burma, for example, has stated that, "In many other countries the use of chlorinated hydrocarbons is being restricted because of their persistent nature. The official position here is that these insecticides are effective, cheap, and, if used properly, are no more hazardous than other newer and more expensive insecticides."[41]

In developing the risk/benefit argument, Frederick J. Rarig, vice president and associate general counsel of Rohm and Haas Company, stated:

Margaret Mead taught us that morality is a relative, cultural concept. I have learned in 35 years of work in the field of hazard analysis that safety is similarly a relative, cultural concept. Safety is never an absolute. It is *not* an *absence* of hazard. Safety is an *acceptable* level of hazard.

Men will not forgo shelter simply because the only shelter they can build is combustible. Mothers will not leave their children naked and exposed to the elements because the only available cloth with which to clothe them is combustible cotton. . . . Men will not starve while insects and rodents flourish simply because there are risks connected with the poisoning of insects and rodents.[42]

Dr. William Hollis, science coordinator of NACA, also pointed out the toxicological risks from crops damaged by pests. He observed: "In this light, the risk versus benefit concept to evaluate pesticides is inappropriate. The ultimate evaluation to be made must consider risk versus risk. That is, the risk of using the pesticide versus the risk of not having optimum production and protection of food, thereby not preventing unnecessary human health hazards.

40. Upholt, p. 35.
41. Robert Oldford, Statement to the Subcommittee on Department Operations Research, and Foreign Agriculture of the Committee on Agriculture, U.S. House of Representatives, June 9, 1983, p. 13.
42. *Proceedings*, p. 29.

Such health hazards include exposure to pest-induced toxins, carcinogens, mutagens, and allergens."[43]

NACA claimed that sometimes the EPA was out of step with other countries in its interpretation of toxicological data. For example, NACA pointed out that whereas the EPA suspended on-food uses of 2,4,5-T based on a study of its health effects, other countries—including the United Kingdom, Canada, New Zealand, and Australia—reviewed the same data and concluded it was acceptable to continue using the herbicide for such purposes.[44]

In trying to place the toxicity of certain pesticides in perspective, Dr. Ram Hamsager, chairman of Hindustan Insecticides Limited, compared the LD_{50} of DDT with nicotine. He indicated the LD_{50} for DDT was about 118 mg. per kilogram of body weight while the LD_{50} for nicotine was about 60 mg. per kilogram of body weight. He asserted: "This proves that nicotine is twice as poisonous as DDT. The toxicity levels of some of the other naturally occurring chemicals which form part of our daily intake, like caffeine found in coffee and thiobromine found in tea, are comparable to safe pesticides like DDT, and BHC."[45]

Defending the export of pesticides that were not approved for use in the United States, Robert Oldford stated: "There are two fundamental reasons why such exports occur. First, products are not usually registered in the U.S. for an agricultural pest crop use which does not exist here—coffee or bananas, for example. Second, developing countries have approval agencies that typically will require valid evidence of registration in a developed country in addition to other information needed to make a decision in the best interest of their citizens."[46]

The industry was trying to minimize pesticide misuse through education and had cooperated with several international organizations such as the FAO, AID, WHO, and the World Bank. Dow Chemical conducted over 400 agricultural

chemicals meetings in South America in 1981, and Monsanto brought union officials of one developing country to the company's U.S. plants to learn of the safety procedures used there. Since 1978 NACA sponsored a series of international conferences between representatives of importing countries and U.S. manufacturers to harmonize registration requirements and develop safety training programs. As a result of a two-year consultation process with industry, consumer, church, and environmental representatives, NACA had adopted a product stewardship code containing voluntary guidelines for its 115 member companies.

It was also argued that 1978 amendments to U.S. law greatly reduced the possibility of inadequate labeling, but that the industry on its own was also trying to develop better labeling procedures. For example, Velsicol had developed a "One World Communication System," using pictographs adapted to different cultures to instruct users in safe handling techniques, supplementing the labels required by U.S. law. Manufacturers, however, had little control over how distributors in developing countries repackaged and labeled pesticides after removing them from bulk shipping containers.

The U.S. pesticide industry showed concern over the rise of thousands of small "pirate" manufacturers of chemicals that were imitations of proprietary pesticides produced in the United States. These companies, usually not closely regulated, sold products in developing countries that were less effective and more dangerous because of contaminants. They were often cheaper, however, than pesticides sold by quality-conscious U.S. companies.

Regulating Pesticides

Jacob Scherr of the Natural Resources Defense Council commented at the 1979 U.S. Strategy Conference on Pesticide Management: "Some developing countries have enacted virtually no legislation to govern the importation, domestic use, and disposal of potentially toxic chemicals. Few maintain any facilities for monitoring the effects of the products on health or the environment. Even where decent laws are on the books, many governments lack the technical and administrative capacity to implement them."[47]

43. Hollis, p. 11. See Wendell Kilgore et al., "Toxic Plants as Possible Human Teratogens," *California Agriculture*, November–December 1981, p. 6; Garnett Wood, "Stress Metabolites of White Potatoes," *Advances in Chemistry*, p. 149, 1976, pp. 369–386; Bruce Ames, "Dietary Carcinogens and Anticarcinogens, *Science*, September 23, 1983, pp. 1256–1262.
44. *Food, Health, Agricultural Chemicals and Developing Countries*, published by NACA, May 1983, p. 4.
45. Hamsagar, p. 8.
46. Oldford, p. 13.
47. *Proceedings*, p. 32.

Regulation in Developing Countries

An Agromedical Approach to Pesticide Management asserted that "a number of developing countries already have strong pesticide laws on their books, but in many cases efforts aimed at enforcing the laws are either negligible or non-existent."[48] Few countries, it was reported, had the necessary regulatory infrastructure for monitoring, testing, setting residue limits, enforcement, and so forth.

The FAO studied the extent of pesticide control among members. Of 144 countries surveyed, 31 had well-developed procedures and enforcement; 26 had well-developed procedures but the degree of enforcement was unknown; 6 were developing control procedures; and 81 had no control procedures or gave no information.[49]

Many developing countries asked the United States and other industrialized countries to help them develop adequate legislation, monitoring, and enforcement mechanisms. In particular, they requested the United States to share its knowledge of the harmful effects of the many chemicals already tested by the U.S. government or corporations. Many also wanted to be kept informed of changes in the status of pesticides registered in the United States.

The following comments made by Samuel Gitonga, agriculture expert for the National Irrigation Board of Kenya, were typical:

> We do not have the necessary machinery to go through an entire testing program to determine whether the product is safe or not. For these reasons, I believe that the U.S. and other developed countries have a responsibility to ensure that the information they have painfully gathered is made available to as many people as possible in the developing world. I certainly reject the idea that the developing countries always know what they want or which pesticides are best to use. Information that a product is not allowed for use in a particular country would be a very useful starting point. The less developed countries must be made aware that there is a problem with using a particular product. These very real dangers of incompletely tested or banned products being used in the less developed countries should be strongly condemned by the international community.[50]

Regulation in the United States

A 1979 report by the General Accounting Office to Congress, entitled *Better Regulation of Pesticide Exports and Pesticide Residues in Imported Food is Essential*, contained the following passage: "The Food and Drug Administration does not analyze imported food for many potential residues. It allows food to be marketed before testing it for illegal residues. Importers are not penalized if their imports later are determined to contain illegal residues. The safety and appropriateness of some residues allowed on imported food has not been determined." In 1977 the United States imported $13.4 billion of agricultural products. Most of these imports were from developing countries with less effective regulatory mechanisms than those in the U.S— 28% of U.S. pesticide exports went to Central American countries from which we obtain 38% of our imported agricultural commodities. The United States imported approximately 600 different food commodities from over 150 countries in 1979.[51]

U.S. pesticide exports and imports were regulated by the Federal Insecticide, Fungicide, and Rodenticide Act of 1947, as amended, and the Federal Food, Drug, and Cosmetic Act of 1938, as amended.

FIFRA required the EPA to register all pesticides before they were distributed, sold, or used in the United States. The EPA registered a pesticide when it determined that the pesticide, when used according to commonly recognized practice, could safely and effectively perform its intended function without unreasonable risk to humans or the environment. If a pesticide was produced for export only, however, it was not required to be registered by the EPA and could be exported regardless of its regulatory status or its intended use. FIFRA required that domestic producers maintain records of shipments and purchasers' specifications for packaging. Amendments made in 1978 required that unregistered pesticides produced solely for export be labeled "Not Registered for Use in the United States of America." Foreign purchasers of unregistered chemicals had to sign statements acknowledging their understanding that these pesticides were not allowed for U.S. use. Copies of foreign purchaser acknowledgements were then sent to the government officials of the importing countries. Labels for exports had to

48. Davies, p. 238.
49. Bull, p. 144.
50. *Proceedings*, p. 41.

51. *Better Regulation*, cover page.

contain the same information as products intended for U.S. use. Among those requirements were the display of a skull and crossbones if highly toxic and a statement of practical treatment, warning or caution statements, and no false representations.

FFDCA required that tolerances be established for pesticide residues. Any food was considered adulterated if it contained residues in excess of these tolerances or if it contained a residue for which the EPA had not established a tolerance.

The EPA and the Food and Drug Administration (FDA) administered these laws. The EPA established tolerances on the basis of the nature, amount, and toxicity of the residue of a pesticide. The FDA was responsible for assuring that all food marketed in the United States, either domestic or imported, met FFDCA residue requirements. The FDA monitored imported food for conformance with these requirements by chemically analyzing samples collected from individual shipments received at various U.S. entry points. Food that was adulterated was required to be denied entry and reexported or destroyed.

In its report, the GAO stated that "pesticide use patterns in foreign countries clearly indicate that a large portion of food imported into the United States may in fact contain unsafe pesticide residues."[52] For example, a 1978 study of coffee imported to the United States showed that 45% (25 out of 55) of the samples contained illegal residues. All of these residues were from pesticides whose use had been canceled or severely restricted in the United States. The cycle of food contaminated by U.S. pesticide exports being imported into the United States was referred to as the *boomerang effect*.

The FDA estimated that approximately one-tenth of the food imported into the United States contained illegal residues. However, the GAO argued that this estimate was probably too low due to inadequacies in the FDA's analytical and sampling procedures. The two multiresidue tests used by the FDA could detect residues of only 73 of the 268 pesticides that had U.S. tolerances. The GAO studied the pesticides allowed, recommended, or used in developing countries on 10 major commodities: bananas, coffee, sugar, tomatoes, tea, cocoa, tapioca, strawberries, peppers, and olives. It

found that an additional 130 pesticides used on these foods had no U.S. tolerances and could not be detected by the FDA's tests. Since the FDA did not know which pesticides were used by other countries on food imported into the United States, it did not know which analytical test to use. This was one reason why the FDA used only *two* of the six multiresidue tests available and *no* single residue test. Without this knowledge, use of other tests would be too costly in terms of time and money. The GAO further concluded that the "anomalies" it found "do not inspire confidence in the validity of the FDA's sampling program."[53]

The report also pointed out that "even when the pesticide residues on imported food are identified as being violative, the food will probably be marketed and consumed rather than detained or destroyed." For example, in Dallas, Texas, Department of Agriculture personnel complained of an insecticide-like smell coming from a shipment of imported cabbage. Despite this complaint and the fact that the importer had a history of shipping adulterated products, the cabbage was allowed to be marketed. The GAO found that "half of the imported food that the Food and Drug Administration found to be adulterated during a 15-month period was marketed without penalty to importers and consumed by an unsuspecting American public."[54]

The Department of Health, Education and Welfare criticized the methodology of the GAO report and disagreed with several of its conclusions and recommendations:

> We believe this draft report neither accurately nor fairly reflects either the degree to which pesticide residues pose a risk to the U.S. consumer or the Food and Drug Administration's (FDA) program for identifying and detaining violative imported products. We recognize the need for improvements in FDA's coverage of imported food for pesticide residues, and several actions are well under way to accomplish these improvements. However, many of the criticisms of FDA programs and professional competence are based upon unsubstantiated conclusions. GAO has posed hypothetical situations without citing sufficient evidence to substantiate their occurrence and thereby may create unfounded apprehensions about

---

52. Ibid., p. 6.

53. Ibid., p. 14.
54. Ibid., pp. 39–40.

the food supply and those charged with assuring its safety.[55]

NACA argued that the safety factor built into the setting of tolerance levels and the Market Basket Surveys carried out by the FDA since 1965 provided adequate safeguards for the American consumer. Tolerances were established by first determining a no-toxic-effect level for a pesticide on test animals and then increasing that many times over, usually by a factor of 100, to set the legal maximum for humans. As part of its yearly surveillance programs, the FDA examined 30 samples, each composed of 117 food items, from different regions and representing the diets of adults and children to determine the average daily intake of pesticide residues. These results were then compared with acceptable daily intake levels. Several studies had consistently shown that actual daily intake was less than ADI levels. For example, the average daily intake of parathion consumed in 1977 was $\frac{1}{5,000}$–$\frac{1}{1,000}$ of the ADI. In no instance was the actual intake of a pesticide as high as the ADI.[56]

NACA asserted that "we are being indicted in the so-called 'circle of poison issue' in spite of the basic fact that, according to the best experts, no one anywhere in the world has suffered illness from pesticide residues in or on food commodities."[57]

The pesticide industry was not in favor of increased government regulation of pesticide exports to alleviate the risks of pesticide use in developing countries and, indirectly, in the United States. About such a proposed change in 1980, Earl Spurrier, director of government relations for Monsanto, said that "the extra restrictions are unduly stringent and they are going to throw much of the export business to foreign competitors, who are not similarly restricted."[58] Instead, the industry favored voluntary efforts by companies to alter the pattern of pesticide misuse that existed worldwide.

57. Jack Early, Remarks of the National Agricultural Chemicals Association Before the Latin American Forum, May 4, 1982, p. 6.
58. "The Unpopular Curbs on Hazardous Exports," *Business Week*, September 1980.

55. Ibid., p. 70.
56. See the ongoing study of the dietary intake of pesticides in the United States in *Pesticide Monitoring Journal*, in Vols. 5, 8, and 9. See, also, J. Frawley and R. Duggan, "Techniques for Deriving Realistic Estimates of Pesticide Intakes," in *Advances in Pesticide Science*, Part III, ed., H. Geissbuhler (New York: Pergammon Press, 1979).

Harvard
Business Review
May-June 1973

Kenneth R. Andrews

Can the best corporations be made moral?

Not by heroic management action,
but by maturity and breadth of perspective in
the design of measurement systems

Foreword

"The overriding master problem now impeding the further progress of corporate responsibility is the difficulty of making credible and effective, throughout a large organization, the social component of a corporate strategy originating in the moral convictions and values of the chief executive." So asserts this author, who then adds that the source of the difficulty is the nature and impact of narrowly designed measurement and reward-and-penalty systems. In this ar-

ticle, he discusses the issue of public responsibility in a private corporation, and suggests the outlines of a management program of action.

Mr. Andrews is Donald K. David Professor of Business Administration, Harvard Business School; Member of the Faculty of Arts and Sciences of Harvard University; and Master of Leverett House. In addition, he is Chairman of the Editorial Board of HBR and a director of four corporations.

Τhe concept of corporate social responsibility has made steady progress during the past 40 years. The words mean in part voluntary restraint of profit maximization. More positively, they mean sensitivity to the social costs of economic activity and to the opportunity to focus

corporate power on objectives that are possible but sometimes less economically attractive than socially desirable. The term includes:

○ The determination of a corporation to reduce its profit by voluntary contributions to education and other charities.

○ The election of an ethical level of operations higher than the minimum required by law and custom.

○ The choice between businesses of varying economic opportunity on grounds of their imputed social worth.

○ The investment for reasons other than (but obviously still related to) economic return in the quality of life within the corporation itself.

This doctrine of corporate social responsibility is vigorously opposed honestly and openly by conservative lawyers and economists and covertly by the adherents of business as usual. Milton Friedman, the conservative economist of the University of Chicago, denounces the concern for responsibility as "fundamentally subversive" to a free society. He argues that "there is one and only one social responsibility of business—to use its resources and engage in activities designed to increase its profits so long as it . . . engages in open and free competition without deception or fraud."[1]

Thus, for example, the manager who makes decisions affecting immediate profit by reducing pollution and increasing minority employment more than present law requires is in effect imposing taxes upon his stockholders and acting without authority as a public legislative body.

Other critics of the doctrine like to point out:

○ How much easier are the platitudes of virtue than the effective combination of profitable and socially responsive corporate action.

○ How little experience with social questions businessmen immersed in their narrow ambitions and technology can be expected to have.

○ How urgent are the pressures of survival in hard times and against competition.

○ How coercive of individual opinion in an organization is a position on social issues dictated by its management.

○ How infrequently in the entire population occur the intelligence, compassion, knowledge of issues, and morality required of the manager presumptuous enough to factor social responsibility into his economic decisions.

Given the slow rate at which verbalized good intentions are being converted into action, many critics of the large corporation suspect that for every chief executive announcing pious objectives there are a hundred closet rascals quietly conducting business in the old ways and taking immoral comfort in Friedman's moral support.

The interventionists question the effectiveness of the "invisible hand" of competition as the ethical regulator of great corporations capable of shaping in significant degree their environments. Interventionists think also that regulation by government, while always to some degree essential under imperfect competition,

---

Readers of this article may be interested in "Profit: Spur for Solving Social Ills" (Thinking Ahead), by David B. McCall, beginning on page 46 of this issue.
                                                    —*The Editors*

---

is not sufficiently knowledgeable, subtle, or timely to reconcile the self-interest of corporate entrepreneurship and the needs of the society being sore-tried and well served by economic activity.

The advocates of public responsibility for a so-called "private" enterprise assert that, in an industrial society, corporate power, vast in potential strength, must be brought to bear on certain social problems if the latter are to be solved at all. They argue that corporate executives of the integrity, intelligence, and humanity required to run companies whose revenues often exceed the gross national product of whole nations cannot be expected to confine themselves to economic activity and ignore its consequences, and that henceforth able young men and women coming into business will be sensitive to the social worth of corporate activity.

To reassure those uneasy about the dangers of corporate participation in public affairs, the social interventionists say to the economic isolationists that these hazards can be contained through professional education, government control, and self-regulation.

This is not the place to argue further against Friedman's simplistic faith in the powers of the market to purify self-interest. We must observe, however, that the argument for the active participation of corporations in public affairs, for responsible assessment of the impact of economic activity, and for concern with the quality of corporate purposes is gaining ground, even as uneasiness increases about the existence of corporate power in the hands of managers who (except in cases of crisis) are answerable only to themselves or to boards of directors they have themselves selected.

Criticism of corporate activity is manifest currently in consumerism, in the movement to in-

---

1. *Capitalism and Freedom* (Chicago, University of Chicago Press, 1962), p. 133.

troduce social legislation into stockholder meetings and to reform board memberships, and (more dangerously) in apathy or antipathy among the young. The most practicable response to this criticism by those holding corporate power is to seek to justify limited government by using power responsibly—the ultimate obligation of free persons in any relatively free society.

We need the large corporation, not for its size but for its capability. Even the vivisectionists of the Justice Department who seek a way to divide IBM into smaller parts presumably have no illusion that the large corporation can or should be eliminated from the world as we know it.

On the assumption, then, that corporate social responsibility is not only here to stay, but must increase in scope and complexity as corporate power increases, I suggest that we look forward to the administrative and organizational consequences of the incursion of private corporations into public responsibility.

Nature of the problem

Among the many considerations confronting the executive who would make social responsibility effective, there are some so well known that we can quickly pass them by. Hypocrisy, insincerity, and hollow piety are not really dangerous, for they are easily detected.

In fact, it is much more likely that genuinely good intentions will be thought insincere than that hypocritical protestations of idealism will be mistaken for truth. "Mr. Ford (or Mr. Kaiser or Mr. Rockefeller) doesn't really mean what he says," as an organization refrain is more Mr. Ford's or Mr. Kaiser's or Mr. Rockefeller's problem than what he should say. Cynicism, the by-product of impersonal bureaucracy, remains one of the principal impediments to the communication of corporate social policy.

I would like to set aside also the problem of choice of what social contribution should be attempted—a problem which disparity between the infinite range of social need and the limits of available corporate resources always brings to mind.

Self-consistent strategy

The formulation of specific corporate social policy is as much a function of strategic planning as the choice of product and market combina-

tions, the establishment of profit and growth objectives, or the choice of organization structure and systems for accomplishing corporate purposes.

Rather than wholly personal or idiosyncratic contributions (like supporting the museum one's wife is devoted to) or safe and sound contributions like the standard charities, or faddist entry into fashionable areas, corporate strategic response to societal needs and expectations makes sense when it is closely related to the economic functions of the company or to the peculiar problems of the community in which it operates.

For a paper company, it would seem a strategic necessity to give first priority to eliminating the poisonous effluents from its mills rather than, for example, to support cultural institutions like traveling art exhibits. Similarly, for an oil company it would seem a strategic necessity to look at its refinery stacks, at spillage, and at automobile exhaust.

The fortunate company that is paying the full social cost of its production function can make contributions to problems it does not cause—like juvenile delinquency, illiteracy, and so on—or to other forms of environmental improvement more appropriate to corporate citizenship than directly related to its production processes.

As leaders of business move beyond conventional philanthropic contributions to strategy-

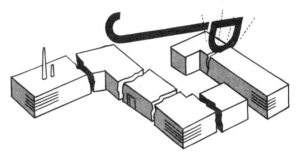

related investments in social betterment, they begin to combine the long-run economic interests of their companies with the priorities (as for pollution) becoming evident in public concern, seeking those points where indeed what is good for the country is good for General Motors.

Once the conscious planning which a fully developed corporate strategy requires is understood, the practical alternatives before any company are not impossibly difficult to identify and to rank according to relevance to economic strategy or to organization needs and resources.

The outcome is an integrated self-consistent strategy embodying defined obligations to society relevant to but not confined to its economic purposes. The top management of a large company, once it elects to, can be expected to have less difficulty in articulating such a strategy than in dealing with the problems of organization behavior to which I now turn.

Organization behavior

The advance of the doctrine of corporate social responsibility has been the apparent conversion of more and more chief executive officers. Change toward responsible behavior and the formulation of strategic intentions are obviously not possible without their concern, compassion, and conviction.

So long as the organization remains small enough to be directly influenced by the chief executive's leadership, certain results can be traced to his determination that they occur—as in centrally decided investments, specific new ventures, cash contributions to charity, and compensation, promotion, and other personnel policies.

But as an organization grows larger and as operations become more decentralized, the power and influence of the chief executive are reinterpreted and diffused. For example:

If a large company is to be sufficiently decentralized to make worldwide operations feasible, power must be distributed throughout a hierarchy inhabited by persons (a) who may not share their chief executive's determination or fervor, (b) who may not believe (more often) that he means what he says, and (c) who may be impelled to postpone action on such problems as management development, pollution, or employment and advancement of minority representatives.

At this point, the overriding master problem now impeding the further progress of corporate responsibility is the difficulty of making credible and effective, throughout a large organization, the social component of a corporate strategy originating in the moral convictions and values of the chief executive.

Quantifiable results: The source of the difficulty is the nature and impact of our systematic planning processes, forms of control, systems of measurement, and pattern of incentives, and the impersonal way all these are administered. The essence of the systematic rational planning

we know most about is quantitative information furnished to the process and quantitative measures of results coming out.

Once plans are put into effect, managers are measured, evaluated, promoted, shelved, or discharged according to the relation of their accomplishments against the plan. In the conventions of accounting and the time scale of exact quantification, performance becomes short-run economic or technical results inside the corporation. Evaluation typically gives full marks for current accomplishment, with no estimate of the charges against the future which may have been made in the effort to accomplish the plan.

Since progress in career, dependent on favorable judgments of quantifiable performance, is the central motivation in a large organization, general and functional managers at divisional, regional, district, and local levels are motivated to do well what is best and most measured, to do it now, and to focus their attention on the internal problems that affect immediate results.

In short, the more quantification and the more supervision of variance, the less attention there will be to such intangible topics as the social role of Plant X in Community Y or the quality of corporate life in the office at Sioux City.

The leaner the central staff of a large organization is kept, the more stress there will be on numbers; and, more importantly, the more difficulty there will be in making qualitative evaluation of such long-term processes as individual and management development, the steady augmentation of organizational competence, and the progress of programs for making work meaningful and exciting, and for making more than economic contributions to society.

The small headquarters group supervising the operations of a conglomerate of autonomous organizations hitherto measured by ranking them with respect to return on equity would not expect to have before it proposals from the subsidiaries for important investments in social responsibility. Such investments could only be made by the corporate headquarters, which would not itself be knowledgeable about or much motivated to take action on opportunities existing throughout the subsidiaries.

Corporate amorality: One colleague of mine, Joseph L. Bower, has examined the process by which corporate resources are allocated in large organizations.[2] Another, Robert W. Ackerman, has documented through field studies the dilemmas which a financially oriented and present-

2. *Managing the Resource Allocation Process* (Boston, Division of Research, Harvard Business School, 1969).

tense accounting system pose for the forward progress of specific social action, like pollution abatement and provision of minority opportunity.[3] Still a third, Malcolm S. Salter, has studied the impact of compensation systems in multinational corporations.[4]

It appears that the outcome of these and other research studies will establish what we have long suspected—that good works, the results of which are long term and hard to quantify, do not have a chance in an organization using conventional incentives and controls and exerting pressure for ever more impressive results.

It is quite possible then, and indeed quite usual, for a highly moral and humane chief executive to preside over an "amoral organization"[5]—one made so by processes developed before the liberalization of traditional corporate economic objectives. The internal force which stubbornly resists efforts to make the corporation compassionate (and exacting) toward its own people and responsible (as well as economically efficient) in its external relationships is the incentive system forcing attention to short-term quantifiable results.

The sensitivity of upward-oriented career executives at lower and middle levels to what quantitative measures say about them is part of their ambition, their interest in their compensation, and their desire for the recognition and approval of their superiors. When, as they usually do, they learn how to beat the system, the margin of capacity they reserve for a rainy day is hoarded for survival, not expended in strengthening their suborganization's future capability or in part-time participation in corporate good works or responsible citizenship on their own time.

With individuals, as with organizations, survival takes precedence over social concern. All we need do to keep even experienced, capable, and profit-producing managers on the ropes of survival is to focus the spotlight on their day-to-day activities and exhaust their ingenuity in outwitting the system by increasing the level of short-term results they are asked to attain.

The isolationists should be quite content with the amorality of an organization motivated by career-oriented responsiveness to narrowly

3. "Managing Corporate Responsibility," scheduled for publication in HBR July-August 1973.

4. "Tailor Incentive Compensation to Strategy," HBR March-April 1973, p. 94.

5. The phrase is Joseph L. Bower's, from *Technology, the Corporation, and the State*, edited by R. Maris and E.J. Mesthene, to be published by the Program on Technology and Society at Harvard University.

designed measurement and reward-and-penalty systems. The interventionists are not. They look for solutions in the experience, observation, and research I have been drawing on in describing the set of problems a new breadth of vision reveals to us.

Thus the art of using the two-edged sword of contribution to society and of stimulation to creative achievement within the corporation becomes even more sophisticated when that institution must not only relate to the societies of different countries and cultures but also attract and keep the dedication of men and women with values and desires not typically American.

Program of action

Inquiry into the nature of the problem suggests the outlines of a program of action. It begins with the incorporation into strategic and operating plans—of subsidiaries, country or area organizations, or profit centers—of specific objectives in areas of social concerns strategically related to the economic activity and community environment of the organization unit.

Since the executive in New York cannot specify the appropriate social strategy for the company in Brazil or the branch in Oregon, or even know what the people there want to work on, intermediate managers who are aware of the social and organization policy of the company, must elicit (with staff help if necessary) pro-

posals for investment of money, energy, time, or concern in these areas.

The review of plans submitted may result in reduction or increase in commitments in all areas; it is essential that the negotiation include attention to social and organization objectives, with as much quantification as reasonable but with qualitative objectives where appropriate.

The development of such strategic and operating plans turns critically on the initiative of responsible corporate individuals, who must be competent enough to accomplish demanding economic and social tasks and have time as well for their families and private affairs.

Financial, production, and sales requirements may be transmitted down rather than drawn upward in an efficient (though often sterilizing) compaction of the planning process. The top-down promulgation of an imaginative and community-centered social and organization strategy, except in terms so general as to be ineffective, is not only similarly unwise in stifling creativity and commitment but also virtually impossible.

Qualitative attention

Once targets and plans have been defined (in the negotiation between organization levels), the measurement system must incorporate in appropriate proportion quantitative and qualitative measures. The bias to short-term results can be corrected by qualitative attention to social and organization programs. The transfer and promotion of managers successful in achieving short-term results is a gamble until their competence in balancing short- and long-term objectives is demonstrated.

Incidentally, rapid rotation virtually guarantees a low level of interest in the particular city through which the manager is following his career; one day it will be seen to be as wasteful as an organization-building and management-development device as it is useful in staffing a growing organization. The alternative—to remain in a given place, to develop fully the company's business in a given city assisted by knowledge and love of the region—needs to become open to executives who do not wish to become president of their companies.

When young middle managers fall short of their targets, inquiry into the reasons and ways to help them achieve assigned goals should precede adverse judgment and penalty. Whenever measurement and control can be directed toward ways to correct problems observed, the shriveling effects of over-emphatic evaluation are postponed. In addition, managers learn that something is important to their superiors other than a single numerical indicator of little significance when detached from the future results to which it relates.

Internal audit: The curse of unquantifiability which hangs over executive action in the areas of corporate responsibility may someday be lifted by the "social audit," now in very early stages of development.[6] In its simplest form, this is a kind of balance sheet and operating state-ment. On it are listed the dollar values of such corporate investments as training programs, individual development activities, time devoted by individuals to community projects, contributions to pollution abatement, transportation, taxes, and the like. All of these investments call the attention of a company and community to the cumulative dollar worth of corporate functions ancillary to production and sales.

But the further evolvement of the social audit, which one day may develop the conventions that make comparison possible, is not essential to immediate qualitative attention to progress being made by managers at all organizational levels toward their noneconomic goals. Consider, for example:

◊ Internal audit groups, necessarily oriented to examining what the public accounting firm must ultimately certify, can be supplemented by adding to their auditors and accountants permanent or temporary personnel, public relations, or general management persons who are qualified to examine, make comment on, and counsel with managers on their success and difficulties in the areas of social contribution and organization morale.

◊ The role in the community of a local branch office, the morale of the work force, clerical and functional staffs, and the expertise and enthusiasm of the salesmen are all capable of assessment, not in hard numbers but nevertheless in valid and useful judgments.

◊ The public relations and personnel staffs of organizations are all too often assigned to superficial and trivial tasks. The employment of such persons in the internal audit function, especially if they have—without necessarily the qualifications or temperament of high-spirited doers—the experience, perspective, and judgment of long service in the organization, would raise the importance of these functions by increasing their usefulness.

Maturity of judgment: Every large corporation develops unintentionally a group of highly experienced but, after a time, uncompulsive managers who are better assigned to jobs requiring maturity of judgment rather than the ability to sprint. The internal qualitative audit, combined with a parallel inquiry by a committee of outside directors, to which I shall allude in a moment, could be an internal counseling, review, and support function epitomizing effective staff

6. See Raymond A. Bauer and Dan H. Fenn, Jr., "What *Is* a Corporate Social Audit?" HBR January-February 1973, p. 37.

support of line operations. It could also provide opportunity for the cadre of older managers no longer motivated by primitive incentives.

Men with executive responsibility, including accountants and controllers, often exercise judgment only distantly affected by numbers; this is not a new requirement or experience. To the extent that managers in the hierarchy are capable of interpreting numbers intelligently, they must be capable of relating results produced to those in gestation and of judging the significance of a profit figure (not to be found in the figure itself) at a given point of time.

Incentive modification: If measurement of performance is to be broad and knowledgeable enough to encompass progress under a strategy containing social and organizational objectives, then the incentive system in a company or organization unit must reward and penalize accomplishments other than those related to economic efficiency.

Moreover, it must become well known in such an organization that persons can be demoted or discharged for failure to behave responsibly toward their subordinates, for example, even if they are successful in economic terms. Career-oriented middle managers must learn, from the response that their organization leadership and community activities receive, how to appreciate the intrinsic worth and how to estimate the value to their own future of demonstrated responsibility.

Management development

Besides liberating the evaluation process by adding qualitative judgment to numbers, the activity which needs expansion in making an organization socially effective and internally healthy is management development—not so much in terms of formal training programs (although I should be the last person to demean the importance of these) as in planned careers.

If organizations elect, as interesting organizations will, high standards of profit and social contribution to be achieved simultaneously, then much is required of the character, general education, and professional competence of managers who must show themselves—whatever their schooling—as liberally educated.

It follows from the argument I am making that, in moderating the amorality of organizations, we must expect executive mid-career education to include exposure to the issues of

responsibility raised here and to the invaluable experience of participating in nonprofit community or government organizations. Under short-term pressures, attention to development

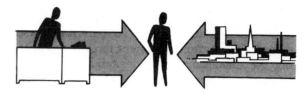

is easily postponed, either as a cost that should be avoided for now or as a process requiring more attention to persons than is convenient or possible.

The management action so far suggested does not constitute innovation so much as reemphasis: it requires not heroic action but maturity and breadth of perspective. Once the aspiration to reach beyond economic to social and human objectives is seen to require extending conventional incentive and performance measurement systems, it is not difficult to avoid imbalance and the unintended organizational consequences of which I have spoken. Awareness of the problem generates its solution.

Audit by directors

But the current move toward revitalization of the board of directors does provide a formal resource to the chief executive who is secure enough and interested enough to avail himself of it. Committees of outside directors are now being formed in a number of companies to meet regularly with the internal audit and outside audit staffs to look closely at the thoroughness and adequacy of the procedures used to ensure that the true condition of the company is reflected in its published accounting statements.

The Penn Central debacle, in the midst of which the board of directors was apparently unaware of approaching disaster, has given considerable impetus to this trend.

If internal audit teams were to extend their counsel, nonpunitive inspection, and recommendations for improvement to social performance and to the quality of organization life as felt by its members, the information they would gather and the problems they would encounter could be summarized for the board committee in the same way as the more conventional subjects of their scrutiny.

In any case, the pervasiveness of the chief executive's posture on social responsibility can be inquired into, and the quality of the management across the organization can be reported on. The board of directors, supposed to provide judgment and experience not available inside the organization, can be—in its proper role of constructive inquiry into the quality of the corporation's management and its support for investment in improving it—a potent force in moderating the management's understandable internal interest in day-to-day achievement.

Conclusion

Nothing will happen, either inward or outward, to further advance the doctrine of social responsibility unless those in charge of the corporation want it to happen and unless their associates share their values and put their backs into solving the organization's master problem. There must be desire and determination first. It must be embodied in a strategy that makes a consistent whole of private economic opportunity and public social responsibility, planned to be implemented in an organization which will be humanely and challengingly led and developed.

A few good guys cannot change the course of a large corporation by their personal influence, but they can arrange that the systems of implementation are appropriate in scope to the breadth of corporate economic and social purpose. Now that enlightened chief executives have made this commitment, it would be tragic to have their will subverted, their determination doubted, and their energy dissipated by bureaucratic organization.

The giant corporation, which in small numbers does half the work of our economic system, is here to stay. It is the dominant force of our industrial society. In its multinational forms it has no higher sovereignty to which it reports; in its national forms it is granted wide latitude. Thus it is important to all of us that its affairs be responsibly conducted and that limited knowledge of the art of managing a large organization not be permitted to thwart us.

If organizations cannot be made moral, the future of capitalism will be unattractive—to all of us and especially to those young people whose talents we need. It is not the attack of the muckrakers we should fear but the apathy of our corporate citizenry.

Harvard
Business Review

January-February 1982

Can a corporation have a conscience?

*Kenneth E. Goodpaster
and John B. Matthews, Jr.*

When making a profit conflicts with respecting the welfare of the community, corporations do not always choose profit as their only goal. Nor do they always decide that such debates of principle are beyond their domain. They look within to their boards of directors and managers, they take the time to hear community representatives, and they choose courses of action carefully geared to the needs of the community as well as their own. Deciding things this way isn't easy, and it bears all the marks of a person trying to decide the right course in a situation that is fraught with conflict. That is why the authors say that conscience can reside in the organization. This opinion represents a change in perspective, for traditionally the notion of conscience has been associated with the

notion of person. Sometimes, stepping outside one discipline with the help of another presents a perspective from which to see how to make conflict manageable and goals clear. Such a new orientation is what this article offers those who are trying to cope with the complexities of corporate management in today's society. With some terminology and insight from moral philosophy, the authors think through the confusion surrounding the concept of corporate responsibility and find a way to define it. By looking closely at the realm in which responsibility is usually understood—the individual's action

and intention—and then projecting the light of this understanding onto the company, they hope to help corporations inform their decisions with moral concerns.

Mr. Goodpaster has come from the discipline of philosophy at the University of Notre Dame to the Harvard Business School, where as lecturer on business administration he teaches a popular course on business and ethics. Mr. Matthews has had a long, successful career of teaching business policy at the Harvard Business School, where he is the Joseph C. Wilson Professor of Business Administration.

During the severe racial tensions of the 1960s, Southern Steel Company (actual case, disguised name) faced considerable pressure from government and the press to explain and modify its policies regarding discrimination both within its plants and in the major city where it was located. SSC was the largest employer in the area (it had nearly 15,000 workers, one-third of whom were black) and had made great strides toward removing barriers to equal job opportunity in its several plants. In addition, its top executives (especially its chief executive officer, James Weston) had distinguished themselves as private citizens for years in community programs for black housing, education, and small business as well as in attempts at desegregating all-white police and local government organizations.

SSC drew the line, however, at using its substantial economic influence in the local area to advance the cause of the civil rights movement by pressuring banks, suppliers, and the local government:

"As individuals we can exercise what influence we may have as citizens," James Weston said, "but for a corporation to attempt to exert any kind of economic compulsion to achieve a particular end in a social area seems to me to be quite beyond what a corporation should do and quite beyond what a corporation can do. I believe that while government may seek to compel social reforms, any attempt by a private organization like SSC to impose its views, its beliefs, and its will upon the community would be repugnant to our American constitutional concepts and that appropriate steps to correct this abuse of corporate power would be universally demanded by public opinion."

Weston could have been speaking in the early 1980s on any issue that corporations around the United States now face. Instead of social justice, his theme might be environmental protection, product safety, marketing practice, or international bribery. His statement for SSC raises the important issue of corporate responsibility. Can a corporation have a conscience?

Weston apparently felt comfortable saying it need not. The responsibilities of ordinary persons and of "artificial persons" like corporations are, in his view, separate. Persons' responsibilities go beyond those of corporations. Persons, he seems to have believed, ought to care not only about themselves but also about the dignity and well-being of those around them—ought not only to care but also to act. Organizations, he evidently thought, are creatures of, and to a degree prisoners of, the systems of economic incentive and political sanction that give them reality and therefore should not be expected to display the same moral attributes that we expect of persons.

Others inside business as well as outside share Weston's perception. One influential philosopher—John Ladd—carries Weston's view a step further:

"It is improper to expect organizational conduct to conform to the ordinary principles of morality," he says. "We cannot and must not expect formal organizations, or their representatives acting in their official capacities, to be honest, courageous, considerate, sympathetic, or to have any kind of moral integrity. Such concepts are not in the vocabulary, so to speak, of the organizational language game."[1]

In our opinion, this line of thought represents a tremendous barrier to the development of business ethics both as a field of inquiry and as a practical force in managerial decision making. This is a matter about which executives must be philosophical and philosophers must be practical. A corporation can and should have a conscience. The language of ethics does have a place in the vocabulary of an organization. There need not be and there should not be a disjunction of the sort attributed to SSC's James Weston. Organizational agents such as corporations should be no more and no less morally responsible (rational, self-interested, altruistic) than ordinary persons.

We take this position because we think an analogy holds between the individual and the corporation. If we analyze the concept of moral responsibility as it applies to persons, we find that projecting it to corporations as agents in society is possible.

1 See John Ladd, "Morality and the Ideal of Rationality in Formal Organizations," *The Monist*, October 1970, p. 499.

Defining the responsibility of persons

When we speak of the responsibility of individuals, philosophers say that we mean three things: someone is to blame, something has to be done, or some kind of trustworthiness can be expected. (See the *Exhibit* on page 138.)

Holding accountable

We apply the first meaning, what we shall call the *causal* sense, primarily to legal and moral contexts where what is at issue is praise or blame for a past action. We say of a person that he or she was responsible for what happened, is to blame for it, should be held accountable. In this sense of the word, *responsibility* has to do with tracing the causes of actions and events, of finding out who is answerable in a given situation. Our aim is to determine someone's intention, free will, degree of participation, and appropriate reward or punishment.

Rule following

We apply the second meaning of *responsibility* to rule following, to contexts where individuals are subject to externally imposed norms often associated with some social role that people play. We speak of the responsibilities of parents to children, of doctors to patients, of lawyers to clients, of citizens to the law. What is socially expected and what the party involved is to answer for are at issue here.

Decision making

We use the third meaning of *responsibility* for decision making. With this meaning of the term, we say that individuals are responsible if they are trustworthy and reliable, if they allow appropriate factors to affect their judgment; we refer primarily to a person's independent thought processes and decision making, processes that justify an attitude of trust from those who interact with him or her as a responsible individual.

The distinguishing characteristic of moral responsibility, it seems to us, lies in this third

For the Confucian—but also for the philosopher of the Western tradition—only law can handle the rights and objections of collectives. Ethics is always a matter of the person.

But is this adequate for a "society of organizations" such as ours? This may be the central question for the philosopher of modern society, in which access to livelihood, career and achievement exists primarily in and through organizations—and especially for the highly educated person for whom opportunities outside of organizations are very scarce indeed. In such a society, both the society and the individual increasingly depend on the performance, as well as the "sincerity," of organizations.

But in today's discussion of "business ethics" it is not even seen that there is a problem.

Peter Drucker

"What Is Business Ethics?"
The Public Interest, No. 64,
Spring 1981, p. 18
© 1981
by National Affairs, Inc.

sense of the term. Here the focus is on the intellectual and emotional processes in the individual's moral reasoning. Philosophers call this "taking a moral point of view" and contrast it with such other processes as being financially prudent and attending to legal obligations.

To be sure, characterizing a person as "morally responsible" may seem rather vague. But vagueness is a contextual notion. Everything depends on how we fill in the blank in "vague for _____ purposes."

In some contexts the term "six o'clock-ish" is vague, while in others it is useful and informative. As a response to a space-shuttle pilot who wants to know when to fire the reentry rockets, it will not do, but it might do in response to a spouse who wants to know when one will arrive home at the end of the workday.

We maintain that the processes underlying moral responsibility can be defined and are not themselves vague, even though gaining consensus on specific moral norms and decisions is not always easy.

What, then, characterizes the processes underlying the judgment of a person we call morally responsible? Philosopher William K. Frankena offers the following answer:

"A morality is a normative system in which judgments are made, more or less consciously, [out of a] consideration of the effects of actions...on the lives of persons...including the lives of others besides the person acting....David Hume took a similar position when he argued that what speaks in a moral judgment is a kind of sympathy....A little later,...Kant put the matter somewhat better by characterizing morality as the business of respecting persons as ends and not as means or as things...."[2]

Frankena is pointing to two traits, both rooted in a long and diverse philosophical tradition:

1   Rationality. Taking a moral point of view includes the features we usually attribute to rational decision making, that is, lack of impulsiveness, care in mapping out alternatives and consequences, clarity about goals and purposes, attention to details of implementation.

2   Respect. The moral point of view also includes a special awareness of and concern for the effects of one's decisions and policies on others, special in the sense that it goes beyond the kind of awareness and concern that would ordinarily be part of rationality, that is, beyond seeing others merely as instrumental to accomplishing one's own purposes. This is respect for the lives of others and involves taking their needs and interests seriously, not simply as resources in one's own decision making but as limiting conditions which change the very definition of one's habitat from a self-centered to a shared environment. It is what philosopher Immanuel Kant meant by the "categorical imperative" to treat others as valuable in and for themselves.

It is this feature that permits us to trust the morally responsible person. We know that such a person takes our point of view into account not merely as a useful precaution (as in "honesty is the best policy") but as important in its own right.

These components of moral responsibility are not too vague to be useful. Rationality and respect affect the manner in which a person approaches practical decision making: they affect the way in which the individual processes information and makes choices. A rational but not respectful Bill Jones will not lie to his friends *unless* he is reasonably sure he will not be found out. A rational but not respectful Mary Smith will defend an unjustly treated party *unless* she thinks it may be too costly to herself. A rational *and* respectful decision maker, however, notices—and cares—whether the consequences of his or her conduct lead to injuries or indignities to others.

Two individuals who take "the moral point of view" will not of course always agree on ethical matters, but they do at least have a basis for dialogue.

Projecting responsibility to corporations

Now that we have removed some of the vagueness from the notion of moral responsibility as it applies to persons, we can search for a frame of reference in which, by analogy with Bill Jones and Mary Smith, we can meaningfully and appropriately say that corporations are morally responsible. This is the issue reflected in the SSC case.

To deal with it, we must ask two questions: Is it meaningful to apply moral concepts to actors who are not persons but who are instead made up of persons? And even if meaningful, is it advisable to do so?

If a group can act like a person in some ways, then we can expect it to behave like a person in other ways. For one thing, we know that people organized into a group can act as a unit. As business people well know, legally a corporation is considered a unit. To approach unity, a group usually has some sort of internal decision structure, a system of rules that spell out authority relationships and specify the conditions under which certain individuals' actions become official actions of the group.[3]

If we can say that persons act responsibly only if they gather information about the impact of their actions on others and use it in making decisions, we can reasonably do the same for organizations. Our proposed frame of reference for thinking about and implementing corporate responsibility aims at spelling out the processes associated with the moral responsibility of individuals and projecting them to the level of organizations. This is similar to, though an inversion of, Plato's famous method in the *Republic*, in which justice in the community is used as a model for justice in the individual.

Hence, corporations that monitor their employment practices and the effects of their produc-

In an interview this week, Robert Kilpatrick, the chairman of the [Business Roundtable's] committee on the federal budget and president of the Connecticut General Insurance Corporation, said that his fellow executives had every intention of taking their "social responsibilities" seriously and working with other groups in the community to solve such national problems as unemployment, inflation, urban decay, stagnating productivity and low living standards.

"We know those problems will not go away," Mr. Kilpatrick said. "The ball is now in the private sector's court. Limited government is going to mean that the problems are going to have to be solved by the private sector alone or working closely with government. If we don't do the job now, we won't have another chance the next time around."

Leonard Silk

tion processes and products on the environment and human health show the same kind of rationality and respect that morally responsible individuals do. Thus, attributing actions, strategies, decisions, and moral responsibilities to corporations as entities distinguishable from those who hold offices in them poses no problem.

And when we look about us, we can readily see differences in moral responsibility among corporations in much the same way that we see differences among persons. Some corporations have built features into their management incentive systems, board structures, internal control systems, and research agendas that in a person we would call self-control, integrity, and conscientiousness. Some have institutionalized awareness and concern for consumers, employees, and the rest of the public in ways that others clearly have not.

2 See William K. Frankena, *Thinking About Morality* (Ann Arbor: University of Michigan Press, 1980), p. 26.

3 See Peter French, "The Corporation as a Moral Person," *American Philosophical Quarterly,* July 1979, p. 207.

If people are going to adopt the terminology of "responsibility" (with its allied concepts of corporate conscience) to suggest new, improved ways of dealing with corporations, then they ought to go back and examine in detail what "being responsible" entails—in the ordinary case of the responsible human being. Only after we have considered what being responsible calls for in general does it make sense to develop the notion of a corporation being responsible.

Christopher Stone

From *Where the Law Ends*
© 1975 by Christopher D. Stone
Reprinted with permission
of Harper & Row, Publishers, Inc.

As a matter of course, some corporations attend to the human impact of their operations and policies and reject operations and policies that are questionable. Whether the issue be the health effects of sugared cereal or cigarettes, the safety of tires or tampons, civil liberties in the corporation or the community, an organization reveals its character as surely as a person does.

Indeed, the parallel may be even more dramatic. For just as the moral responsibility displayed by an individual develops over time from infancy to adulthood,[4] so too we may expect to find stages of development in organizational character that show significant patterns.

Evaluating the idea of moral projection

Concepts like moral responsibility not only make sense when applied to organizations but also provide touchstones for designing more effective models than we now have for guiding corporate policy.

Now we can understand what it means to invite SSC as a corporation to be morally responsi-

ble both in-house and in its community, but *should* we issue the invitation? Here we turn to the question of advisability. Should we require the organizational agents in our society to have the same moral attributes we require of ourselves?

Our proposal to spell out the processes associated with moral responsibility for individuals and then to project them to their organizational counterparts takes on added meaning when we examine alternative frames of reference for corporate responsibility.

Two frames of reference that compete for the allegiance of people who ponder the question of corporate responsibility are emphatically opposed to this principle of moral projection—what we might refer to as the "invisible hand" view and the "hand of government" view.

The invisible hand

The most eloquent spokesman of the first view is Milton Friedman (echoing many philosophers and economists since Adam Smith). According to this pattern of thought, the true and only social responsibilities of business organizations are to make profits and obey the laws. The workings of the free and competitive marketplace will "moralize" corporate behavior quite independently of any attempts to expand or transform decision making via moral projection.

A deliberate amorality in the executive suite is encouraged in the name of systemic morality: the common good is best served when each of us and our economic institutions pursue not the common good or moral purpose, advocates say, but competitive advantage. Morality, responsibility, and conscience reside in the invisible hand of the free market system, not in the hands of the organizations within the system, much less the managers within the organizations.

To be sure, people of this opinion admit, there is a sense in which social or ethical issues can and should enter the corporate mind, but the filtering of such issues is thorough: they go through the screens of custom, public opinion, public relations, and the law. And, in any case, self-interest maintains primacy as an objective and a guiding star.

The reaction from this frame of reference to the suggestion that moral judgment be inte-

4 A process that psychological researchers from Jean Piaget to Lawrence Kohlberg have examined carefully; see Jean Piaget, *The Moral Judgment of the Child* (New York: Free Press, 1965) and Lawrence Kohlberg, *The Philosophy of Moral Development* (New York: Harper & Row, 1981).

grated with corporate strategy is clearly negative. Such an integration is seen as inefficient and arrogant, and in the end both an illegitimate use of corporate power and an abuse of the manager's fiduciary role. With respect to our SSC case, advocates of the invisible hand model would vigorously resist efforts, beyond legal requirements, to make SSC right the wrongs of racial injustice. SSC's responsibility would be to make steel of high quality at least cost, to deliver it on time, and to satisfy its customers and stockholders. Justice would not be part of SSC's corporate mandate.

The hand of government

Advocates of the second dissenting frame of reference abound, but John Kenneth Galbraith's work has counterpointed Milton Friedman's with insight and style. Under this view of corporate responsibility, corporations are to pursue objectives that are rational and purely economic. The regulatory hands of the law and the political process rather than the invisible hand of the marketplace turns these objectives to the common good.

Again, in this view, it is a system that provides the moral direction for corporate decision making—a system, though, that is guided by political managers, the custodians of the public purpose. In the case of SSC, proponents of this view would look to the state for moral direction and responsible management, both within SSC and in the community. The corporation would have no moral responsibility beyond political and legal obedience.

What is striking is not so much the radical difference between the economic and social philosophies that underlie these two views of the source of corporate responsibility but the conceptual similarities. Both views locate morality, ethics, responsibility, and conscience in the systems of rules and incentives in which the modern corporation finds itself embedded. Both views reject the exercise of independent moral judgment by corporations as actors in society.

Neither view trusts corporate leaders with stewardship over what are often called non-economic values. Both require corporate responsibility to march to the beat of drums outside. In the jargon of moral philosophy, both views press for a rule-centered or a system-centered ethics instead of an agent-centered ethics. In terms of the *Exhibit,* these frames of reference countenance corporate rule-following responsibility for corporations but not corporate decision-making responsibility.

Since we may have only weak confidence in our intuitions and judgments about the justice of the whole structure of society, we may attempt to aid our judgment by focusing on microsituations that we do have a firm grasp of. For many of us, an important part of the process of arriving at what [philosopher John] Rawls calls "reflective equilibrium" will consist of thought experiments in which we try out principles in hypothetical microsituations....Since Plato, at any rate, that has been our tradition; principles may be tried out in the large and in the small. Plato thought that writ large the principles are easier to discern; others may think the reverse.

Robert Nozick

From *Anarchy, State and Utopia*
© 1974 by Basic Books Inc.
Reprinted with permission of
the publisher

The hand of management

To be sure, the two views under discussion differ in that one looks to an invisible moral force in the market while the other looks to a visible moral force in government. But both would advise against a principle of moral projection that permits or encourages corporations to exercise independent, non-economic judgment over matters that face them in their short- and long-term plans and operations.

Accordingly, both would reject a third view of corporate responsibility that seeks to affect the thought processes of the organization itself—a sort of "hand of management" view—since neither seems willing or able to see the engines of profit regulate themselves to the degree that would be implied by taking the principle of moral projection seriously. Cries of inefficiency and moral imperialism from the right would be matched by cries of insensitivity and illegitimacy from the left, all in the name of preserving us from corporations and managers run morally amok.

Better, critics would say, that moral philosophy be left to philosophers, philanthropists, and politicians than to business leaders. Better that corporate morality be kept to glossy annual reports, where it is safely insulated from policy and performance.

Exhibit	Three uses of the term *responsible*	
The causal sense	"He is responsible for this." Emphasis on holding to account for past actions, causality.
The rule-following sense	"As a lawyer, he is responsible for defending that client." Emphasis on following social and legal norms.
The decision-making sense	"He is a responsible person." Emphasis on an individual's independent judgment.

The two conventional frames of reference locate moral restraint in forces external to the person and the corporation. They deny moral reasoning and intent to the corporation in the name of either market competition or society's system of explicit legal constraints and presume that these have a better moral effect than that of rationality and respect.

Although the principle of moral projection, which underwrites the idea of a corporate conscience and patterns it on the thought and feeling processes of the person, is in our view compelling, we must acknowledge that it is neither part of the received wisdom, nor is its advisability beyond question or objection. Indeed, attributing the role of conscience to the corporation seems to carry with it new and disturbing implications for our usual ways of thinking about ethics and business.

Perhaps the best way to clarify and defend this frame of reference is to address the objections to the principle found in the ruled insert on pages 139-141. There we see a summary of the criticisms and counterarguments we have heard during hours of discussion with business executives and business school students. We believe that the replies to the objections about a corporation having a conscience are convincing.

Leaving the double standard behind

We have come some distance from our opening reflection on Southern Steel Company and its role in its community. Our proposal—clarified, we hope, through these objections and replies—suggests that it is not sufficient to draw a sharp line between individuals' private ideas and efforts and a corporation's institutional efforts but that the latter can and should be built upon the former.

Does this frame of reference give us an unequivocal prescription for the behavior of SSC in its circumstances? No, it does not. Persuasive arguments might be made now and might have been made then that SSC should not have used its considerable economic clout to threaten the community into desegregation. A careful analysis of the realities of the environment might have disclosed that such a course would have been counterproductive, leading to more injustice than it would have alleviated.

The point is that some of the arguments and some of the analyses are or would have been moral arguments, and thereby the ultimate decision that of an ethically responsible organization. The significance of this point can hardly be overstated, for it represents the adoption of a new perspective on corporate policy and a new way of thinking about business ethics. We agree with one authority, who writes that "the business firm, as an organic entity intricately affected by and affecting its environment, is as appropriately adaptive...to demands for responsible behavior as for economic service."[5]

The frame of reference here developed does not offer a decision procedure for corporate managers. That has not been our purpose. It does, however, shed light on the conceptual foundations of business ethics by training attention on the corporation as a moral agent in society. Legal systems of rules and incentives are insufficient, even though they may be necessary, as frameworks for corporate responsibility. Taking conceptual cues from the features of moral responsibility normally expected of the person in our opinion deserves practicing managers' serious consideration.

The lack of congruence that James Weston saw between individual and corporate moral responsibility can be, and we think should be, overcome. In the process, what a number of writers have characterized as a double standard—a discrepancy between our personal lives and our lives in organizational settings—might be dampened. The principle of moral projection not only helps us to conceptualize the kinds of demands that we might make of corporations and other organizations but also offers the prospect of harmonizing those demands with the demands that we make of ourselves.

5 See Kenneth R. Andrews,
The Concept of Corporate Strategy.
revised edition
(Homewood, Ill.:
Dow Jones-Irwin, 1980),
p. 99.

Is a corporation a morally responsible 'person'?

Objection 1
to the analogy:

Corporations are not persons. They are artificial legal constructions, machines for mobilizing economic investments toward the efficient production of goods and services. We cannot hold a corporation responsible. We can only hold individuals responsible.

Reply:

Our frame of reference does not imply that corporations are persons in a literal sense. It simply means that in certain respects concepts and functions normally attributed to persons can also be attributed to organizations made up of persons. Goals, economic values, strategies, and other such personal attributes are often usefully projected to the corporate level by managers and researchers. Why should we not project the functions of conscience in the same way? As for holding corporations responsible, recent criminal prosecutions such as the case of Ford Motor Company and its Pinto gas tanks suggest that society finds the idea both intelligible and useful.

Objection 2:

A corporation cannot be held responsible at the sacrifice of profit. Profitability and financial health have always been and should continue to be the "categorical imperatives" of a business operation.

Reply:

We must of course acknowledge the imperatives of survival, stability, and growth when we discuss corporations, as indeed we must acknowledge them when we discuss the life of an individual. Self-sacrifice has been identified with moral responsibility in only the most extreme cases. The pursuit of profit and self-interest need not be pitted against the demands of moral responsibility. Moral demands are best viewed as containments – not replacements – for self-interest.

This is not to say that profit maximization never conflicts with morality. But profit maximization conflicts with other managerial values as well. The point is to coordinate imperatives, not deny their validity.

Objection 3:

Corporate executives are not elected representatives of the people, nor are they anointed or appointed as social guardians. They therefore lack the social mandate that a democratic society rightly demands of those who would pursue ethically or socially motivated policies. By keeping corporate policies confined to economic motivations, we keep the power of corporate executives in its proper place.

Reply:

The objection betrays an oversimplified view of the relationship between the public and the private sector. Neither private individuals nor private corporations that guide their conduct by ethical or social values beyond the demands of law should be constrained merely because they are not elected to do so. The demands of moral responsibility are independent of the demands of political legitimacy and are in fact presupposed by them.

To be sure, the state and the political process will and must remain the primary mechanisms for protecting the public interest, but one might be forgiven the hope that the political process will not substitute for the moral judgment of the citizenry or other components of society such as corporations.

Objection 4:

Our system of law carefully defines the role of agent or fiduciary and makes corporate managers accountable to shareholders and investors for the use of their assets. Management cannot, in the name of corporate moral responsibility, arrogate to itself the right to manage those assets by partially noneconomic criteria.

Reply:

First, it is not so clear that investors insist on purely economic criteria in the management of their assets, especially if some of the shareholders' resolutions and board reforms of the last decade are any indication. For instance, companies doing business in South Africa have had stockholders question their activities, other companies have instituted audit committees for their boards before such auditing was mandated, and mutual funds for which "socially responsible behavior" is a major investment criterion now exist.

Second, the categories of "shareholder" and "investor" connote wider time spans than do immediate or short-term returns. As a practical matter, considerations of stability and long-term return on investment enlarge the class of principals to which managers bear a fiduciary relationship.

Third, the trust that managers hold does not and never has extended to "any means available" to advance the interests of the principals. Both legal and moral constraints must be understood to qualify that trust – even, perhaps, in the name of a larger trust and a more basic fiduciary relationship to the members of society at large.

Objection 5:

The power, size, and scale of the modern corporation – domestic as well as international – are awesome. To unleash, even partially, such power from the discipline of the marketplace and the narrow or possibly nonexistent moral purpose implicit in that discipline would be socially dangerous. Had SSC acted in the community to further racial justice, its purposes might have been admirable, but those purposes could have led to a kind of moral imperialism or worse. Suppose SSC had thrown its power behind the Ku Klux Klan.

Reply:

This is a very real and important objection. What seems not to be appreciated is the fact that power affects when it is used as well as when it is not used. A decision by SSC not to exercise its economic influence according to "noneconomic" criteria is inevitably a moral decision and just as inevitably affects the community. The issue in the end is not whether corporations (and other organizations) should be "unleashed" to exert moral force in our society but rather how critically and self-consciously they should choose to do so.

The degree of influence enjoyed by an agent, whether a person or an organization, is not so much a factor recommending moral disengagement as a factor demanding a high level of moral awareness. Imperialism is more to be feared when moral reasoning is absent than when it is present. Nor do we suggest that the "discipline of the marketplace" be diluted; rather, we call for it to be supplemented with the discipline of moral reflection.

Objection 6:

The idea of moral projection is a useful device for structuring corporate responsibility only if our understanding of moral responsibility at the level of the person is in some sense richer than our understanding of moral responsibility on the level of the organization as a whole. If we are not clear about individual responsibility, the projection is fruitless.

Reply:

The objection is well taken. The challenge offered by the idea of moral projection lies in our capacity to articulate criteria or frameworks of reasoning for the morally responsible person. And though such a challenge is formidable, it is not clear that it cannot be met, at least with sufficient consensus to be useful.

For centuries, the study and criticism of frameworks have gone on, carried forward by many disciplines, including psychology, the social sciences, and philosophy. And though it would be a mistake to suggest that any single framework (much less a decision mechanism) has emerged as the right one, it is true that recurrent patterns are discernible and well enough defined to structure moral discussion.

In the body of the article, we spoke of rationality and respect as components of individual responsibility. Further analysis of these

components would translate them into social costs and benefits, justice in the distribution of goods and services, basic rights and duties, and fidelity to contracts. The view that pluralism in our society has undercut all possibility of moral agreement is anything but self-evident. Sincere moral disagreement is, of course, inevitable and not clearly lamentable. But a process and a vocabulary for articulating such values as we share is no small step forward when compared with the alternatives. Perhaps in our exploration of the moral projection we might make some surprising and even reassuring discoveries about ourselves.

Objection 7:

Why is it necessary to project moral responsibility to the level of the organization? Isn't the task of defining corporate responsibility and business ethics sufficiently discharged if we clarify the responsibilities of men and women in business as individuals? Doesn't ethics finally rest on the honesty and integrity of the individual in the business world?

Reply:

Yes and no. Yes, in the sense that the control of large organizations does finally rest in the hands of managers, of men and women. No, in the sense that what is being controlled is a cooperative system for a cooperative purpose. The

projection of responsibility to the organization is simply an acknowledgement of the fact that the whole is more than the sum of its parts. Many intelligent people do not an intelligent organization make. Intelligence needs to be structured, organized, divided, and recombined in complex processes for complex purposes.

Studies of management have long shown that the attributes, successes, and failures of organizations are phenomena that emerge from the coordination of persons' attributes and that explanations of such phenomena require categories of analysis and description beyond the level of the individual. Moral responsibility is an attribute that can manifest itself in organizations as surely as competence or efficiency.

Objection 8:

Is the frame of reference here proposed intended to replace or undercut the relevance of the "invisible hand" and the "government hand" views, which depend on external controls?

Reply:

No. Just as regulation and economic competition are not substitutes for corporate responsibility, so corporate responsibility is not a substitute for law and the market. The imperatives of ethics cannot be relied on — nor have they ever been relied on – without a context of external sanctions. And this is true as much for individuals as for organizations.

This frame of reference takes us beneath, but not beyond, the realm of external systems of rules and incentives and into the thought processes that interpret and respond to the corporation's environment. Morality is more than merely part of that environment. It aims at the projection of conscience, not the enthronement of it in either the state or the competitive process.

The rise of the modern large corporation and the concomitant rise of the professional manager demand a conceptual framework in which these phenomena can be accommodated to moral thought. The principle of moral projection furthers such accommodation by recognizing a new level of agency in society and thus a new level of responsibility.

Objection 9:

Corporations have always taken the interests of those outside the corporation into account in the sense that customer relations and public relations generally are an integral part of rational economic decision making. Market signals and social signals that filter through the market mechanism inevitably represent the interests of parties affected by the behavior of the company. What, then, is the point of adding respect to rationality?

Reply:

Representing the affected parties solely as economic variables in the environment of the company is treating them as means or resources and not as ends in themselves. It implies that the only voice which affected parties should have in organizational decision making is that of potential buyers, sellers, regulators, or boycotters. Besides, many affected parties may not occupy such roles, and those who do may not be able to signal the organization with messages that effectively represent their stakes in its actions.

To be sure, classical economic theory would have us believe that perfect competition in free markets (with modest adjustments from the state) will result in all relevant signals being "heard," but the abstractions from reality implicit in such theory make it insufficient as a frame of reference for moral responsibility. In a world in which strict self-interest was congruent with the common good, moral responsibility might be unnecessary. We do not, alas, live in such a world.

The element of respect in our analysis of responsibility plays an essential role in ensuring the recognition of unrepresented or underrepresented voices in the decision making of organizations as agents. Showing respect for persons as ends and not mere means to organizational purposes is central to the concept of corporate moral responsibility.

In the first part of the 17th century, Sir Edward Coke, one of Great Britain's most eminent jurists, concluded that a corporation was but an impersonal creation of the law—not a being, just a product of written rules and government fiat. But times have changed. Sir Edward could not have foreseen the results of the Industrial Revolution. He certainly did not foresee that 350 years after his pronouncements corporations would be the largest employers on earth, would generate the preponderance of the world's goods and services, and would be owned on a worldwide basis by millions of shareholders.

Although it may be true that Conoco remains an inanimate being for legalistic purposes, the company has a very personal existence for its shareholders, employees, officers, and directors. The success or failure of Conoco affects most of them during their working lives, and may affect them during their retirement. And to the employees, officers, and directors, Conoco's reputation concerns their reputation as well.

No one can deny that in the public's mind a corporation can break the law and be guilty of unethical and amoral conduct. Events of the early 1970s, such as corporate violations of federal law and failure of full disclosure, confirmed that both our government and our citizenry expect **corporations** *to act lawfully, ethically, and responsibly.*

Perhaps it is then appropriate in today's context to think of Conoco as a **living corporation;** *a sentient being whose conduct and personality are the collective effort and responsibility of its employees, officers, directors, and shareholders....*

The Conoco Conscience.
inhouse booklet on moral standards
© 1976
Continental Oil Company